1

8

CPP	CLN 12/06
CBA	CLO 7/07
CFU	CMI
CIN	CPE
CKI	CRI
CLE	CSA
CLH 1/06	CSH
CLHH	

Railway Milestones and Millstones:
Triumphs and Disasters in British Railway History

Railway Milestones and Millstones:
Triumphs and Disasters in British Railway History

Stanley Hall

Ian Allan
PUBLISHING

First published 2006

ISBN (10) 0 7110 3110 X
ISBN (13) 978 0 7110 3110 4

Published by Ian Allan Publishing

an imprint of Ian Allan Publishing Ltd, Hersham, Surrey
KT12 4RG.
Printed in England by Ian Allan Printing Ltd, Hersham,
Surrey KT12 4RG.

Code: 0610/B1

Visit the Ian Allan Publishing website at
www.ianallanpublishing.com

Front cover, top: Hull Trains Class 222 Pioneer No 222104
Sir Terry Farrell and GNER Class 43 powercar No 43120
London 2012 at the King's Cross buffer stops on 6 September
2005. *Brian Morrison*

Front cover, bottom: Built at the Great Western Railway's
Swindon works, 'Iron Duke' class 4-2-2 *Tartar* was designed
by Sir Daniel Gooch specifically for the broad-gauge railway,
which ultimately turned out to be a millstone. *Ian Allan Library*

Back cover, top: Newly-built 'Merchant Navy' class No 21C2
Union Castle with a short train on 4 July 1941. *Southern Railway*

Back cover, bottom: A fully-loaded Motorail train stands in Crewe
on 25 May 1985. *M. F. Haddon*

Title page: The Waverley route was doomed to close in the
struggle to cut costs, but whilst it was still open it was possible
to see stirring sights such as this with Class A3 Pacific No 60041
Salmon Trout climbing from Shankend to Hawick with a fully
fitted freight on 4 November 1965. *Paul Riley*

Contents

PART 2 — 1914 to 1947

PART 3 — 1948 to 1970

PART 4 — 1971-2005

Preface

This book is a personal selection of the successes and failures, from both internal and external causes, in Britain's railway history over the period 1825 to 2005. Milestones are projects or developments which had a major, successful impact, usually with lasting effect. Examples are G. J. Churchward's 'Saint' and 'Star' class locomotives and the Absolute Block System of Signalling, and readers will find that almost all the successes have been created by railway engineers and managers.

Millstones are at the opposite end of the spectrum. Some were self imposed, such as Francis Webb's obsession with compounding and the newly nationalised British Railways' failure to continue the former companies' development of main line diesel locomotives. But many, indeed most, sprang from the actions, or lack of action, of successive governments, dating almost from the beginning of railways and continuing to the present day.

Some readers may criticise my selection, and we all have our favourites. Others may question my judgement of the importance of my choices, and that is a fruitful field for debate. And my arguments and conclusions will please some and infuriate others. Reviewers will have a field day, and whilst I have taken every care with factual accuracy it is inevitable that errors may have crept in here and there, or that some of my sources may have been less than reliable.

A book that casts its net as widely as this one requires extensive research through a huge range of available material, and I freely acknowledge the help I have received, in the collection of data, from the books, journals and other documents listed in the bibliography. However, the judgements and conclusions which I express in these pages, whilst based on such data, are my own, but I have taken note of the views expressed by those authors and writers whose judgement, knowledge and experience I respect.

Many of my views have been formed over a period of at least 60 years, not only whilst working on the railway in positions which finally took me to the British Railways Board's headquarters (a place full of views and opinions of varying quality), but also since retirement, when I have had the opportunity both to study current railway affairs in great depth and to browse through historical sources. Railway history is a fascinating subject.

Stanley Hall, FCILT, FIRO, Hon.FIRSE
Skipton
North Yorkshire
2006

PART 1
1825 to 1913

Chapter 1

Mechanical engineering 1825 to 1913

Milestones — Locomotives

Above right: 'Star' class
No 4056 *Princess Margaret,*
built at Swindon in 1914 and
seen here in its original form.
This engine remained in
service until 1957 and
was the last of the class
to be withdrawn. *IAL*

Below: 'Star' class No 4003
Lode Star, the first of the class
and built at Swindon in 1907.
These were four-cylinder
engines and considerably more
powerful than the two-cylinder
'Saints'. This engine has been
preserved. *IAL*

George Jackson Churchward's 4-6-0s — the 'Saints' and 'Stars' — and 2-8-0s

George Churchward was born in 1857 and, when he was 16 years old, he became a pupil of John Wright, the Locomotive Superintendent of the South Devon Railway at Newton Abbot. Four years later, he entered the drawing office at Swindon, Great Western Railway (GWR), and he was destined to spend the rest of his working life at Swindon. He became Locomotive Works Manager in March 1896, then Chief Assistant to the Locomotive, Carriage and Wagon Superintendent in September 1897.

At that time, William Dean was the superintendent, but when he retired on 31 May 1902, after 25 years in the post, Churchward was appointed to succeed him. This was the milestone. He had had a long apprenticeship. Churchward recognised that the increasing weight of trains, and the demands of the passenger business for higher speeds of the expresses, required more powerful locomotives, and he therefore set about designing locomotives which would meet those requirements. It was a golden opportunity.

Apart from some minor designs, he produced in 1903 an express passenger locomotive which was considered to be technically in advance of any other such locomotive in the country. It had a 4-6-0 wheel arrangement and two outside cylinders 18in x 30in. The driving wheels were 6ft 8½in diameter and the boiler pressure was 225psi. Tractive effort was 23,090lb. Thus the 'Saints' were born, and eventually, over the next 10 years or so, 77 were built. The earlier locomotives did not have superheaters when built, but a few years later they were equipped with them and had other minor changes. The later locomotives were equipped with superheaters when new. The class was numbered in the 29XX series. In 1924, C. B. Collett, Chief Mechanical Engineer at the time, rebuilt No 2925 as a prototype for the 'Hall' class. The 'Saints' were very long-lived, and several engines survived well into BR days, the last one, No 2920 *Saint David,* not being withdrawn until 1953.

However, the Great Western proposed to develop its high speed, long distance expresses even further, and Churchward was ready with a development of the 'Saints'. By 1906 he had gained sufficient experience with that class, and with his 4-4-2s. He had also experimented with

compounding, but concluded that it was of no value to the GWR. However, he had been impressed with a French four-cylinder locomotive and decided to incorporate four cylinders in his next design, which became the 'Star' class, appearing in 1907. They were similar in many respects to the 'Saints', but had four cylinders 15in x 26in, and tractive effort was increased to 27,800lb. 73 of these splendid engines were built between 1906 and 1923. Like the 'Saints' they were extremely long-lived, and many survived to be taken over by BR, the last one, No 4056 *Princess Margaret,* not being withdrawn until 1957. Fortunately, a member of the class has been preserved, No 4003 *Lode Star.* The class was numbered in the 40XX series. It could be said that the 'Stars' were 20 years ahead of express passenger locomotives on most other railways. Some were subsequently rebuilt by Collett as 'Castles'.

The secret of Churchward's success lay in a number of advanced features in his designs. Swindon, under his guidance, had developed a very free-steaming high-pressure tapered boiler, and the steam was used economically and efficiently by long-lap, long-travel valves. To many eyes, his 4-6-0s were the finest express locomotives of any railway company in the years leading up to World War 1. He was a British pioneer in introducing superheating, along with George Hughes of the Lancashire & Yorkshire Railway. He is widely regarded as being the outstanding British locomotive engineer of his time, and the graceful lines of his engines could rival those of any other company. His post was retitled Chief Mechanical Engineer in 1916, and he retired in 1921. George Jackson Churchward ranks high in the Pantheon of great locomotive engineers, and why he did not receive a knighthood — along with his contemporaries John Aspinall of the Lancashire & Yorkshire Railway and Vincent Raven of the North Eastern — remains a mystery.

Another of Churchward's successes was his '28XX' class 2-8-0 design for heavy freight haulage. Building commenced in 1903 and continued until 1919, by which time 84 had been built. Building restarted in 1938/39 with only slight modifications, which is a tribute to the excellence of the original design. It continued until 1942, by which time another 82 engines had been built. The GWR had hoped that the standard wartime heavy freight locomotive in World War 2 would be the '28XX' class, but Stanier's LMS 2-8-0 was chosen instead. It might be argued that they both came from the same stable.

The '28XX' class engines were the first successful 2-8-0 heavy freight engines in Britain,

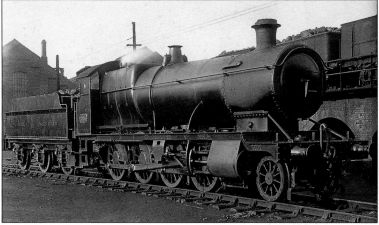

and were considered to be a huge advance on other freight engines on any railway. Their dimensions were eventually standardised as follows: two cylinders 18½in x 30in, boiler pressure 225psi, wheel diameter 4ft 7½in, giving a high tractive effort of 35,380lb. It is a tribute to the excellence of the design that the first member of the class was not withdrawn until 1958, and several have been preserved.

The Midland compounds

Around the turn of the 19th into the 20th century, several railway companies were experimenting with compounding, some of them, such as the London & North Western and the North Eastern, on quite a large scale and on a range of locomotive designs. Locomotive engineers were constantly striving to design a locomotive that was more efficient in operation and more economical in coal and water consumption than current designs. However, none of the experiments was judged to be sufficiently successful to justify being adopted for long-term production, except one — the Midland Railway's 4-4-0 design of 1902.

Top: Aspinall, of the Lancashire & Yorkshire Railway, produced a series of sturdy and powerful 2-4-2 passenger tank engines, examples of which could be seen at work for over 70 years between 1889 and 1961. After the Grouping in 1923 quite a few went to the Midland Section, especially in the Leeds District. LMS No 10795 was built at Horwich in 1898 and withdrawn in 1959. Here it waits at Ilkley with a Skipton to Bradford train in 1946. *F. W. Smith*

Above: An example of Churchward's heavy freight engine: 2-8-0 No 2883, built at Swindon in 1919. The class had been introduced as far back as 1903 and they were highly successful and very powerful engines. *IAL*

Right: The mainstay of the Midland Railway's passenger services, a 4-4-0, No 406, seen here at Ilkley in 1946 with a Skipton to Bradford train in its final form dating from 1920, after several nominal rebuildings. It was in fact virtually a new engine, but classified as a rebuild for accountancy purposes. Its predecessor was originally built in 1892 by Sharp, Stewart & Co when Samuel Johnson was Locomotive Engineer. These small, Class 2P, engines were chosen as a standard class by the LMS and 136 were built after the Grouping. No 406 remained in service until 1951.
F. W. Smith/Transport Treasury

Right: A fine-looking Midland Railway Johnson 'Belpaire' 4-4-0 No 767 (original No 857) built in 1905 on a down express. It is coupled to No 761's tender. *IAL*

Below: The second of Samuel Johnson's 4-4-0 compounds, No 1001 (old 2632), heads a smart-looking set of carriages on a down express near Elstree. *IAL*

The Midland Railway's success might be thought all the more unusual, as it was the only compound locomotive designed by that company, whereas the NER and particularly the LNWR produced several designs. Samuel Johnson had been locomotive engineer of the Midland Railway since 1873, and had provided that company with a range of serviceable express passenger locomotives of the 4-4-0 wheel arrangement, many of which were rebuilt by his successors more than once. By 1900 he was already 69 years old and might have been expected to be contemplating retirement but he knew that the Midland Railway needed a more powerful express passenger locomotive for its hilly routes used by Anglo-Scottish and St Pancras-Manchester expresses, and for the increasing weight of passenger trains in general. He therefore produced his '2606' class of 4-4-0s with distinctive Belpaire boilers, always known as the 'Belpaires'. Over the next few years 80

Top: A brand new L&Y 'Dreadnought' four-cylinder 4-6-0 No 1662, seen in 1923 a few weeks after Grouping. It was renumbered 10433 by the LMS and was a handsome and powerful-looking machine, but the class was not the success that the L&Y had hoped for, and 10433, like most of the other members of the class, had a life of less than 20 years. One of the 'Dreadnoughts' took part in the Carlisle-Preston trials in 1924 but did not do well, being heavy on coal consumption. *IAL*

Left: The LMS standard compounds were fine-looking machines and a great favourite with Scottish drivers. Even the LNWR men finally began to like them when they had mastered the art of driving them, which required quite different skills from driving 'George the Fifths' etc. No 1169 is seen at the head of a lightweight Birmingham to Euston express in 1933, near Bletchley. *M. W. Earley*

were built, incorporating various modifications, and were renumbered 700 to 779 in the 1907 renumbering scheme.

But more was to come. Johnson was planning an even more powerful 4-4-0, and in 1902 it appeared — a compound. Initially, two were built, numbered 2631 and 2632, with two low-pressure outside cylinders and a single high-pressure cylinder between the frames. This arrangement was known as the 'Smith' system. W. M. Smith was an old 'Derby' man employed as chief draughtsman at Gateshead on the North Eastern Railway, and had been involved in the development of compounding.

Three more were built before Samuel Johnson retired in 1903, to be replaced by R. M. Deeley. Deeley obviously liked what he saw and built 40 more between 1905 and 1909, with changes to cab, splashers and running plate design. Their dimensions were the same, except for the boiler pressure, which was raised from 195psi to

220psi. The driving wheels were 7ft in diameter and tractive effort in the final form was 21,840lb. The class was numbered 1000-1044. The Johnson engines subsequently received the Deeley design changes, and these changes established a visual styling which lasted for many years. Deeley also introduced an ingenious type of regulator which provided live steam directly to all three cylinders on starting, but when the regulator was fully opened, the live steam supply to the outside cylinders was cut off, and they then received their steam from the inside cylinder. The Midland compounds could always be recognised audibly by their exhaust beat when starting. There was initially a strong beat with live steam being supplied to all three cylinders, but it changed to a noticeably softer beat when compounding took place as speed increased. All the compounds subsequently received superheated boilers, but it was a surprisingly leisurely process, starting in 1914 and

Darlington Works built 10 electric locomotives for the Shildon–Newport electrification just after the start of World War 1. LNER No 26510 rests in a siding at an unknown location.
F. W. Day

not being completed until 1928. The whole class of Midland compounds was very long-lived and survived World War 2, although they were withdrawn rapidly a few years later. No 1004, a Manningham (20E) favourite, could still be seen at work in 1951, and the last of the class was withdrawn in 1953.

To take the story forward, at the Grouping in 1923 the LMS railway was faced with the need to decide its locomotive policy, given the multiplicity of types it had acquired. The most pressing question concerned express passenger locomotives. None of the pre-Grouping types was an obvious winner, therefore trials were held to determine which of the existing types to adopt. Wasting no time, the first set of trials began on 10 December 1923, on the Settle-Carlisle line, and the following locomotives were used — a superheated Midland compound No 1008, a '990' class Midland 4-4-0 No 998, and an LNWR 'Prince of Wales' 4-6-0. The compound won hands down, but the LNW men cried 'foul', complaining that the compound was in tip-top condition, having just been outshopped, whereas their engine had run a fair mileage. A further series of trials was therefore carried out between 18 November and 10 December 1924, using both ex-Midland and LMS standard compounds, an LNW 'Claughton' 4-6-0 *Sir Francis Dent*, and a Caledonian 4-4-0. The LNW men cried 'foul' again, complaining that they had been given the worst engine at Edge Hill shed, whilst the Caledonian engine was clearly inadequate. The LMS standard compounds came out top, and large orders were placed for more of them.

However, George Hughes, the Chief Mechanical Engineer, was convinced that the compounds were not the ultimate answer to future requirements for main line express passenger haulage. Yet another set of tests was therefore

soon organised, this time between Carlisle and Preston, using a dynamometer car. The locomotives selected were a Hughes 4-6-0, a 'Prince of Wales' class 4-6-0 *Kestrel*, a 'Claughton' 4-6-0 and an LMS standard compound No 1065. Again the compound proved its superiority when measured by coal consumption per drawbar horsepower. The Hughes 4-6-0 did not do at all well in that respect. However, the end of the story was the hurried orders to the North British Locomotive Co for 50 'Royal Scots', which fortunately turned out to be winners from the first day. The compounds were clear winners on moderate loads on their own railway, but were thought to be not really suited to the sustained express running on the LNWR, although it might be mentioned that shortly before the LNER began non-stop running with the 'Flying Scotsman' between King's Cross and Edinburgh on 1 May 1928, the LMS stole its thunder a little by running non-stop between the two cities with compound No 1054 on a six-coach portion of the 'Royal Scot' on the preceding Friday. The Glasgow portion also ran non-stop behind one of the new 'Royal Scot' class locomotives, No 6113 *Cameronian*, with nine coaches.

Arguments will rage for ever on the validity of the trials, and there was undoubtedly a Midland bias, Midland men having taken over the key roles after Grouping, but there is no denying the excellence of the compounds on all but the heaviest loads and when driven efficiently. The LNW men naturally hated them. They thrashed their engines whenever necessary, but compounds had to be handled intelligently. The compounds performed well enough on the Birmingham-Euston two-hour expresses, but it was in Scotland that the compounds really came into their own. Drivers there loved them. Perhaps the last word should belong to Roland Bond, who was actually present at the trials. In his book *A Lifetime with Locomotives*, he states that the tests established beyond question the economic superiority of the compounds over all other contenders, even when hauling and keeping time with loads a good deal heavier than the normal permitted maxima.

The compounds eventually numbered 240. Nos 900 to 939 were built in 1927 by the Vulcan Foundry (except for the last few which were built later). Nos 1000 to 1044 were built by the Midland Railway, and Nos 1045 to 1199 were built between 1924 and 1927 at Derby and Horwich, and by contractors Vulcan Foundry and the North British Locomotive Co. Massive withdrawals took place during the second half of the 1950s, the last one being withdrawn in 1960. They were very handsome engines.

The Shildon-Newport electrification (North Eastern Railway)

In 1910 Vincent Raven became Chief Mechanical Engineer of the North Eastern Railway, and the following year the General Manager, Sir Alexander Kaye Butterworth, appointed Messrs Merz & MacLellan as consulting engineers to report on railway electrification. Raven and Merz visited the USA to see main line electrification at first hand, and the outcome was a decision by the NER board to embark upon a pilot scheme. The Shildon to Newport route was chosen for evaluation because it was reasonably self-contained, was mainly a freight route, and carried a heavy, stable traffic of coal to the large Newport marshalling yards, near Middlesbrough.

Infrastructure work started on 16 June 1913. It was decided to adopt the high tension dc system at 1,500 volts, with power being transmitted to the locomotives through overhead contact wires. The contractors were Siemens-Schuckert, but due to the outbreak of war in 1914 they were obliged to withdraw, and the contract was taken over by the British Insulated Helsby Cable Company. Some delay ensued, but by 1 July 1915 it was possible to achieve a partial introduction of electric operation. Full operation began on 10 January 1916 of Britain's first main line electrification — a milestone.

A fleet of 10 electric locomotives was designed and built at the company's works at Darlington North Road, with electrical equipment being supplied and fitted by Siemens Bros Dynamo Works Ltd, Stafford. The locomotives had two separate electric motive power units, one at each end, with the cab in between, and power was provided by four electric motors of 275hp each. The locomotives weighed 74 tons and were of the 0-4-4-0 wheel arrangement. The designed load was 1,400 tons at 25mph on level track.

The trade recession and resultant slump which followed the end of World War 1 seriously affected the railways of southwest Durham and Teesside. The traffic levels of 1913 on which the economics of the scheme were based were never realised after the war, and dropped alarmingly by 1930. An investigation in 1933 indicated that savings could be made by reverting to steam operation, and electric operation ceased on 31 December 1934. Direct train working from collieries to steelworks and other industrial users reduced the use of marshalling yards, and Shildon yard closed a few days later. A bold but initially justified experiment had come to an end, the victim of changed circumstances arising from the war.

Superheating

Until early in the 20th century, all steam locomotives in Britain used what became known as 'saturated' steam, in which the steam raised in the boiler is taken directly to the cylinders to propel the engine. Saturated steam contains moisture, and has a tendency to condense when in contact with cooler surfaces on its journey from the boiler to the cylinders, thus producing small droplets of water.

Experiments in Germany to raise the temperature of the steam above that which is possible with saturated steam were carried out on Prussian Railways by Wilhelm Schmidt, and in 1896 he equipped a number of locomotives with an early form of superheating. These experiments led him to design a boiler with tubes lying within the normal boiler flue tubes. Saturated steam was passed through these extra tubes, which had the effect of raising it to a higher temperature and converting the steam almost into a gas.

This had two advantages — first, superheated

Churchward was one of the first British locomotive engineers to fit his engines with superheaters, and they became standard equipment from 1913. GWR 'Star' class No 4053 *Princess Alexandra*, built at Swindon in 1914, heads an express in BR days, looking every inch a champion. *IAL*

An ex-LMS mixed traffic 4-6-0 No 45495 takes water at Lea Road troughs with a Manchester–Blackpool relief express on 24 July 1965. *Ron Fisher*

steam was found to have greater expansive properties than saturated steam, leading to power increases of up to 25%; and second, the condensation problem was reduced, or even avoided altogether. There were some initial problems with carbonisation of cylinder lubricants, until improved lubricants were devised.

Two of Britain's most progressive locomotive engineers recognised the potential of superheating — Churchward, of the Great Western Railway, and George Hughes, of the Lancashire & Yorkshire Railway. Churchward began experimenting with the Schmidt superheater in 1906 by fitting it to one of the new 'Saint' class 4-6-0s, and whilst it was a success as a superheater, it had disadvantages with both lubrication and increased maintenance. After further trials, Churchward designed his own superheater, and by 1909 he had produced a standard version, employing low-degree superheat to overcome the disadvantages already mentioned. George Hughes, who had become Chief Mechanical Engineer of the L&YR in 1904, rebuilt four of Aspinall's 7ft 3in 4-4-0s with piston valves, forced feed lubrication for cylinders and steam chests, and Schmidt superheaters. Although there were initial problems, the work of these modified locomotives was recorded as 'little short of marvellous'. He also applied superheating to 20 locomotives of the final series of 2-4-2 tank engines in 1911 and to a large number of 0-8-0 heavy freight engines in 1912.

After these early developments, superheating soon became standard practice to all new builds of locomotives on all railways, resulting in improved performance and lower coal consumption.

The provision of water troughs

In the 20th century, water troughs were a common sight on most long-distance main lines, enabling water to be taken into the tender without the necessity of stopping the train at a water column. The troughs became necessary as longer non-stop journeys became a commercial requirement.

The first water troughs, several hundred yards long, were laid in the 'four-foot' between the rails on the North Wales main line of the London & North Western Railway in 1860, under the direction of John Ramsbottom, the Locomotive Superintendent. In order to replenish the water in the tender, the fireman had to lower a scoop into the trough. The speed of the train then forced the water up a pipe into the tender tank. A lineside sign indicated the start of the troughs, so that the fireman knew exactly where to lower the scoop. He then had to stand by to raise the scoop, before the tank overflowed and deluged the front coaches. Regular travellers knew where the troughs were and took care to close the windows in good time.

The troughs were fed from a lineside tank, and in hard water areas the water was specially softened before being fed into the tank. The highest troughs in the country were between Dent and Garsdale, on the Midland Railway, at a height of over 1,000ft — and one of the few places on the Settle-Carlisle line where there is a sufficiently long, level stretch. They were a quarter of a mile in length, and laid down on both lines in 1907. The water was taken off the fells and did not need softening. At one time the troughs were steam-heated against freezing, but the frequent passage of trains was generally sufficient to prevent other than thin, surface freezing.

Millstones — Locomotives

Francis Webb's express passenger compound locomotives

Francis William Webb was born in 1836 and joined the London & North Western Railway in 1851 as an apprentice to Francis Trevithick, the Locomotive Superintendent at Crewe Works. He was to spend almost all his working life at Crewe and rose through the various stages to become Chief Mechanical Engineer in 1871. He spent the next few years equipping the LNWR with a large fleet of cheap, efficient, simple and sturdy machines which were typical of the era and very long-lived, including 0-6-0 freight engines, 2-4-0 passenger engines, 2-4-2 passenger tank engines and 0-6-2 tank engines primarily for coal traffic. All told there were 1,400 of these engines, an early example of standardisation. He also modernised the very extensive Crewe Works.

He then began to develop an interest in compounding and produced a whole series of designs, starting in 1882, most of which were not generally regarded as successful, nor did they improve as each new design appeared. There are many contemporary accounts to this effect. The various batches were:

1882 — The 'Experiments', 2-4-0 passenger engines, of which 30 were built between 1882 and 1884. They had two outside cylinders and one low-pressure inside cylinder, and 6ft 7$\frac{1}{2}$in diameter driving wheels. Ahrons, a contemporary reporter, wrote that 'The high pressure engine would slip and choke the receiver without moving the locomotive, and if the ports of the low-pressure cylinder were not open the engine would not start at all.' Men with pinchbars gave the trains a start. Rous-Marten, another contemporary and an expert on the subject, described the 'Experiments' as being 'hopelessly sluggish, and deficient in speed'. They were generally regarded as unsuccessful, being bad starters and uneconomical, and were quickly scrapped when George Whale succeeded Webb in 1903.

1884 — The 'Dreadnought' class of three-cylinder 2-4-0 compounds was introduced. They were generally similar to the 'Experiments' but the driving wheels were reduced to 6ft 3in in diameter and boiler pressure was increased from 150psi to 175psi. Ahrons said that 'those who had to handle them inwardly seethed during such periods as had not to be devoted to official enthusiasm'. Occasionally they would produce a good performance, but frequently they were mediocre and sometimes very bad. 40 were built

between 1884 and 1888. They too were quickly scrapped by George Whale.

1889 — The 'Teutonics' were introduced: three-cylinder 2-4-0 engines with 7ft 1in diameter driving wheels. Only 10 were built (1889/90), which is a pity as they were regarded as being head and shoulders above the rest. The renowned *Jeannie Deans* worked the 2.0pm Scotch express from Euston to Crewe daily from 1890 to 1899 and almost always kept time. *Adriatic* averaged over 64mph from Euston to Crewe with a 70-ton train during the Aberdeen Races in 1895. *Ionic* made a non-stop run from Euston to Carlisle the same year at 51mph with a 150-ton train. It must have seemed that Webb had finally perfected his compound designs.

1891 — The 'Greater Britains' appeared, of which 10 were built between 1891 and 1894 in a 2-2-2-2 wheel arrangement. As usual there were two high-pressure outside cylinders and one low-pressure inside cylinder, and they might be regarded as enlarged 'Teutonics'. They put up some very good performances, but unfortunately they were a very small class.

Top: One of Francis Webb's first class of compounds, the 'Experiments', dating from 1882, stands on the turntable. This one is No 315 *Alaska*. *IAL*

Above: The 'Teutonics' date from 1889 and were among the most successful of Webb's 2-4-0 compounds. No 1306 *Ionic* poses for the camera. This is the locomotive which made an historic non-stop run at 51mph average speed from Euston to Carlisle on 8 September 1895 during the famous races to Aberdeen. *IAL*

1894 — 10 members of the 'John Hick' class, with a 2-2-2-2 wheel arrangement, appeared between 1894 and 1898. They had been built for the Crewe-Carlisle section and had 6ft 3in diameter driving wheels, but were poor performers and were generally regarded as Webb's worst locomotives.

1897 — Webb now produced a larger express passenger engine, the 4-4-0 'Jubilee' class of four-cylinder 4-4-0 compounds. 40 were built between 1897 and 1900. They were regarded on the whole as erratic and unreliable. They could pull well uphill but were sluggish on the level and had to be piloted even with comparatively light loads. Then, in 1901-03 Webb built 40 of a similar type, the 'Alfred the Great' class. Their performance was also regarded as unsatisfactory, and a rule was issued that they must be piloted for loads over 270 tons. However, in 1903, the year in which Webb retired, the 'Alfreds' were converted to 'Benbows' with modified valve gear, which improved them considerably. In the same year, Webb's successor, George Whale, began wholesale scrapping of the three-cylinder compounds.

It is significant that Webb, as one of the longest-serving CMEs ever, and of the greatest and proudest railway in Britain, the LNWR, was never knighted. Perhaps he was just too autocratic and made too many enemies in high places on the LNWR. His reputation inevitably has been blighted by his persistence with compounds, but he equipped the LNWR with a huge fleet of small engines which were perfectly satisfactory and cheap. Even as late as 1902 his 'Jumbos' (non-compound) 2-4-0s (the 'Precedents') undertook the lion's share of express work, especially north of Crewe. When double-heading occurred, it was said that not even a 'Jumbo' could hurry up a four-cylinder compound. Fortunately for the LNWR, they had a very large stock of 'Jumbos'.

Perhaps his greatest legacy was Crewe Works, which he had made modern and efficient. His successor, George Whale, gave short shrift to Webb's compounds, rebuilding the 4-4-0s as simple two-cylinder engines. Their power was enhanced, maintenance costs were reduced, and high speeds were attained. It will remain a mystery as to why Francis Webb continued building compounds with such zeal, but seemed not to learn the lessons from those classes which were successful. Was it partly because no one dared to contradict him and point out where improvements could be made?

Webb was a member of a powerful team at the head of LNWR affairs for many years, the other members being Sir Richard Moon, chairman from 1861 to 1891, Sir George Findlay, General Manager from 1880 to 1893, and the redoubtable George Potter Neele, Superintendent of the Line from 1862 to 1895. If the three of them had still been in harness after 1891, might they have curbed Francis Webb's enthusiasm for compounds before he

Right: The 'Alfred the Great' class of four-cylinder compounds with a 4-4-0 wheel arrangement was introduced in 1901. Their dimensions were the same as the 'Jubilees', except for a slight increase in heating surface, but they were no more successful than the 'Jubilees' until they received modified valve gear in 1903. Modified engines became known as the 'Benbow' class. No 1973 *Hood* stands at the head of an express in Euston No 14 platform. It did not survive long enough to receive an LMS number. *H. Gordon Tidey*

Below right: In 1904 Webb's successor, George Whale, introduced his 'Precursor' Class of 4-4-0 two-cylinder engines, of which 130 were built in four years. They were simple and reliable, but rather heavy on coal. No 622 *Euphrates* seen here was part of the first batch in 1904 and was withdrawn in 1927. *IAL*

Bottom right: Webb's zeal for compounding was not confined to passenger engines, for in 1892 Crewe Works produced the first of a long line of heavy goods engines with an 0-8-0 wheel arrangement. They were three-cylinder engines, and 111 were built up to 1900. George Whale converted them to simples. A four-cylinder example hauls a long up goods train. *H. Gordon Tidey*

went on to build some of the least successful — the 'John Hicks', the 'Jubilee' 4-4-0s and the 'Alfred the Great' 4-4-0s?

During 1942/43 there was a very interesting debate in the monthly periodical *The Railway Magazine* about the compounds, particular in the articles written each month by Cecil J. Allen in his celebrated and exceptionally long-lived series 'British Locomotive Practice and Performance'. The general consensus appeared to be that whilst some compounds would produce excellent performances in the right hands, this did not reflect the general standard. The LNWR consistently worked its engines far harder than other companies, and the 'Precedent' 2-4-0s often had to take over trains which were much too heavy for them, due to frequent failures of compounds. LNWR express passenger locomotives were never really big enough for the work they had to do, so they had to be 'thrashed', or double-headed with reluctance. The Midland also had a small engine policy, but they happily double-headed. That was the difference. A knowledgeable contributor, T. Lovatt Williams, considered that the 'Benbows' did good work with moderate loads all over the system, but that their steaming was extremely erratic. He felt that Webb gained nothing from his 4-4-0 compounds and would have been better with a simple, straightforward 4-4-0 design.

Like many other locomotive engineers, Francis Webb was always striving for the more economical and efficient use of steam through compounding, but success largely eluded him

and it appears to have become an obsession. Nonetheless, he provided the LNWR with a whole range of sturdy, simple machines. It is also significant that several young men became his pupils and went on to achieve eminence in locomotive engineering.

The London & North Western Railway 'Claughton' Class 4-6-0s

C. J. Bowen Cooke became Chief Mechanical Engineer of the LNWR in 1909, when he succeeded George Whale. Bowen Cooke, who was born in 1859, trained at Crewe under Francis Webb, like many other locomotive engineers, and became Southern Area Running Superintendent. By the time he came to Crewe, it was obvious that the LNWR needed more powerful engines, and he quickly introduced the renowned 'George the Fifth' class 4-4-0s, of which 90 were built between 1910 and 1915. Apart from 10 of the first batch, the whole class was built with superheaters, and the engines were a great success. In typical LNWR style, they could be worked very

hard and pull big loads, and they rapidly displaced George Whale's 'Experiment' class 4-6-0s. However, with a tractive effort of only 20,639lb, it was evident that a more powerful locomotive was needed.

This appeared in 1913, a superheated four-cylinder 4-6-0 of very handsome appearance. Its cylinders were 16in x 26in, boiler pressure 175psi and tractive effort 23,683lb. The class became known as 'Claughtons' after the name of the first one *Sir Gilbert Claughton,* LNWR No 2222, later London, Midland & Scottish Railway No 5900. 130 were built between 1913 and 1921 (70 of them in 1920/1). It was soon realised that the boiler was inadequate to supply four cylinders of such size, and the cylinder diameter was reduced to 15$\frac{1}{2}$in. This did not completely solve the problem, but first World War 1 and then the grouping in 1923, by which time H. P. M. Beames had succeeded Bowen Cooke on his early death, possibly prevented the necessary attention being given to improving the performance of the 'Claughtons'.

The question has to be asked as to why Bowen Cooke failed to provide a boiler of adequate size. He is reported to have said in an interview with Chas S. Lake, a technical writer for the *Railway Gazette,* that he had to keep down the weight of the engine to meet the civil engineer's requirements in respect of one of the old London & Birmingham bridges at Camden. However, it was also suggested that the size of the boiler had been determined by the decision to use the forming blocks already in existence, rather than make new blocks for bending the boiler plates. In view of the legendary parsimony of the LNWR, that could well be the explanation. But would a larger boiler have made the 'Claughtons' much more successful? Later experience when 20 of the class were reboilered did not appear to provide grounds for such optimism.

After the Grouping in 1923, George Hughes

Above: 'Claughton' class 4-6-0 No 42 *Princess Louise* had the distinction of being the last of the class, as LMS No 6004, surviving until 1949. It had been rebuilt with a larger boiler in 1928, and is seen opposite at Willesden shed in 1939. Almost all the others had been withdrawn in the 1930s
F. R. Hebron/J. P. Wilson

Left: Large-boilered 'Claughton' No 5962 waits for the right-away at Birmingham New Street in 1929. It was withdrawn in 1935 after a life of only 15 years. *A. Flowers*

Below left: 'Claughton' No 5971 (LNW No 2511 *Croxteth*) is also a noteworthy engine. It was nominally converted to be the first member of the 'Patriot' class in 1930, but it was actually scrapped and only a few parts were used for the new engine, which became LMS 5500 in 1934. Incidentally, *Croxteth's* early demise was caused by severe damage resulting from a head-on collision in Waste Bank tunnel, on the Settle-Carlisle line, on 6 March 1930. It was hauling a local passenger train from Hellifield to Carlisle. The metamorphosed 'Claughton' No 5971 became 'Patriot' class No 5971, and is seen at Nottingham Midland. It has provision for a name, but is unnamed in this photograph.
J. N. Hall/
Rail Archive Stephenson

of the Lancashire & Yorkshire Railway became CME of the newly formed London, Midland & Scottish Railway. There was some tinkering with two of the 'Claughtons', but they were replaced on front rank duties by the hurriedly built 'Royal Scot' 4-6-0s in 1927. Fortunately the 'Royal Scots' were a great success, and at long last the West Coast main line had an engine that was completely master of the job when working heavy expresses. However, there were still 130 'Claughtons' and in 1928, under Beames' supervision, 20 of them were rebuilt with larger boilers of 200psi. Ten had Caprotti valve gear and ten had conventional Walschaert's. Some of the surplus unrebuilt 'Claughtons' were sent to the Midland Division, where for a while they worked the Anglo-Scottish expresses.

In 1930 a decisive step was taken to deal, at least partly, with the problem of the less than wholly satisfactory 'Claughtons'. Between 1930 and 1933, 42 were scrapped and replaced by the same number of engines of a new class, the 'Patriots'. The 'Claughtons' were officially 'rebuilt', and the new 'Patriots' took the names and numbers of withdrawn 'Claughtons', but little material was reused. The 'Patriots' were really scaled down versions of the 'Royal Scots', and were very successful. When William Stanier came to the LMS, he very rapidly scrapped the remaining 'Claughtons', the last unrebuilt engine being withdrawn in November 1935. The large-boilered engines soon followed to the scrapheap, but the last one, No 6004, was saved by World War 2, to afford another generation of trainspotters a view of a handsome failure.

The Midland Railway's small engine policy

For its passenger expresses, the Midland relied on a fleet of 45 compound 4-4-0s, with a tractive effort of 21,840lb, and, whilst they were excellent, they had to undertake a lot of hard

Above: The Great Central built a whole range of 4-6-0s from 1902 onwards. No 1169 *Lord Faringdon,* built in 1917, became LNER Class B3 No 6169. They were four-cylinder handsome-looking machines. *IAL*

Left: In 1907 Deeley built 10 very fine 4-4-0s of the '990' class for the Leeds–Carlisle section. They were contemporary with the compounds but were all withdrawn after about 20 years' life as they were a non-standard class. *IAL*

Below left:
Built in the 1860s by Matthew Kirtley, a Midland Railway double-framed 0-6-0 carries its post-1907 No 2462. There were over 500 of these engines. *IAL*

Right: In many ways the Midland Class 3F 0-6-0s were the mainstay of its freight business. There were nearly 500 of them, dating from 1885, and most of them survived to be taken over by BR in 1948 after various rebuildings. They were still to be seen in the 1960s and were very sturdy and serviceable machines, quite at home on local passenger trains. No 3260 stands ready for departure at Bournemouth West with the 3.30pm for Templecombe on 29 June 1946. *G. O. P. Pearce*

Above: The largest of the Midland's freight engines, the Class 4F 0-6-0s, did not appear in volume production until 1917, but ultimately the class numbered 192 engines. No 3989, built at Derby just before the Grouping, heads a mixed freight. Undated, but probably late 1920s. *IAL*

work on the Anglo-Scottish expresses and over the Peak to Manchester. Although they were at least the equal of any other company's 'Atlantic' 4-4-2s, several companies had begun to build larger and more powerful locomotives of the 4-6-0 wheel arrangement, among them principally the Great Western with its 'Star' class, the Great Central with a whole series of engines, the LNWR 'Claughtons', the L&Y Hughes 'Dreadnoughts' and the North Eastern Raven's 4-6-0s. Not all these designs were as successful as the compounds, but they were potentially stronger. There were no other Midland engines in power class 4P except the 10 of the '990' class 4-4-0s, and reliance had then to be placed on the 'Belpaire' 4-4-0 simple engines in power class 3P, which dated back to 1901.

Matters were even worse on the freight side.

The Midland had a very heavy coal traffic from the Yorkshire and Midlands coalfields, some of which travelled very long distances, northwards to Leeds and beyond, northwestwards to Manchester and beyond, southwestwards to Bristol and southwards to London. For these heavy flows of traffic, the Midland had nothing more powerful than the Class 4F 0-6-0s, of which only two were built before World War 1. Work did not start on the remainder of the class until 1917, therefore for all but six years during the Midland's separate existence, the company had nothing larger than a motley collection of Class 2F and 3F 0-6-0s of varying vintage, some of them extremely elderly. Expensive double-heading was, inevitably, rife.

Other companies had been building large fleets of heavy freight engines since the beginning of the century. Again, the Great Western led the field in 1903 with its powerful and long-lived '28XX' class 2-8-0s. Robinson, on the Great Central had also begun to build 2-8-0s, starting in 1911. These became LNER Class O4. Gresley, on the Great Northern, followed suit in 1913 with the (LNER) 'O1' class. Other companies standardised on 0-8-0s, the North Eastern in 1901 and the LYR also in 1901.

The reason for the persistence with which the Midland pursued its small-engine policy, for both passenger and freight trains (the only large company to do so), remains a mystery, although the Midland paid good dividends. But in view of its favourable location in the middle of huge coalfields, it might have been expected to have paid even higher dividends. Perhaps it spent too much acquiring small companies, such as the Northern Counties Committee in Northern Ireland and the London, Tilbury & Southend, when it ought to have been modernising and upgrading its locomotive stock.

The Midland's policy was a rod only for its own back, but the matter became serious after the Grouping in 1923 when the policy was inflicted on the whole of the LMS.

Whilst the Midland had no freight engines larger than the Class 4F 0-6-0s, other companies had been building more powerful machines for many years. As we have seen earlier, Churchward introduced his excellent '28XX' class of very powerful 2-8-0s in 1903. No 2813 stands on shed at Severn Tunnel Junction. *IAL*

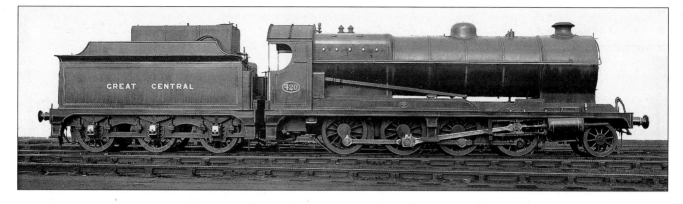

This page: The North Eastern Railway had used 0-8-0s since 1901, when they were introduced by W. Worsdell (LNER Class Q5), and were developed by Vincent Raven in his Classes Q6 and Q7. The North Eastern never had any 2-8-0s. Robinson, on the Great Central, introduced 0-8-0s in 1902 and went on to build 2-8-0s in 1911. Gresley on the Great Northern, introduced 2-8-0s in 1913 and the Lancashire & Yorkshire Railway had been using 0-8-0s since 1901, when Aspinall was CME. In this series of four photographs ex-GCR Class 8M 2-8-0 No 420 (LNER Class O5) poses for its photograph on 26 April 1919 (*Modern Transport*); a Gresley Class O2/3 2-8-0, No 63973, heads a southbound freight near Retford in BR Days (*J. Davenport*); NER Class Q6 0-8-0 No 3456 waits at York for its next working on 29 July 1947 (*G. C. B. Herbert*); and an L&Y 0-8-0, No 12721, built in 1902, hauls a long rake of apparently identical wagons. *IAL*

Passenger rolling stock

Chapter 2

Introduction

When trains replaced stagecoaches, the vehicles provided for the carriage of passengers on the railway had no form of heating; indeed it is quite possible that the question never arose. Stagecoaches had no heating and passengers were accustomed to 'wrapping up well' in cold weather. Third Class passengers fared even worse — they had to travel in open vehicles with no roofs, rather like the 'outside' passengers of stagecoaches.

As the decades passed after 1830, coach construction gradually improved and passenger vehicles became totally enclosed. This at least had the advantage of keeping out most of the draughts, but little or nothing was done for 50 years to provide passengers with some degree of heating, which might actually be regarded as a millstone. It certainly did nothing to make train travel in winter a pleasure. Passengers had to rely on footwarmers containing hot water, at first available only in the First Class. They could be obtained at stations and it is reported that as late as 1905 the Midland Railway had a stock of 27,000.

The early trains had no lighting, but eventually a form of illumination was provided by rape-oil roof lights, known as stink pots. All that can be said about them was that it was better than nothing, but not much.

Lavatory accommodation was unknown for many years, and passengers on long distance journeys had to avail themselves of facilities at those stations where the train stopped for several minutes.

Dining cars, sleeping cars, corridors were for the future. From 1825, for the next half century, little was done to provide passengers, even in the First Class, with what 20th century passengers would regard as essentials, and long distance train journeys were to be endured rather than enjoyed, except perhaps on warm summer days. It might have been expected that competition between companies for traffic between the same pair of towns might have been a spur to the provision of better facilities in order to attract passengers from the rival route, but nothing happened.

The Midland Railway was the first company to unleash what was almost a revolution in the provision of better facilities, and it had its genesis in North America.

The Pullman revolution

James Allport, general manager of the Midland Railway, was unhappy with the poor facilities and wretched accommodation provided for Third Class passengers on all railways, and he set out on the road to reform. In 1872 he undertook an extensive tour of North America, travelling thousands of miles in the parlour and sleeping cars which George M. Pullman had built in large numbers after the American Civil War.

Passengers on the Midland Railway must have been astonished when they first saw this Pullman coach in 1874. They would have been even more astonished, and no doubt delighted, to discover that it provided lavatories and heating, unknown on Britain's railways at that time. Despite those amenities, these day coaches (drawing room cars) were not popular because they had open accommodation, American style, rather than compartments. However, the First Class Pullmans and sleeping cars were immediately popular. *British Railways*

He could not fail to be impressed, even though Pullman's cars had been designed to cater for journeys which might last for two or three days, or even longer. On his return to England, he persuaded the Midland Board to receive George Pullman, and to allow him to make a presentation to the Midland shareholders at the half-yearly meeting. Pullman undertook to design and build a number of sleeping cars, parlour cars and day coaches and to operate them at his own risk on the Midland Railway. On 25 January 1874 — a milestone — the Pullman sleeping car *Midland* made its appearance, having been shipped from the USA in parts and assembled at Derby. It was nearly 60ft long and of typical American appearance, with open canopied platforms at each end. It contained 24 sleeping berths in an upper and lower berth arrangement, had much improved lighting and was warmed by an oil-fired hot water heater. It was nothing short of a revolution. More vehicles were built, including parlour cars, and all Pullman cars had lavatories.

On 1 June, the Midland ran a special express from St Pancras to Bradford Forster Square, composed of two First Class Pullmans and three American day coaches for Second and Third Class passengers. All passengers had access to lavatories, and heating was available throughout the train. Unfortunately the day coaches, of completely open saloon accommodation rather than in compartments, did not find favour with passengers, but the First Class Pullmans and sleepers were at once popular, and were used on services between St Pancras and Liverpool and the West Riding. The morning service left Bradford at 8.30am and arrived in London at 2.5pm, returning from St Pancras as a sleeping car service at midnight. When the Settle-Carlisle

line opened to passengers in May 1876, a Pullman service was introduced between St Pancras and Glasgow.

The Pullmans were taken into Midland stock in 1888, and at the end of the century the Midland ordered some new carriages from America, which were erected at Derby. They remained in service until after World War 1. The Pullman bodies then gave many more years' service as staff mess rooms and store rooms in yards and sidings, and were a common sight.

Heating

It may seem astonishing now to recall that for half a century or more passengers had no other form of heating than portable foot-warmers, which were basically flat, metal containers full of hot water. Long winter journeys must have been an ordeal, with no respite from the cold until the next station at which a new foot-warmer could be obtained. How passengers must have crowded round them to thaw out their frozen hands and feet.

Towards the end of the century, a number of systems were being developed, which were eventually standardised using a system of low-pressure steam heating, fed from the engine through pipes along the length of the train to radiators underneath the seats. This was a real blessing to passengers, and can properly be regarded as a milestone in the development of improvements in passenger comfort. The system was introduced in the St Pancras to Manchester expresses of the Midland Railway in 1897, but five years earlier the Great Western had provided steam heating (and lavatory accommodation) for all three classes on a new corridor service — the 1.30pm from Paddington to Birkenhead. By 1898 the old-fashioned 'hot water cans' were being rapidly superseded on the GWR by steam heating. The East Coast companies introduced steam heating in 1895.

Lighting

Mention has already been made of the smoky, stinking oil pots which were placed in the roofs of carriages by a man walking along the roof. The degree of illumination provided was perhaps better than nothing, but not by a great deal. The Pullman cars introduced by the Midland Railway (see above) had Argand burners using kerosene, which was quite effective, but by then a German inventor and engineer, Julius Pintsch, had developed a system of gas lighting, fed from pressurised oil gas stored in tanks under the floor.

Carl Friedrich Julius Pintsch was born in Berlin in 1815 and saw the first gas lamps installed in Berlin in 1826. He established a business in Berlin in 1843 manufacturing oil lamps and lanterns, and went on to develop the oil gas, produced from purified naphtha, which bears his name. It was soon installed on some German railways, and Pintsch established a business in the USA, after which his lighting system was widely used there.

G. P. Neele records in his 'Railway Reminiscences' that Pintsch visited the LNWR in 1879 to describe his system of oil-gas lighting for railway carriages. It was recognised to be a vast improvement on the existing oil roof-lamps 'which were too often badly trimmed and reduced at the end of a journey to a mere speck of light'. Pintsch's plan appeared to provide what was required, but Francis Webb, the CME, already had a scheme in hand with a Mr Pope. It was a very similar system and was adopted by the LNWR, which never believed in outsourcing its needs if they could possibly be met in-house. However, the other companies were quick to adopt Pintsch's method in the 1870s. By 1882 the GWR had begun to replace the rape-oil roof lamps. The gas burners initially had fish-tail jets, but the incandescent mantle later invented gave the system a new lease of life.

Unfortunately, the natural propensity of the gas to either directly cause, or subsequently add to, the conflagration which sometimes followed a serious accident, especially those on the Midland Railway at Hawes Junction (1910) and Ais Gill (1913), brought gas lighting into a certain degree of disrepute. Electric lighting had been available since the 1890s and was generally adopted later in new builds. By 1913 there were 12,000 electrically-lit carriages in service, but there were still over 40,000 gas-lit carriages and gas lighting continued in use for many years, despite pressure from the Board of Trade

Inspectors to speed up the process of conversion to electricity. Even by the time of the Charfield accident in 1928, in which gas-lit vehicles were involved in the subsequent fire, half of the carriages on the LMS had gas lighting, whilst the figure for the GWR was two-thirds.

Lavatory accommodation

Only elderly readers will remember certain anxieties which were felt when being required to travel in non-lavatory accommodation on journeys lasting some hours. The trains concerned were usually excursion trains or holiday reliefs, but in the 19th century, at least until the 1870s, it was the normal practice. Lavatory accommodation was not provided, and opportunity had to be taken to visit the lavatory at those stations where dining stops of 20 minutes or so were made. The larger stations, and important junctions, had commodious suites of toilets for that purpose.

Not a great deal has been written about this somewhat delicate topic, but Ackworth in his 'Railways of England' (1889) records that the North Western standard 42ft tri-composite eight-wheeler carriage had two First Class compartments with lavatories between them. However, the LNWR's largesse did not extend to Second and Third Class passengers. The Great Western had been providing lavatories on a few trains for First Class passengers since 1884 as had the Midland on its Pullman services since the 1870s, and this was probably *the* milestone, although both East Coast and West Coast companies had been providing a measure of lavatory accommodation in their sleeping cars (First Class only, of course). The tri-composites of the LSWR in 1898 had lavatories for each class, but the fact that the standard provision of lavatory accommodation for all three classes in Britain's longer-distance trains did not occur until the 20th century might be considered a serious millstone.

Dining facilities on trains

The essentials for a comfortable journey, apart from the track and the riding of the carriage, are lighting (during darkness and through tunnels), heating (in cold weather), and lavatory accommodation (on long journeys). Eating and sleeping are non-essentials. They just happen to increase the pleasure of the journey.

The first train to run regularly in Britain conveying a dining car is said to be a Leeds–King's Cross service of the Great Northern Railway, which commenced to run on 26 September 1879. It was First Class only and a milestone, setting an example for what was to follow, when

The luxurious interior of a Midland dining car, designed by David Bain.
British Railways

the provision of dining cars for both (or all three) classes of passenger eventually became a regular practice on long-distance expresses. Ackworth reports that in 1899 'hardly an express leaves or arrives at Euston without breakfast or luncheon or dining cars attached', but the LNWR had started to provide six-wheeled dining cars on its Euston to Manchester and Liverpool trains in 1889. In 1891, luncheon and dining car were provided on the 2.0pm 'Corridor'. The Great Western had begun to provide dining cars in May 1896, when they were attached to two trains between Paddington and Bristol, and Cardiff. They were First Class only, but by 1903 dining facilities were being provided for all three classes. The Midland provided sumptuous dining cars in its St Pancras to Manchester trains in 1897, whilst the LSWR began to provide them in 1901. A luncheon car was introduced into the 'Flying Scotsman' in 1900, which allowed the York stop to be reduced from 20 minutes to 10 minutes.

The provision of dining cars was not done by the companies out of consideration for the well-

being or comfort of their passengers, but because it allowed the lengthy station stops at places such as York, Swindon, Wolverton, Preston and Normanton to be reduced (or abolished altogether). And it was only practicable when there was sufficient lavatory accommodation on trains. The imperatives of competition prompted the provision of dining cars where there were competing routes. A warm, comfortable dining car was an important inducement to travel on that company's trains. The reluctance of some companies to provide them earlier stemmed from the increase in train weight which resulted, and taken together with the provision of lavatory accommodation, and heavier, more comfortable carriages, often with corridors, necessitated the provision of more powerful engines. It also reduced the seating capacity of trains.

As an alternative to eating in the dining car, passengers could avail themselves of luncheon baskets which were widely available at major stations. They are thought to have been first provided at Chester in March 1876 for the Irish

Mail trains, priced at 5s (25p) and 2s 6d (12^{1}/$_{2}$p). In January 1878 they began to be available at Perth for the Scotch expresses. Luncheon baskets provided a very good meal and at some places both hot and cold fare was available. In 1903 the Midland was advertising luncheon baskets at its major stations and junctions for 2s 9d (approx 14p). For an extra sixpence (2^{1}/$_{2}$p) you could have half a bottle of wine. Cutlery, crockery, condiments, corkscrew and napkins were included.

Sleeping cars
Half a century after the Stockton & Darlington Railway opened, the railway companies began to turn their minds to improving the lot of the luckless passenger on an unheated overnight long distance express train. The Midland Railway was one of the first to do so, with the introduction of Pullman car sleeper services in 1875 and 1876. The contrast in the levels of passenger comfort which resulted, compared with what had gone before, can only be imagined, yet other companies were slow to follow suit.

The Great Western made a half-hearted effort in December 1877 when it introduced two six-wheeled sleeping cars on its Paddington-Plymouth services. One car had a dormitory with seven beds for gentlemen and the other car had four beds for ladies. Lavatory accommodation was provided. However, the dormitory arrangement was unpopular; therefore the GWR built some eight-wheeled sleeping cars in 1881 which had a side corridor giving access to dou-

ble berth compartments and lavatories. The LNWR followed suit in 1883 when it began to run 42ft long 'corridor sleeping saloons' by the night train between Euston and Glasgow Central. They were specially designed to ensure comfort and privacy, the saloons being supplied with hot water and heating. Lavatory accommodation was provided, and an attendant accompanied the vehicle throughout the journey. They were First Class only.

The sleeping car services proved very popular, and by the end of the 19th century, sleeping cars were provided not only on the Anglo-Scottish services but also between London and provincial cities in England.

The abolition of Second Class
Paintings depicting passenger trains on the Liverpool & Manchester Railway, opened in 1830, show trains of all three classes. First Class coaches are closely modelled on stagecoaches, the Second Class is rather more crowded and spartan, whilst Third Class passengers are conveyed in open trucks, with or without seats. However, journeys on the LMR were quite short.

It is evident that the railway companies did not expect large numbers of Third Class passengers, but they were soon to be proved wrong. This did not lead to an immediate improvement in Third Class accommodation, because the companies were concerned that such action would lead to a transfer of former Second Class travellers into the Third Class, with a consequent loss of rev-

The LNWR also built some fine carriages, such as this 65ft 6in dining car. *IAL*

29

Sleeeping cars of a later era. BR Mark 1 stock on an Aberdeen–King's Cross train at Stevenage on 11 April 1978. *D. L. Percival*

enue. Third Class passengers were not generally conveyed on express trains, and they continued to have wretched journeys on slow trains running at times which were often inconvenient. An excursion train in the Glasgow area in 1850 consisted of 18 covered carriages, three open cattle trucks and three open sheep trucks. The open trucks had been provided to accommodate passengers *who refused to get off the roofs of the covered carriages.*

In an effort to improve the lot of Third Class passengers, parliament had taken action as early as 1844 in the Regulation of Railways Act (known as the Cheap Trains Act). It introduced a requirement for the running of one train daily in each direction on every line for Third Class passengers in closed carriages with seats, at a fare of not more than a penny a mile, and stopping at all stations. Such trains became known as 'Parliamentary Trains'.

Gradually, Third Class travelling conditions improved, but only slightly. By the early 1870s, James Allport, General Manager of the Midland Railway, was determined to improve the lot of the Third Class passenger. In 1872, he caused a revolution by requiring all Midland passenger trains to convey Third Class passengers. A milestone. He was supported by the Great Eastern, but the rival LNWR was not at all happy at this development. Then, on 1 January 1875, Allport abolished Second Class bookings throughout its system. Another milestone. All Second Class carriages were made Third Class, and the old wooden Third Class carriages were broken up as soon as they could be replaced. It was also announced

that in future all Third Class carriages would have upholstered seats and reasonably spacious compartments. It was nothing less than another revolution and it laid the foundations of the Midland's well-earned reputation for the high quality and comfort of its carriages. It was also an astute business decision. By now, Third Class passengers were predominant, and by 1888 the numbers of passengers carried in the different classes on Britain's railways were as follows:

First Class	30 million
Second Class	63 million
Third Class	682 million

Revenue was as follows:

First Class	£3 million
Second Class	£3 million
Third Class	£20 million

Despite this, other companies were slow to abolish Second Class. G. P. Neele records that from May 1893 Second Class bookings between England and Scotch stations would no longer be given and concurrently the following companies would cease to convey Second Class passengers — Caledonian, Cambrian, Highland, North Eastern and Great Northern. However, the LNWR declined to take such action generally and the Great Western did not do so until 1910. Second Class was generally abolished in 1917, by which time it accounted for only 2% of passenger traffic, but it was retained for many years on certain continental boat trains.

Civil and signalling engineering

Chapter 3

Civil engineering — Milestones

Bridges and viaducts

The confidence, energy and skill of Britain's 19th century civil engineers is epitomised in the magnificent structures which still embellish our landscape, and they are so numerous that only a small selection can be dealt with in the pages at our disposal. Any selection can therefore be only a personal one, but I have attempted to provide examples of the work of the eminent civil engineers of the day exemplified in both stone and steel. They are not listed in any particular order.

The Britannia tubular bridge

The civil engineer in charge of the Britannia Bridge was Robert Stephenson (1803-59), the son of the great George Stephenson. He had been appointed engineer for the building of the Chester & Holyhead Railway, which entailed bridging both the River Conway and the Menai Strait. His design of the Conway tubular bridge, which was completed in 1848, provided the template for the bridge over the strait, but the latter was a much bigger challenge. In the strait there was only one rocky islet for intermediate support, and Stephenson conceived the idea of two wrought iron tubes resting on three stone piers, with smaller tubes from the outer piers to the land. The design of the tubes was worked out during a series of experiments on a 75ft model of a tube at William Fairbairn's shipyard at Millwall.

Work began on the masonry piers in spring 1846 and the first wrought iron plates were delivered in June 1847. The tubes, of oblong section and weighing over 1,500 tons, were constructed on the banks of the strait and were then floated into position between the piers. Hydraulic pumps were used to raise the tubes into their final positions. Two million rivets were used, and the last one was driven home by Robert Stephenson himself, to the deafening cheers of his workmen. As a final touch, four magnificent lions couchant were sculpted by John Thomas from limestone blocks to symbolically guard the entrances to the bridge.

The first train passed through the bridge on 9 March 1850, and the bridge was then examined by Captain Simmons, a Government Inspector, for the Railway Commissioners.

A diesel multiple-unit destined for Llandudno Junction leaves the Britannia Bridge and passes between the two guardian lions on 28 September 1965. The inscription over the entrance reads 'Erected Anno Domini MDCCCL Robert Stephenson Engineer'. *G. M. Cashmore*

One of Brunel's masterpieces, the Royal Albert Bridge over the River Tamar linking Devon with Cornwall. It was opened in 1859. A 'Western' class diesel-hydraulic eases the 'Cornishman' on to the bridge on 30 August 1972.
Ian R. Smith

Various tests and measurements took place whilst heavy trains passed through the bridge, and Captain Simmons declared himself satisfied. The bridge was then officially opened for traffic on Monday, 18 March 1850.

The Royal Albert Bridge, Saltash
The name of Isambard Kingdom Brunel was revered throughout the length and breadth of the Great Western Railway, and still is in many parts today. He was born at Portsmouth in 1806, the son of Marc Isambard Brunel, and worked with his father on the construction of the Thames tunnel. He was a man of many talents, as demonstrated by his wide range of achievements, among which were:

- He was Chief Engineer of the Great Western Railway between Bristol and London, completed in 1841 including the two-mile long Box tunnel;
- He produced the accepted design for the Clifton Suspension Bridge;
- He designed Paddington station with its beautiful triple-arched train shed;
- He designed railways in Italy, Austria and India;
- He designed the *Great Britain,* the first major ship to use a screw propeller, in 1843

However, his most outstanding visible achievement must be the Royal Albert Bridge at Saltash, which bears his name and the date of opening — 1859. It was built to enable the Cornwall Railway to run through from Plymouth. Preliminary work began in 1848, but owing to the impoverished state of the Cornwall Railway, little progress was made for the next four years. Eventually work was resumed in 1852 for a single-track bridge. The bridge has two central spans, each 455ft long, resting on a central pier, and the bridge deck is suspended from two wrought iron tubes in the shape of a flat arch. The whole bridge, with its approach viaduct at each side, is 2,200ft long.

The tubes were constructed on the shore and floated into position on pontoons, before being raised into their final position by hydraulic rams, following a similar procedure to that adopted by Robert Stephenson on his Britannia Bridge. The bridge was opened on 3 May 1859 by Prince Albert, but illness caused Brunel to be absent. He was, in fact, fatally ill and died later that year at the age of only 53, robbing the engineering world of a man of great and inventive genius. The bridge is a suitable monument to his life, and he has a worthy place among that great triumvirate of engineers of the mid-19th century which includes Joseph Locke and Robert Stephenson.

The Royal Border Bridge, Berwick on Tweed
The Royal Border Bridge is a masonry arch bridge crossing the River Tweed and was built for the York, Newcastle & Berwick Railway by

Robert Stephenson. It consists of 28 arches, each of 61ft 6in span and was opened by Queen Victoria on 29 August 1850. Earlier on the same visit she had opened the Central station at Newcastle. The previous year, another of Robert Stephenson's famous bridges had been opened over the River Tyne at Newcastle — the High Level bridge, a two-level structure, with the railway on the top deck and the road below.

The Forth Bridge

Given the ingenuity and drive of British engineers in the 19th century, it is no surprise to learn that there were several schemes for a bridge across the Firth of Forth to shorten the distance between Edinburgh and Dundee/Aberdeen. Before the bridge was built, trains had to travel inland for many miles to cross the river near Alloa.

The East Coast companies (Great Northern, North Eastern and North British) were at a considerable disadvantage compared with the West Coast group (LNWR and Caledonian) for the London to Aberdeen passenger business, and they commissioned Sir Thomas Bouch to design and build a bridge across the firth. His plan consisted of a stiffened suspension bridge, upon which the firm of William Arrol started work in 1878, but work was quickly halted when Bouch's Tay Bridge collapsed in December 1879 in a gale, and 75 passengers and traincrew were killed. Bouch had been knighted for his Tay

bridge, but its collapse is thought to have led to his early death in 1880. Work on his Forth Bridge, of which just one pier had been built, was finally abandoned in 1881.

No time was lost in inviting fresh proposals, and in 1881 John Fowler and Benjamin Baker were instructed to complete their design based on three double cantilevers with suspended spans in between. This was developed into the present bridge design, with main spans of 1,700ft — greater at the time than any other bridge in the world. The design appears to have been wholly Baker's idea and he took the lead on project design until its completion. The design was based on the most thorough structural analysis possible and it was the first major British bridge to be built in steel. The firm of Sir William Arrol was chief contractor. Once the foundation caissons had been made and sunk in 1886, erection of the steelwork began, and in little over three years the bridge — fully tested — was officially opened by the Prince of Wales on 4 March 1890. It had been first used on 21 January 1890, when two test trains each comprising a locomotive and 50 wagons, and each weighing 900 tons, ran onto the bridge side by side from the south entrance.

The Forth Bridge has an overall length of over 8,000ft, the trains cross the river at a height of 158ft and the towers reach a height of 361ft. It ranked as the largest man-made construction in the world of its time and cost £3.2 million to

The Forth Bridge was an incredible adventure, and is a monument to man's vision and engineering genius.
W. A. Sharma/IAL

The interior view of the Forth Bridge is no less impressive as BR Standard Class 5 No 73106 takes an up express across it on 31 July 1958.
W. A. Sharma/IAL

build. More than 50,000 tons of steel and 6$\frac{1}{2}$ million rivets were used in its construction, employing 5,000 workers. However, the maintenance of a bridge of this size, made almost entirely of steel, is a major and costly undertaking, and one of its best known features is the need to keep on repainting it, which was normally done every three years. This is the time it takes to paint from one end to the other, giving rise to the well-known saying about 'painting the Forth Bridge'.

The bridge was owned by the East Coast Consortium, plus the Midland Railway, and they formed the Forth Bridge Company, to own and maintain the structure. Incidentally, it is believed that the construction cost was somewhat defrayed through the fares and rates structure. For charging purposes, the Forth Bridge was counted as being several miles longer than it actually was. The shorter distance between King's Cross and Aberdeen led within a few years to the well-known 'races' when East Coast competed with West with their overnight services in 1895. These were really prestige stunts and had little lasting effect.

The Midland Railway's interest in the Forth Bridge derived from the facility it gave, in conjunction with the North British Railway, to run through coaches from London St Pancras to Aberdeen. In its 1903 timetable, the 9.30am train from St Pancras to Edinburgh Waverley, forerunner of the 'Thames-Forth Express', conveyed through coaches to Aberdeen, which was reached at 10.5pm. The advertised Luncheon and Dining Cars would no doubt be appreciated.

John Fowler was created a baronet in the year that the bridge was opened, although he had already been made KCMG by Queen Victoria in 1885. His partner, Benjamin Baker, was also knighted.

The Ribblehead viaduct
The story of the building of the Ribblehead viaduct is well known. A lengthy wrangle with the London & North Western Railway led the Midland Railway directors in 1865 to authorise the building of a railway from Settle Junction to a junction with the North Eastern Railway at Petteril Bridge on the approach to Carlisle. However, various developments then caused the Midland to attempt to obtain parliamentary powers to abandon the project. That attempt

failed, and in 1869 the Midland had to go ahead and build the line. In the main, it was glad to do so, but we are not concerned here with the details of that wrangle.

It is also the story of John Sydney Crossley, who was the Midland Railway's Engineer-in-Chief. To him was given the task of building what has become one of the best-known viaducts in the country, on a line popular now for its magnificent wild scenery, its breathtaking viaducts and its many deep tunnels. On 3 August 1869 applications were invited for tenders for the contract covering the Settle Junction to Dent Head section, and resident engineers were appointed. The contract stipulated that the contract had to be completed by 1 May 1873, and it included the major works at Ribblehead and Blea Moor. An entire town, Batty Green, suddenly appeared in this desolate spot on the empty moor. It was renowned for bad weather, for high winds and rain and snow.

The viaduct consists of 24 masonry arches of 45ft span, the height of the loftiest being 165ft. The foundations were carried down through peat and clay to rest on rock. One and a half million bricks were used in the arches. Every sixth pier is larger than the others, and of enormous strength. The first stone was laid by William Ashwell, the contractor's agent, on 12 October 1870 and the last arch was completed in 1874. On 3 August 1875, John Crossley wrote to the Board of Directors' Construction Committee, 'I have the pleasure to report that goods trains have this day travelled over the line', but passenger trains did not commence running until 1 May 1876, following approval of the works by Colonel F. H. Rich, an Inspecting Officer of the Board of Trade.

Signalling — Milestones

It might well be said that signalling systems and equipment have progressed through a whole series of milestones almost from the inception of railways until the present day. Here is a selection of the more important ones.

The electric telegraph

The telegraph was a very important milestone because, among many other benefits, it enabled messages to be passed down the line regarding the safe running of trains. Experiments with the instantaneous exchange of messages over a distance using electricity were being carried out at the same time as the first main line railways were being built, but no really practical device for the purpose was produced until 1837. In that year the physicists Charles Wheatstone and William Fothergill Cooke conducted satisfactory trials between Euston and Camden on the London & Birmingham Railway, using an electro-magnetic, five needle telegraph instrument operated by

Ribblehead viaduct, with a BR/Sulzer Type 4 heading the Down Thames-Clyde express on 1 June 1970. *J. H. Cooper-Smith*

primary batteries. Although Robert Stephenson was impressed by the trials, the company decided not to adopt the system.

The newly-opened Great Western Railway installed this apparatus between Paddington and West Drayton in 1839, and extended it to Slough, in an improved, simpler and cheaper form in 1843. This improved form was known as the double-needle instrument and was widely adopted. There was also another variation, the single needle instrument, which was used on a large scale by the railway companies.

Another early installation took place on the London & Blackwall Railway. Robert Stephenson was one of the engineers of that railway, and he had already witnessed the potential of Cooke's telegraph system on the London & Birmingham Railway. On the Blackwall Railway, the telegraph equipment was actually used to control train movements, and this was the milestone which eventually formed the basis of all train signalling throughout the British Isles for the next 100 years. Indeed, the electric telegraph is still in use today on some quieter lines whose signalling has not been modernised.

The electric telegraph soon found a valuable application to the operation of trains through long tunnels. One of the first of such applications was through the Clay Cross tunnel, south of Chesterfield, on the North Midland Railway, reputedly as early as 1841. The GWR installed the telegraph system through Box tunnel in 1847.

Space interval signalling — the Absolute Block system
For 20 years or so, trains had been worked on a time-interval system, in which a train was allowed to follow another train after a set interval of time had elapsed since the first train departed. The inherent dangers of such a system

are readily apparent, especially during darkness and bad weather. A driver entering a section on line worked under such a system had always to expect that he might find a train moving slowly, or even be at a stand, just round the next bend — and that applied at every bend.

As trains became more frequent, and ran at higher speeds, the inadequacies of such a system were obvious, and the existence of the electric telegraph provided the answer, although the railway companies were very slow to adopt it, being unwilling to make the investment and afraid that it might reduce line capacity. It was a system based on a space interval between trains, rather than a time interval, and the electric telegraph allowed a signalman to send a message to his colleague further back down the line that a train had arrived safely at his signalbox and that he could now allow another train to proceed. The driver of that second train could now proceed with full confidence that there was no other train in the section of line between the two signalboxes. It was a significant milestone.

The system was called the Absolute Block System of signalling and its object was to prevent more than one train being in a block section between two signalboxes on the same line at the same time. It was called 'absolute' because it provided certainty, and the term 'block' possibly derives from the fact that the line was divided into blocks, called sections. As early as 1851, the Board of Trade Railway Inspecting Officers were advocating the use of the block system, using the immortal words 'so that no two trains shall be on the same line at the same time'.

One of the first known applications was on the South Eastern Railway in 1852, and the London & North Western Railway installed a quite sophisticated two-mile telegraph system on its southern section in 1855. As the years passed, the Absolute Block System was refined in several ways to increase safety, but some railway companies, to their shame, refused to install it or did so very slowly, until finally compulsion had to be applied through the Regulation of Railways Act of 1889. That act was one of the very rare instances in which force had to be applied to compel the railway companies to take the required action.

The fixed signal
To put it at its simplest, because train drivers cannot steer round a train in front, they must be given instructions as to whether they must stop, because there is a train in front; or whether they can proceed, because there isn't. Such instructions can be given to a driver by a variety of means — by hand signals, by written authority,

An array of instruments in the signalbox at Oakham. On the shelf are the instruments which control the working of the Absolute Block System of signalling. Below them are indicators which repeat the indications of the lineside signals. *D. C. Hall*

or by equipment mounted at the lineside.

On the early railways the instructions were given to a driver by hand signals, indicated by the policeman holding his arms in different positions. At night different coloured lights were used. Quite quickly, recourse was made to various forms of equipment mounted at the lineside, enabling the policeman to cover a wider area and avoid delay. Such forms of equipment became known as fixed signals, because they were fixed in the ground at a particular location. As early as 1834, a very simple form of fixed signal, for night use only, started to be used on the Liverpool & Manchester Railway. It consisted of a red or white light placed on the top of a post by the policeman or pointsman, who had to climb a ladder to do so. In its way, it was a milestone.

By 1838 the need for fixed signals was becoming more apparent, and the Grand Junction Railway, opened that year, was equipped with them from the start. The signals took the form of a circular or D-shaped board fixed on a spindle with a handle to turn it through a horizontal arc of 90 degrees. The disc when facing the driver indicated danger, and was turned edge-on to indicate safety. A lamp was provided for night use. Similar signals were erected on the Newcastle & Carlisle Railway in 1840. When the Great Western Railway opened in 1838, it used fixed signals in which a ball was hoisted to the top of a post to indicate safety. When lowered it indicated danger.

Semaphore signalling apparatus using wooden arms had been in use by the military and other authorities for many years as a means of transmitting messages over long distances, but the first use as a railway signal took place at New Cross on the Croydon Railway in 1841. The railway's engineer, Charles H. Gregory, erected one, a three-position signal. When the arm was horizontal it meant danger; when it was inclined downwards at 45 deg it indicated caution; and when it disappeared into a slot in the post it signified clear. This was also a milestone, as the forerunner of the standard railway semaphore signal still in use today in some areas.

The Distant signal

In the early days, it was readily apparent that a driver had to approach a station cautiously, even if he had no need to stop there for traffic purposes, in case the signal at the station (known as the 'Home' signal) was at danger. If the driver could be given advance information about the state of the Home signal, he could then proceed with confidence if it was showing 'proceed', and the concept arose of a signal several hundred yards back which would repeat the indication of the

Left: A fine array of Great Western signals at Worcester Shrub Hill. The upper red arms indicate danger — stop, and there is one for each diverging line at the junction ahead. The fish-tail yellow arms are Distant signals. *D. C. Hall*

Below: At one time there were over 10,000 signalboxes and they were a familiar feature of any train journey. Most of them have now gone, including this one at Gisburn (L&Y) between Blackburn and Hellifield. The line is still open as a valuable diversionary route. *IAL*

Home signal. It became known a Distant signal, and with such an arrangement a driver would know positively whether he had to brake or whether he could continue at full speed. This was a milestone and became one of the fundamental building blocks of signalling systems, including today's modern colour-light installations.

The track circuit

Accidents happened from time to time in which a signalman overlooked the presence of a train or an engine standing on the line under the control of his signals, and allowed another train to approach, with the risk of a serious collision. It was a real risk too; the worst accident in the history of Britain's railways had as its main cause the forgetfulness of the signalman. It happened at Quintinshill, on the Caledonian main line near Gretna on 22 May 1915, when a southbound special troop train ran head-on, engine to engine, into a local passenger train. The local train had been shunted across from the northbound main line to the southbound main line out of the way of a northbound Scotch express. The signalman then overlooked the presence of the local passenger train, cleared his signals for the troop train, and 227 lives were lost. There were many other instances.

The use of electrical circuits to detect the presence of a train had been the subject of experiments as far back as the 1860s by both W. R. Sykes at Crystal Palace station, and by W. Robinson in the USA. Sykes' experiments were inconclusive owing to poor ballast conditions causing current leakage, but Robinson persevered and installed track circuits at New York in the 1870s. They were intended to act as a safeguard against a signalman's forgetfulness, but did not find favour in Britain for many years.

Track circuits indicate to a signalman the presence of a train. They are operated by passing a weak electric current through the running rails. When a train comes along it diverts the electric current through the wheels and axles of the train and short-circuits the current. It then actuates an indicator in the signalbox and can electrically lock signals at danger.

The objections to its use in Britain were two:

It was believed in some quarters that providing signalmen with safeguards against one hazard might cause them to be less careful in dealing with other operations which did not have safeguards, thus increasing rather than decreasing danger. The considerable cost of providing track circuits throughout the railway.

The first application in Britain is thought to have been on the London, Chatham & Dover Railway in 1886, at St Paul's station between Blackfriars and Farringdon. It was an important milestone, because track circuits became another essential building block in modern signalling installations, as well as improving safety. However, the railway companies did not rush forward to emulate the Chatham Railway. The next installation did not take place until 1894, when the Great Northern Railway installed track circuits through Gasworks tunnels just outside King's Cross station. It took another serious collision and fire to galvanise the Midland Railway into action, following an accident at Hawes Junction on Christmas Eve in 1910.

Automatic train control (ATC)

The two main sources of accident were signalmen's errors and drivers wrongly passing signals at danger. The fundamental requirement of a driver was (and still is) that he should observe and obey all signals. Failure to do so could, and did, cause serious collisions, resulting in multiple fatalities and wreckage. Nineteenth-century history was littered with such events, and railway officers on several companies began to consider the installation of devices which would remind a driver that he was passing a Distant signal at 'caution'. Arguments against taking any action were put forward with conviction (the same arguments as in the case of track circuits), but experiments and trials continued. They began in the 1870s when Captain Tyler, one of the Board of Trade's Railway Inspecting Officers, proposed a form of automatic warning for use at Distant signals during fog. During 1887, the Rules & Regulations Committee of the Railway Clearing House reported that several railway companies were experimenting with an audible signal, either mechanical or electrical, as a guide to drivers during fog, and some companies, notably the North Eastern and the Great Central, carried out extensive trials.

The Great Western held aloof, buttressed by its excellent safety record, but its confidence was shaken by a collision in 1900, when one of its drivers ran past several Stop and Distant signals at danger in broad daylight, into the rear of another passenger train standing in Slough station. The railway company's officers responded positively by designing what became the most effective automatic train control (ATC) system. It was operated by a ramp laid longitudinally between the rails which engaged with a spring-loaded shoe underneath the engine. When the Distant signal was Off (clear), an electric current sounded a bell on the engine, but when the signal was at caution no current passed and an alarm was sounded on the engine by the raising of the shoe. Prolonged experiments were carried out, and by 1910 the system had been installed between Paddington and Reading. By this time the equipment on the engine had been modified to give an automatic application of the brake unless the driver intervened.

It was the most practicable system of all the experiments, and a milestone. After the Great War, the GWR extended the system to all its main lines and engines. It was the only company to do so.

The Midland Railway's Rotary Block and similar systems

Many collisions were caused when signalmen overlooked the presence of a train in the rear section (the section of line between their signalbox and the preceding signalbox) and allowed another train to approach. W. R. Sykes developed his well-known 'lock and block' system in the late 19th century and it found great favour, especially on the busy suburban lines south of the Thames. It was designed to ensure that a signalman could not allow a train to pass his signalbox into the next section until the previous train had been proved by the equipment to have passed through that section. It was equally designed to ensure that a signalman could not allow a second train to approach from the signalbox in rear until the previous train had been proved to have cleared that section.

It was a very valuable safeguard, and its introduction into service was a milestone in railway safety, but it suffered from one defect. It was necessary to have a release mechanism in the system to enable trains to move during a failure of the equipment and to provide for a situation in which a train which had been signalled forward was no longer going to travel forward. The release mechanism was provided by a key which was available to the signalman, and it was too easy for the signalman to assume that the equipment had failed when in fact it was doing its job of protecting a train still in the section. There were a number of serious collisions from this cause.

The Midland Railway's Rotary Block system was also designed to prevent a second train from entering a section whilst there was still a train in it. This was achieved through electrical locking, making it impossible for a signalman to allow a second train to approach, until the previous train had been proved to have arrived at his signalbox by the operation of a mercury treadle, which released the locking. The same electrical locking also made it impossible for a signalman to clear his signal to allow a train to enter a section whilst there was still a train in it.

The name 'Rotary Block' is derived from the handle on the signalling instrument, which can only be rotated in one direction and can only be released from the 'Train in Section' position (other than by the normal operation of the mercury treadle) by the signalman pressing a can-

The Midland Railway developed its rotary block system to guard against signalmen's errors, and the Leeds–Carlisle section was one of the routes equipped. Denthead signalbox stood in lonely isolation and split the block section between Blea Moor and Dent station. It was particularly useful when snow clearance operations were in progress on this vulnerable section. The photograph is dated 11 August 1968, after the signalbox had been permanently closed for some years. *David Wharton*

The interior of Crewe Station A signal cabin in 1983, showing its Webb-Thompson all-electric locking frame. Note the absolute block signalling instruments on the top shelf. *Jack Winkle*

celling button in a small glass covered case. Both signalmen concerned have to press the cancelling buttons simultaneously to effect the release. The glass cover is a psychological barrier because it can only be replaced by a signalling technician and has to be reported. It is a very effective deterrent to hasty action, and the 'Rotary Block' system has been proved to be very safe since it was first installed early in the 20th century.

The development of power operation of points and signals

The invention of the track circuit enabled signalmen to control a much larger area, even though most of it was out of sight, but initially the railway companies were unable to take advantage of this facility because a signalman's ability to control a greater area was limited by his ability to operate points and signals by hand over long distances. A limit of 200 yards was stipulated by the Board of Trade for the manual operation of points. Some form of power operation was therefore required.

The same problem had become equally apparent on the European railway systems and in the USA, and it was in the latter that power began to be applied to the operation of points and signals. The first power signalling system, designed by George Westinghouse in 1884, was operated by compressed air and installed on the Philadelphia & Reading Railroad. Two years later a Bianchi-Servettaz hydraulic system was installed in Italy at Abbiategrasso, on the Mediterranean Railway. The Westinghouse system was improved in 1892

by the introduction of an electro-pneumatic system, in which the points were moved by high-pressure compressed air, actuated by electrically operated valves.

Britain's railway companies were slow to adopt power operation, despite the emerging need, and were worried about the cost of maintaining the new system and the need to employ skilled workmen to do it. Three systems ultimately found favour in Britain in the early 1900s: the Westinghouse electro-pneumatic system; a low-pressure pneumatic system; and an all-electric system. The Westinghouse system was installed by the North Eastern Railway, one of the most progressive companies, at Newcastle, Hull and Tyne Dock. The Caledonian company installed it at Glasgow Central station, covering the whole of the enlarged station area, and the Lancashire & Yorkshire company did so at a triangular junction at Bolton Trinity Street. The latter installation continued in use until the 1980s. However, the distinction of being the first, and a milestone in railway signalling, belongs to the Great Eastern Railway, which had a small installation at Granary Junction, Bishopsgate, opened in 1899. The operating frame of this signalbox is preserved in the National Railway Museum at York.

The London & South Western employed a low-pressure system for working points and signals, and combined this with the installation of a large number of automatic sections, with 16 between Barton Mill and Hook, 12 between Grateley and Andover and 10 between Brookwood and Woking. Altogether, the LSWR had 62 automatic sections on its main line and was very progressive in its policy of signalling modernisation. The low-pressure system was also used by the Great Central Railway over seven miles between Manchester London Road and Newton.

Typically, the LNWR preferred to manufacture its own equipement as far as possible. Webb and Thompson devised an all-electric system, which became known as the 'Crewe' system because it was installed in nine signalboxes there, and also at Euston and Camden. Hybrid systems were installed by the Glasgow & South Western Railway in the Glasgow area and by the London, Brighton & South Coast Railway in the London area.

Many companies were installing power signalling of various types extensively during the late 1890s and up to World War 1, but other companies, such as the Midland, the L&YR and the Great Eastern, did very little, whilst the Great Northern and the North British did nothing at all. In some cases, such as at London Victoria, Edinburgh Waverley and York, the signalling had recently been renewed in mechanical form, at considerable expense.

Government and legislation

Chapter 4

Milestone

Formation of the Railway Inspectorate of the Board of Trade

Following the success of the Liverpool & Manchester Railway, which opened in 1830, many more lines were opened in the next few years, including those which provided the genesis of some of our most important railway companies, such as the London & North Western, the London & South Western, the Great Western and the Midland. 71 acts were passed for new railways between 1831 and 1837, and the rapidly developing railway system soon attracted the attention of parliament. It was felt that some control over the working of the railways was necessary in the public interest and a parliamentary select committee was therefore appointed in 1839 to consider the question. No less a personage than George Stephenson gave evidence in support of a bill for the management and better regulation of the railways. He said: 'When I see so many young engineers and such a variety of notions I am convinced that some system should be laid down to prevent wild and visionary schemes being tried, at the great danger of injury or loss of life to the public.'

The committee's recommendations led to the Regulation of Railways Act of 1840. This short act came into force on 10 August 1840 and commenced: 'Whereas it is expedient for the safety of the public to provide for the due supervision of the railways . . .'

Its main provisions, so far as the Railway Inspectorate was concerned, were:

- No railway may be opened for the public conveyance of goods or passengers without a month's notice being given (Section 1);
- The Board of Trade may appoint persons to inspect railways (Section 5);
- Returns of traffic, charges, and accidents causing personal injury are to be made by the railway companies (Section 3);

This was the milestone which created the Railway Inspectorate, with powers to inspect any railway. Civil engineers might have been used to form the Railway Inspectorate but there were two objections to this. First, all the available civil engineers were heavily involved in railway construction or other civil engineering schemes; and second, it might prove impracticable to ensure that civil engineers had the required status among their peers, were completely professionally objective, and were free from pressures from their paymasters.

For these reasons, the Corps of Royal Engineers was approached to provide Inspectors, an admirable practice which continued unchanged until recent years. The first Inspector General of Railways was Lt-Col Sir J. M. Frederic Smith, and two other officers were appointed to assist him. At first the inspectorate had no powers other than to inspect railways, and it could do nothing if it found that a new railway had not, for instance, been built to a standard that would allow passengers to be carried safely, other than to use its powers of persuasion. A similar situation arose so far as the discovery of unsafe working practices in the operation of railways was concerned. The inspecting officers had no powers to insist on changes, nor had they any powers to inquire into accidents, but in practice they did carry out such inquiries without any authority. However, this omission was partly rectified by Gladstone's act of 1842, which gave the Board of Trade powers to postpone the opening of a new line if an inspector reported that the opening 'would be attended with danger to the public using the same'.

For the next 150 years, the inspectorate, never more than four or five strong, continued to ensure that new lines were of an acceptable standard, that all accidents were inquired into, with the more important ones being the subject of public inquiry and report, and that the necessary improvements in the operating of the railway were adopted. It was wholly a force for good and became one of the finest government inspectorates. The inspectors were men of high repute and standing, and by the end of the 19th century a considerable degree of mutual co-operation and respect had developed between members of the inspectorate and railway officers.

Millstones

Almost from the very inception of railways, they quickly became a vital part of the country's industry and commerce. Without the railways there would have been little or no progress throughout the 19th century. However, this powerful position gave the government cause for concern that the railways might exploit their monopoly position through unreasonably high charges and inadequate facilities and service. This concern was shared by industry as a whole, which supported the provision of competitive lines as a means of securing a good service. All this was very understandable. But it led to a number of developments which hampered the railways and restricted their profits, with the result that funds for modernisation in the 20th century were limited. They became millstones.

The heavy costs incurred in obtaining a Private Act to build a railway

In order to obtain powers to build a railway and acquire the necessary land, the promoters of a new line had to go through the following stages:

- After preliminary surveys had been carried out, a prospectus had to be issued, inviting members of the public and others to subscribe for shares.
- When sufficient capital had been raised a detailed survey had to be undertaken and a route planned. The ownership of land had to be discovered and negotiations had to be undertaken with landowners. Opposition, real or contrived, had to be overcome, sometimes with offers of free shares. These negotiations might result in the route having to be amended, with additional surveys being required. Opposition from existing railway companies had to be met by, for example, offering those companies facilities over the new line.
- When the route had finally been agreed, a bill had to be drawn up for presentation to a parliamentary committee. Parliamentary procedures could result in further changes to the proposed line.
- If and when parliamentary approval was given in the shape of an act, more money had to be raised so that building work could commence.

During the course of these lengthy procedures, considerable legal, accountancy and survey costs arose even before the first sod could be dug. And these costs had to be remunerated throughout the lifetime of the railway company. In international comparisons of costs Great Britain suffered notoriously through the heavy initial outlay in lands and parliamentary expenses to enable a railway to be built.

The Great Western built several long cut-offs around the turn of the 19th/20th century to improve its competitive position by speeding up journey times. One of the best known ran between Reading and Taunton, on which 'Hall' class No 5923 *Colston Hall* makes a vigorous attack of Brewham Bank with an up August Bank Holiday extra on 30 July 1960. Note that even though this is an extra train, all the carriages are properly roof-boarded. The neat and tidy permanent way and cess are enough to make present-day track engineers (and locomen) weep. The Great Western was a proud railway, and had every reason to be. *Richardson Bros*

Over-capitalisation and the lack of a planned network

Apart from the capital costs incurred as explained above, costs also arose from the lack of a planned national network of railways. Railways were built wherever promoters thought they could make a profit, not necessarily along the best route. The West Coast route omitted Northampton and Kendal; it should have gone through Birmingham and Manchester. The East Coast direct route omitted Lincoln and Leeds. Many lines were built purely for competitive reasons, for example:

- The Great Western cut-off between Reading and Taunton, which ran mainly through open country and was built to improve the GWR's competitive position with the London & South Western Railway for the Exeter and Plymouth traffic.
- The Great Central route through Nottingham to Marylebone.
- The Great Northern Railway's extensions into the Nottinghamshire and Derbyshire coalfields and across to Burton and Stafford, in competition with the Midland Railway.
- The competition between the Caledonian and Glasgow & South Western railways to the southwest of Glasgow.
- Competition in the South Wales valleys.

The list is endless. Government and industry welcomed it, but it led to gross over-capitalisation of the railway industry. Industry never ceased to complain about high freight charges and compared them unfavourably with those in Western Europe, but they were caused by the building of what on a rational network might be regarded as unnecessary lines. However, it has to be borne in mind that some of these schemes were promoted in the belief that traffic on the railway would continue to increase so far as could be foreseen, set against a background of continuous decade by decade increases, as shown by the following table.

Year	Passengers carried (millions)	Freight tonnage (millions)
1860	163	94
1870	337	169
1880	604	235
1890	818	303
1900	1,142	423
1910	1,307	514

Given this continuing and remarkable rate of

Sir Edward Watkin's ambitious scheme to give the Manchester, Sheffield & Lincolnshire Railway its own line to London nearly bankrupted the company. When it was opened in 1899, the MS&LR changed its name to the Great Central Railway. One of Robinson's 4-6-0s, No 33, built by Beyer-Peacock in 1922, heads a stopping passenger train of elderly carriages along the line near Leicester. *IAL*

increase, any prudent railway manager would want to be sure that he had the capacity to deal with it, and would be expected to plan ahead to do so. No one can reasonably have anticipated the enormous effect that World War 1 would have on railway traffic levels, nor subsequent developments.

Government regulation

Passenger fares and freight charges were always regulated, but as the years went by many millions of 'exceptional' charges (which were lower than standard) for specific freight traffics between specific points came into use. Schedules of charges were embodied in the acts authorising the construction of the various railways, but as the piecemeal system of railways expanded to cover the whole country, the absence of a common schedule gave rise to many anomalies. By the 1880s, traders complained bitterly about the complexity of the charges structure, and the government passed the Railway & Canal Traffic Act of 1888. Every railway company was required to submit to the Board of Trade a revised classification of merchandise traffic and a revised schedule of maximum rates and charges. A three-sided war of great complexity broke out between the railway companies and traders, while the government floundered.

The new charges were confirmed by the Rates & Charges Order Confirmation Acts of 1891-2, but there was inadequate time to deal with all the millions of rates. Revised charges were due to come into force on 1 January 1893, but they could not be examined in time, and neither the traders nor the railway companies knew what they were. The companies therefore took the drastic step of charging the new statutory rates in all cases where the existing exceptional rates had not been examined as regards their legality. Heated complaints and objections from traders led to the Railway & Canal Traffic Act of 1894, under which any rate which had been increased after 31 December 1892 was open to challenge. This created a situation in which all rates that existed at December 1892 became the new legal maximum. These proceedings provided a field day for accountants and lawyers, but the effect was that the railway companies were unable in practice to increase any rates to cover increased costs in the future. This situation continued until World War 1, and partly accounts for the reduction in railway profits which became evident in the 1900s. A full description of these issues would occupy many pages, such was their labyrinthine complexity, but the whole saga is one of the many examples of government bungling and ineptitude that pepper railway history. The apparent inability of successive governments to thoroughly examine their own proposals and think through the possible unexpected and unintended consequences of any course of action is a situation not unknown even today.

Government intervened quite early in the life of railways. It passed the Railway Clauses Consolidation Act of 1845, which prohibited 'undue preference' and required all railway charges to be equal between different traders. The Railway & Canal Traffic Act of 1854 obliged the railway companies to provide 'reasonable facilities' for 'receiving forwarding and delivering traffic upon their railways' both goods and passengers. It sounds innocuous enough, but the detailed list of facilities became a millstone, especially after World War 1, and gave generous grounds for disputes and arguments. The government of the day felt that these provisions were necessary even though competition, encouraged

by the government, should have resulted in these provisions being met without legislation.

An earlier requirement imposed by parliament, which was not replicated in mainland Europe, was the duty to fence the railway. This duty had existed from the earliest days of private railways, and empowered justices of the peace to require those undertakings to erect, maintain and repair sufficient fences. The requirement to fence was given statutory force by the Regulation of Railways Act 1842, and was replaced three years later by Section 68 of the cumbrously titled Railway Clauses Consolidation Act, which stated:

'The company shall make and at all times thereafter maintain the following works for the accommodation of the owners and the occupiers of lands adjoining the railway . . . sufficient posts, rails, hedges, ditches, mounds, or other fences for separating the land taken for the use of the railway from the adjoining lands not taken, and protecting such lands from trespass, or the cattle of the owners or occupiers thereof from straying thereout . . .'

Note, therefore, that a fence is not just something constructed of wooden posts and rails, but includes all the other forms of barrier. Note also that the fence is provided to prevent trespass *from* the railway onto the landowner's estate and to protect the owner or occupier of such land from the consequences of his cattle straying on to the railway. Fences were not for the benefit of

The LNWR would have liked to amalgamate with both the Midland and the L&Y at the turn of the 19th/20th century but Parliament refused to sanction such a proposal. Twenty years later it was compelled to do so by the 1921 Railways Act. The 'Claughtons' were the pride of the line of the LNWR, and No 5948 *Baltic* was rebuilt by the LMS with a larger boiler and Caprotti valve gear. It stands proudly at Willesden on 17 September 1932 but was withdrawn only three years later. *E. R. Wethersett*

the general public (the law in this respect has changed in recent years in respect of children). Fences are also required alongside lines electrified on the third rail for the safety of the general public. This simple subject has given rise to astonishing amounts of litigation over the years.

The government's views on amalgamations

For many years the government was content to allow mergers, takeovers and absorptions of companies as the railway map developed. It was logical to do so, especially with end-on mergers and larger companies absorbing smaller ones. However, in the last two decades of the 19th century, some of the larger companies wished to merge, and the government of the day was concerned that such mergers would create overpowerful companies and reduce competition. Even though these were private companies, the government refused to sanction such proposals. It would have enabled those companies to reduce their costs, with potential benefits to passengers and traders alike. It is ironic that, two or three decades later, the mergers were forced through by the government under the 1921 Railways Act.

Local authority rates

Throughout the history of railways, local municipal authorities have levied rates on the railway companies. Railways are almost unique in one respect, owing to the very nature of the system, with 20,000 route miles of track passing through thousands of different authorities, large and small. Local authorities tended to look upon the companies as a convenient source of revenue, and there were many arguments and legal battles, which continued until 1929. The companies always felt that they were being unfairly treated. Apart from the actual cost of the rating assessments, there was the very considerable cost of employing an army of surveyors and legal experts to dispute them. It was a substantial burden and a millstone. In 1929 a Local Government Act relieved the railways of 75% of their rating bill, but the companies received no benefit whatsoever, as the whole of the 75% was swallowed up in rebates required to be given on freight charges to subsidise coal, iron, steel and agriculture. It was a pump-priming exercise to ease unemployment. The railway companies, although in some financial difficulty themselves, received no assistance from the government, which was as duplicitous as usual in its treatment of railways. We will look at this subject again in Chapter 9.

The Railway Passenger Duty (tax)

Chancellors of the Exchequer have always had to raise revenue from whichever quarter they can, and, as we have seen above, the railways have always been regarded as an easy target. The attack started as early as 1832, when a duty of a halfpenny a mile was imposed on every four passengers carried. It was vigorously opposed, and in 1844 a clause in the Regulation of Railways Act (known as Gladstone's Cheap Trains Act) exempted from the duty all fares of a penny a mile or less on passengers carried in what became known as Parliamentary Trains. These were trains which companies were obliged to provide at least once daily over each line, which stopped at each station and had an overall speed, including stops, of 12mph. Covered carriages with seats had to be provided.

The railway companies, assisted by passenger associations, continued to oppose the passenger duty, and it was varied in 1883 when the Cheap Trains Act was passed, reducing the duty where workmen's trains were run. The passenger duty was finally abolished in 1929, but was subject to conditions which will be examined in Chapter 9.

Chapter 5

General

Milestones

The opening of the world's first public steam-worked main-line passenger railway

The description 'the world's first public steam-worked main-line passenger railway' is very carefully worded, because there were many railways in existence before the Liverpool & Manchester Railway opened on 15 September 1830, and some are claimed to be 'firsts'.

For example, the Middleton Railway, which ran from collieries at Middleton to Leeds, dates from 1758, when it received its act of parliament, the first railway company to do so. The Surrey Iron Railway, which ran from Wandsworth to Croydon, received its act in 1801, and is claimed to have been the world's first public railway. Users supplied their own wagons and horses. However, one of the strongest contenders for the title of the world's first public railway is the Stockton & Darlington, which received parliamentary powers for the carriage of both goods and passengers, and opened on 27 September 1825. But coal was the main business of the S&DR, whilst passengers were conveyed in horse-drawn vehicles operated by contractors. Finally, there was

the Canterbury & Whitstable Railway, which opened for the conveyance of both passengers and freight on 4 May 1830. For most of its length, haulage was by means of a stationary engine, and the remaining mile was by locomotive. However, it is not really a strong contender, as the locomotive was subsequently replaced by a horse.

The Liverpool & Manchester Railway was the first railway to be operated exclusively by steam locomotives, and was the first to lay the foundations for all the railway companies which followed — a very significant milestone.

The Travelling Post Office trains

The creation of a national network of railways enabled the movement of mails to be considerably improved and speeded up. One of the earliest acts of parliament applicable to railways was the Railways (Conveyance of Mails) Act of 1838 which obliged the railway companies to provide facilities for the conveyance of mails at reasonable prices. The facilities included conveyance by ordinary or special trains at such hours of the day or night as were required. Carriages could be required exclusively for the carriage of mails or for sorting letters while in transit. The railway companies welcomed this

Right and far right: The picking up and dropping off of mail bags at the lineside is now a distant memory, but for many years was very common. In these two photographs we see (1) the postman fixing bags to the pick-up apparatus. The net alongside caught the bags which were swung out from the train; (2) a LNWR mailvan with pick-up net extended and mailbags swung out. *IAL*

traffic, of course. It was customarily handled by postmen, and all the railway companies had to do was to provide transport. Two years later Rowland Hill, the Postmaster General, introduced his Penny Post, resulting in huge increases in the volume of mail traffic.

Immediately after the passing of the Act in 1838, travelling post office vehicles were introduced on the West Coast main line and their use rapidly spread to other lines. The first trains operated exclusively for mail began running between Paddington and Bristol in 1855 and this might be regarded as a milestone. The famous 'West Coast Postal' from Euston to Glasgow and beyond, which was the subject of the celebrated film 'Night Mail' made by the GPO Film Unit in 1936, began running in 1885. G. P. Neele refers to it as 'a Grand Night Postal train for mails and parcel post, entirely independent of and separate from any public passenger traffic; the train to run as an arterial service through Great Britain, from London to Glasgow, to Edinburgh, Perth and Aberdeen and vice versa, with a connection at Crewe for Ireland'. For mail purposes, it replaced the old 'Limited Mail', which also conveyed passengers. The 'Limited Mail's many cross-country connections, which formed part of a comprehensive national network, were retimed to connect with the new train.

The introduction of parcels post in 1883 led to a considerable increase in post office traffic by rail. Parcels post was handled by railway staff to and from trains, unlike the mails.

The lineside pick-up and set-down apparatus dates from the earliest days of railways, and must be regarded as another milestone in the expeditious carriage of the mails. The first trials appear to have been held as early as 1838 on the newly opened London & Birmingham Railway at Boxmoor, but it was not long before equipment was installed at Berkhamsted, Leighton Buzzard and six more locations northwards towards Preston. By 1860 there were 101 locations at which the apparatus was installed throughout Britain, and the number had increased to 243 by 1911.

Suburban electrification

At the end of the 19th century, a number of companies were considering electrifying some of their more intensively worked suburban services, mainly to combat electric tramway and other competition. The first one to do so, and a significant milestone, was the Mersey railway, which opened its electrified service from Liverpool to Birkenhead and Rock Ferry in 1903, using the third rail system with electricity at 650 volts dc. The incentive to electrify in this case came from competition by the Birkenhead ferries.

The Lancashire & Yorkshire Railway rapidly followed suit, when in March 1904 it inaugurated a service of electric trains between Liverpool Exchange station and Southport. Thirty-eight motor cars and 53 trailers were provided for the service. A branch from Marsh Lane Junction to Aintree was opened in 1906. Electric power at 600 volts dc was supplied by the company's generating station at Formby and was fed to the

trains by the third rail system. The L&YR with the North Eastern Railway (see below) share the honour of being the first main line railway companies to introduce suburban electrified trains in Britain; another milestone.

The popular residential areas to the north of Manchester in the Heaton Park/Prestwich areas developed rapidly from 1900, and this caused the L&YR to consider electrifying the line from Manchester Victoria to Bury Bolton Street. Electric services began to operate in April 1916, using multiple-unit trains. Electricity was supplied through the third-rail system, using 1,200 volts dc current generated by the company in its plant at Clifton Junction.

The North Eastern Railway was also suffering severely from tramway competition in the Newcastle area and it decided to electrify what became eventually a circular route from Newcastle Central to North Shields and Whitley Bay, and back via Monkseaton and Benton, terminating at Newcastle New Bridge Street. The first passenger service commenced running on 29 March 1904, and by the end of the year the

Right: The Midland Railway never showed much interest in suburban electrification, but it installed an experimental overhead system between Lancaster, Morecambe and Heysham in 1908, using electricity at 3,300 volts, which lasted for many years and provided a connection between Lancaster Green Ayre and Castle stations. *IAL*

Below: An LB&SCR electric multiple-unit stands in Victoria station. These trains used the overhead system of current collection. *British Railways*

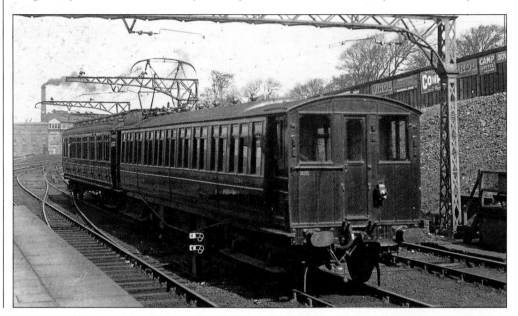

whole scheme was in operation. This was also a third-rail scheme.

In 1906 the Midland Railway decided that it needed to have experience in the operation of an electrified suburban service, and in consequence it announced in July 1906 that it intended to electrify the service between Lancaster, Morecambe and Heysham. This was done in two stages — Heysham to Morecambe on 13 April 1908 and on to Lancaster on 8 June 1908. The line was electrified on the overhead system using electricity at 6,600 volts ac, the first of that type of installation, and a milestone.

South of the River Thames, two companies developed electrified suburban schemes before 1914. The London, Brighton and South Coast Railway (LB&SCR) obtained powers to electrify the South London line in 1904, although electric trains did not run until 1 December 1909. Further schemes on the LB&SCR followed in 1911 and 1912. They used the overhead line system, with electricity being supplied at 6,600 volts ac. The London & South Western Railway, also stung by expanding tramway competition, planned in 1913 to electrify some of its suburban services. The first one, Waterloo to East Putney, opened on 25 October 1915, and further schemes followed in 1916.

Main line electrification
The credit for introducing the first main-line electrification belongs to the North Eastern Railway. That company had introduced subur-

ban electrification in 1904 on the Newcastle to Whitley Bay loop, but the company's Chief Mechanical Engineer, Vincent Raven, had his sights set on main line electrification. Supported by his General Manager (the NER was very progressive), Messrs Merz & MacLellan were appointed as the company's consulting engineers, with a remit to report on railway electrification, with particular reference to the North Eastern Railway's main routes. As a result of their findings, the NER board decided to embark on a pilot scheme, and the Shildon to Newport (Middlesbrough) line was selected as a trial site. The line opened for electric traction in 1915.

It proved to be a very successful venture and after the war Raven (now Sir Vincent) turned his attention to the possible electrification of the main line between York and Newcastle. In 1922 he built a large 4-6-4 electric locomotive intended to work the passenger expresses, and, but for the advent of the Grouping in 1923, the scheme might well have gone ahead. The North Eastern was a very prosperous company and could have afforded to do so, but the newly formed London & North Eastern Railway, with Nigel Gresley as its Chief Mechanical Engineer, quietly dropped the scheme. Gresley was a steam man to his fingertips. In any event, the LNER was never as prosperous as the North Eastern had been, lumbered as it was by a collection of companies that were barely viable. East Coast electrification had to wait for another 70 years.

Sir Vincent Raven's express electric locomotive, No 13, built in 1922 for the North Eastern Railway and intended for use between York and Newcastle, a scheme which was abandoned after the LNER was formed in 1923. If Sir Vincent had been chosen as CME of the LNER in preference to Gresley, would the scheme actually had been carried through, giving Britain its first main-line electric railway? It was to be another 70 years before the East Coast main line was electrified. *F. R. Hebron*

Millstones

The Midland St Pancras Grand Hotel

This magnificent edifice in High Victorian Gothic style fronting the Euston Road marked the Midland Railway's proud entrance into London. C. Hamilton Ellis described it as a vast Gothic pile, flamboyant and tremendous beside the Cromwellian dignity of King's Cross next door. It was designed by Sir George Gilbert Scott and opened in 1873, and it must have made a sizeable dent in the Midland company's bank balance. Such extravagance when the Midland was heavily involved in promoting expensive extensions to Manchester and Carlisle is odd, but perhaps the directors wanted to cock a snook at what they no doubt considered to be the slum of Euston just down the road, a station of no architectural merit whatsoever, apart from its magnificent Doric Arch which was in any case completely out of keeping with its surroundings.

The hotel was the last word in opulence and magnificence, but by 1935 it needed internal modernisation and its very heavy running costs were a considerable burden. It was too expensive to refurbish or modernise in the financial conditions of the day, and it closed its doors as a hotel. However, as it formed the frontage to the station, it could not just be demolished and swept out of the way, so it lingered on until the 1990s, forlorn and unloved, and yet a splendid reminder of those gracious, confident, late-Victorian days, when the railway companies exuded prosperity and greatness, even though they were never very prosperous. But their confidence in the future was boundless.

After 1935 the hotel found a use as railway offices, until by the 1980s it was no longer suitable for such purpose. In the 1960s, the hawks in British Railways had considered demolition during its retrenchment period but did not actively pursue the subject. Perhaps the outcry over the demolition of the Doric Arch dissuaded it. However, in the mid-1990s a new pride had arisen in the country's industrial history, and part of the hotel was restored at a cost of £10 million, partly funded by a heritage grant. But for 70 years it has been a millstone, and has prevented the frontage of the station and its approaches from being remodelled on modern lines. Now it will stand incongruously amid the rebuilt King's Cross/St Pancras complex, to be marvelled at by passengers arriving from the continent on Channel Tunnel trains, who will look in astonishment at such a splendid folly. The French, no doubt, will say *'C'est magnifique, mais ce n'est pas la gare'*, unable to believe that such architectural extravagance could possibly be a railway station.

The restricted loading gauge

The British loading gauge (the height and width restrictions on trains) must have seemed adequate when it was first adopted by George Stephenson, but gradually became an inescapable millstone. Ultimately it imposed restrictions on the boiler size of locomotives, and the width of freight vehicles and coaches. The height restriction has made it impossible to design a suitable double-deck commuter passenger coach, and more recently the advent of freight containers with a height of over 8ft has created expensive difficulties, requiring the headroom under bridges on certain routes to be increased. No one can be blamed for this unfortunate legacy, although the continental loading gauge is more generous and passengers enjoy more spaciousness.

During most of the 19th century, no thought

Sir George Gilbert Scott's gothic extravaganza — the Midland St Pancras Grand Hotel in pre-Grouping days. *BR*

was given to the likelihood of Britain's railways being joined to the continental network. However, Sir Edward Watkin had a vision of his Manchester, Sheffield & Lincolnshire Railway (which became the Great Central Railway) being joined to the continent by an extension towards London, thence over the lines of the Metropolitan Railway and the Southern railway companies, and a tunnel under the Channel. Thus the London extension was constructed to continental gauge standards. Work on the Channel Tunnel had actually been started earlier, in the 1870s, but the War Office was uneasy at the prospect of a foreign army using it as an invasion route, and the project was stopped. However, work could easily have been restarted in the early 1900s when relationships with France were improved.

But Watkin's idea was always a pipe dream — the cost of converting to continental standards the whole of the route from a point south of Chesterfield to the Channel coast (except for the London extension) would have been quite beyond the limited financial resources of the Great Central Railway.

The Great Western Railway's broad gauge
The universal adoption of Brunel's broad gauge, in which the rails were laid 7ft apart instead of George Stephenson's 4ft 8½in, would undoubtedly have been beneficial, were it not for the fact that the additional land required for building a railway (including goods and passenger stations, yards and sidings, together with the additional cost of constructing the railway) would have imposed considerable financial burdens upon railway companies which many would have found hard to bear. In practice, the extra capital required would have been impossibly hard for most railway companies to service.

It became a millstone in another respect, when the expansion of the railway network caused increasing problems at junctions and locations where the two gauges met, and eventually persuaded the GWR to face the cost of converting all its broad gauge track to what had become known as the standard gauge, and converting or scrapping its broad gauge rolling stock. A Royal Commission studied the gauge problem and recommended that George Stephenson's gauge be adopted as standard, and the 1846 Gauge Act made it compulsory for all new railways.

Brunel was a man of vision and not necessarily wrong in adopting his broad gauge, but eventually he was out of step with most of the European railways and the North American railways.

The lack of through communication for passenger trains in major cities
As has been mentioned before, Britain's rail network developed piecemeal with little or no thought being given to the creation of a sensible, logical network rather than, as happened, a whole series of dead-end lines ending near the centre of our large cities, and leading to a multiplicity of stations in them. There were exceptions, such as Bristol, used by the GWR and the Midland; Leeds (New, later renamed Leeds City South), used by the North Eastern and the LNWR; and York, owned by the North Eastern but used also by the Midland from Sheffield and the L&Y from Normanton. But the list of cities with several stations or where through running was impossible or limited is larger.

Top: Broad gauge carriages assembled at Swindon following the final conversion of the track to standard gauge in May 1892. *GWR*

Above: The L&YR's Victoria station at Manchester allowed through running in an east/west direction, providing the same facility for the LNWR which had its Exchange station alongside. Unfortunately it did not provide through running in a north/south direction, even though the provision of such facilities was discussed from time to time. *NRM*

Millstones on the East Coast main line. The 20mph dog-leg at Peterborough for all main line trains, whether calling at Peterborough or not, was not eradicated until the early 1970s. In 1960 Class A3 Pacific No 60049 *Galtee More* enters Peterborough station gently with an up express from Sunderland. *IAL*

Examples of stations where through running was impossible are:

Bradford (Forster Square and Exchange) preventing the Midland from running Anglo-Scottish expresses via Bradford.
Glasgow (Central and Buchanan Street) preventing the Caledonian from running through trains from English stations to stations north of Glasgow.
Almost all the London termini.
Manchester (London Road), which until recently prevented West Coast main line trains from running via Manchester.

Examples of cities which had several stations are:

Birmingham New Street (Midland & LNWR Joint), Moor Street (GWR) and Snow Hill (GWR).
Glasgow Buchanan Street (Caledonian), Central (Cal), Queen Street (North British) and St Enoch (G&SW).
Leeds Central (GNR and L&YR), New (LNWR and NER) and Wellington (Midland).
Liverpool Central (CLC), Exchange (L&YR) and Lime Street (LNWR).
Manchester Central (GCR & Midland), Exchange (LNWR), London Road (GCR & LNWR) and Victoria (L&YR).
And, of course, London.

The result of this lack of planning was increased land-take, with all its associated costs, together with the cost of provision and operation of duplicate lines, stations, depots, yards, engine sheds, carriage sidings, etc. Passenger fares and freight rates were higher than they would otherwise have been, and the profitability of railway companies was lower. It was a huge millstone.

Millstones on the Great Northern main line
The worst millstone on the Great Northern main line was Peterborough, where the main lines had severely speed-restricted curves of 20mph approaching the station from both north and south. This was of no consequence in the 19th century, when almost all trains stopped at Peterborough, but became an increasing millstone in LNER days, continuing until the station was rebuilt and the tracks realigned in 1973. This at last allowed non-stop trains to bypass the station and travel through Peterborough at 105mph.

The tunnels through London's Northern Heights and at Welwyn, together with the Welwyn viaduct, became increasingly a millstone in the 20th century. The LNER had plans to quadruple the line but could not afford to do so, and quadrupling, with additional tunnelling, had to wait until the 1950s following nationalisation. Even then, there were insufficient funds to build a second Welwyn viaduct and two new tunnels at Welwyn North and they continue to be millstones.

The failure to universally adopt the Westinghouse air brake
In the 19th century, the railway companies were unaccountably slow to design effective braking systems for use on their passenger trains, with the result that collisions were not infrequent. The companies professed that they could not find a braking system that was suitable, which resulted in the formation in 1874 of a Royal Commission under the chairmanship of the Duke of Buckingham & Chandos. He was appointed to inquire into the whole question of the safe working of the railways, and as part of that review the commission arranged for brake trials to be held near Newark, on the Midland Railway line from Nottingham. They took place in June 1875.

Eight companies participated, and eight different braking systems were tested. They included the LNWR Clarke & Webb chain brake, Fay's system used on the L&YR, Smith's simple vacuum used by the GNR, and the Westinghouse brake used by the Midland and the LB&SCR. Unfortunately, the results were considered to be inconclusive, with each company professing that its own system was the best one. A glorious opportunity was lost of standardising on the Westinghouse air brake throughout Britain, a situation that was not to be achieved until almost a century later. All the other braking systems tried at Newark failed to meet the Board of Trade's requirements, issued in 1876, that the brake should operate on all vehicles on the train, that it should be capable of being operated by both the driver and the guard, and that it should be applied automatically in the event of a train breaking in two. However, the Board of Trade was reluctant to apply compulsion, not wishing to appear to be taking over some of the companies' responsibility to operate their trains safely. Compulsion had to wait until 1889, with the Regulation of Railways Act.

George Westinghouse was born in New York in 1846 and became a prolific inventor. He devised the air brake in 1868/69, in which the brakes were held off by air pressure. It was a simple ('non-safe') system at first, but following a visit to Britain in 1875 he developed an automatic, fail-safe, system which fully met the Board of Trade's requirements. It was adopted by a number of pre-Grouping companies in Britain, notably the Great Eastern, the Caledonian, the LB&SCR and the North British. The other companies eventually adopted Smith's automatic vacuum brake. George Westinghouse formed a Westinghouse Continuous Brake Company in Britain in 1876. He had no success with the LNWR, who firmly believed that if it wasn't built at Crewe it was no good. In fact the LNWR, to its discredit, persisted with its lamentable chain brake until compelled to fall into line by the 1889 Act.

Personality

Sir Richard Moon

Richard Moon was one of the outstanding railway personalities of the 19th century. He was born in 1814, the son of a Liverpool merchant, and the history of his life is practically the 19th century history of the London & North Western Railway. He joined the Board in 1847 when the company had just come into existence, with the amalgamation of the London & Birmingham, the Manchester & Birmingham and the Grand Junction lines. During his long connection with it, first as a director and then (from 1861 to 1891) as chairman, the LNWR became the largest, most successful and most powerful railway in Britain.

Throughout his career, Richard Moon's powers of organisation and his genius for railway diplomacy were of the greatest advantage to the company, and to him it owed its commanding position. He was a clear thinker, a good administrator and a strong advocate of economy (he considered that 45mph was fast enough) and his

policies resulted in the LNWR consistently paying its shareholders higher dividends than any other railway company. He believed that everything that the company did was subservient to the size of the rewards to the shareholders. Every penny spent had to be justified, which is why the LNWR became self-sufficient as far as possible and did not employ contractors where it could be avoided.

Richard Moon was a good judge of character and was assisted by a number of very efficient chief officers. Francis Webb was Chief Mechanical Engineer from 1873 to 1903. George Findlay was Goods Manager from 1864 to 1874, Chief Traffic Manager from 1874 to 1880, and General Manager from 1880 to 1893. George Neele was Superintendent of the Line from 1862 to 1895. This very long-serving triumvirate paralleled Richard Moon's tenure as chairman and gave the LNWR considerable stability and steady growth.

Richard Moon was created a baronet during Queen Victoria's Golden Jubilee in 1887 and died at Coventry in 1899.

Historians are fortunate that both Findlay and Neele wrote about their railway lives. Findlay published *The Working and Management of an English Railway* in 1889, which ran to six editions, and is probably the best account of the administration of a British railway company ever produced. He was also knighted (in 1892). G.P. Neele published his memoirs in 1904 under the title *Railway Reminiscences — Notes on a Railway Superintendent's Life*, in which he sets out year by year all the developments and events in a superintendent's career. It is an invaluable treasure trove. Both books are required reading for anyone who wishes to acquire a deeper understanding of railways in the 19th century.

PART 2
1914 to 1947

Mechanical engineering

Chapter 6

Milestones — Locomotives

Sir Herbert Nigel Gresley's Pacifics and Class V2 2-6-2s

Nigel Gresley, as he is universally known, was born in Edinburgh on 19 January 1876 (which might be considered a landmark in itself, in view of what followed). From 1893 to 1897 he served an apprenticeship as a pupil of Francis Webb at Crewe, then he moved to the Horwich Works of the Lancashire & Yorkshire Railway to find his fortune under John Aspinall, the Locomotive Superintendent. After a spell in the Drawing Office he was appointed Running Shed Foreman at Blackpool in 1900. Two years later he found himself at Newton Heath carriage works as Works Manager, and in 1904 he became Assistant Carriage & Wagon Superintendent of the L&YR. Then fate played its part. In 1905 a vacancy arose on the Great Northern Railway for a carriage & wagon superintendent. Aspinall recommended Gresley to his friend H. A. Ivatt, who was Locomotive Engineer of the GNR, and Gresley was accord-

ingly appointed. Ivatt was due to retire in a few years' time and in 1911 Gresley succeeded him.

Gresley's subsequent career is well known, and he produced many excellent designs in his 30 years service, firstly as Locomotive Engineer of the GNR, and then as Chief Mechanical Engineer of the London & North Eastern Railway, but today he is best remembered for his Pacifics and especially for his streamliners. However, one might mention his Class O1 and O2 2-8-0s, his Class K3 2-6-0s, his 'Shires' and his 'Hunts' (4-4-0s), and especially his 'Green Arrow' class 2-6-2s. But we must start with his Pacifics, because they dominated the LNER East Coast main line for 40 years.

At the end of World War 1 the East Coast main line expresses were still hauled by Ivatt Atlantics (4-4-2s). Whilst they were excellent engines, some of which had been rebuilt by Gresley, a more powerful engine was needed, and in 1922, just before the Grouping, Gresley produced his *chef-d'oeuvre*, a big Pacific, GNR No 1470 *Great Northern*, quickly followed by No 1471 *Sir Frederick Banbury*. This was to be a major milestone and the beginning of a long production line

Before turning his mind to Pacifics, Gresley produced these very powerful and efficient 2-6-0 mixed traffic engines, known as Class K3. They had 5ft 8in diameter driving wheels and a tractive effort of 30,031lb. No 120 heads south with a fully fitted freight train (No 552) from Scotland to King's Cross Goods. The first of the class appeared in 1921 and building continued until 1937. They were very versatile engines. *C. R. L. Coles*

Right: The 'V2' 2-6-2s were a mixed traffic version of the Pacifics with their 6ft 2in driving wheels and they were equally as powerful. The first one appeared in 1936 and building continued until 1943. No 60975 stands under a coaling tower in very early BR days. *Eric Treacy*

Below: After World War 1 Nigel Gresley set to work to provide the Great Northern Railway with express passenger locomotives that were more powerful and faster than Ivatt's Atlantics. The first example was a 4-6-2, No 1470, aptly named *Great Northern,* which emerged from Doncaster Works in 1922. *IAL*

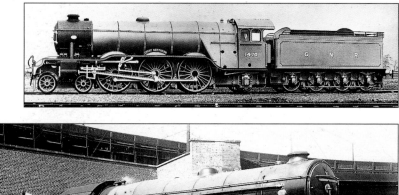

Above: In LNER days, No 1470 *Great Northern* in splendid condition stands on the turntable waiting to be photographed. *IAL*

of Pacifics. They were beautifully proportioned and elegant, and looked like racehorses: indeed, they were named after racehorses, which was very appropriate, as day after day they raced up and down the East Coast main line. The LNER classified the original Pacifics as 'A1'. They had three cylinders 18in x 26in, 6ft 8in diameter driving wheels and a boiler pressure of 180psi. Tractive effort was 29,835lb. 52 were built over the next few years.

Was this an engine to beat the Great Western's 'Castle' class? Both engines had been exhibited on adjacent stands at the British Empire Exhibition at Wembley in 1924, and then in the following year the two companies arranged exchange trials, the LNER being represented by No 4474 *Victor Wild* and the GWR by No 4079 *Pendennis Castle.* The LNER locomotive acquitted itself well, but the 'Castle' was thought to have performed even better. Gresley studied the results and realised that there were lessons to be learned from the front-end design of the 'Castle' and its higher boiler pressure. He applied those lessons to a new series of Pacifics in 1928, with improved valve gearing and a higher boiler pressure of 220psi. Tractive effort was increased to 32,909lb. It did the trick. The new locomotives were classified 'A3' and were nicknamed 'Super-Pacifics'. There were 27 of them, and all the earlier Class A1s were rebuilt in due course. The alterations turned a very good engine into a world-beater, which many people regard as one of the finest express engines ever built in Britain.

But even the 'A3s' were to be eclipsed, if that were possible. The catalyst was perhaps the 'Fliegende Hamburger', a new high-speed diesel train which ran between Berlin and Hamburg. The LNER considered the merits of introducing such a train on the East Coast main line but Gresley persuaded them that an improved 'A3' with a light train could produce equally good performances. Trials with *Flying Scotsman* and the 'A3' No 2750 *Papyrus* on light loads showed great promise, the latter achieving 108mph, a new speed record, with a seven coach train. Four more 'A3' Pacifics had been included in the building programme for 1935, but Gresley took the opportunity to include improvements. The most obvious was a streamlined casing, but underneath it Gresley provided a boiler of

250psi, improved steam passages and draught-ing. A new high speed train, the *Silver Jubilee,* was introduced in the timetable for winter 1935 and Doncaster Works turned out the first streamlined engine, No 2509 *Silver Link,* just in time. At the inaugural press run, 112^{1}/$_{2}$mph was recorded, with an average of 100mph being achieved continuously for 43 miles. It was an unprecedented performance and another mile-stone. Three more of these silver-grey streamlin-ers were built, and the quartet worked the King's Cross to Newcastle four-hour service. They were known as Class A4.

However, even better was to come. Aided by low-interest government loans, a further 30 were built in 1936/37, and new high-speed trains were introduced — the 'Coronation', King's Cross to Edinburgh in six hours, and the 'West Riding', Kings Cross to Leeds in 2hr 43min, and Bradford in 3hr 5min. Success followed success. In 1938, *Mallard* set a world record for steam when it achieved 126mph whilst descending Stoke Bank north of Peterborough. The stream-lined trains were a huge publicity success for the LNER and a great morale boost for the staff, who had lived through tight economic pressures. But primarily, the 'A4s' had technically out-classed even the 'A3s'. They were the glory of the East Coast expresses for the next 30 years and Gresley's crowning achievement. He was quite properly knighted in 1936.

And yet, and yet. . . High-speed expresses and streamliners are only a part of the story, and in economic terms only a small part. Freight traffic is also important, and the acceleration of mer-chandise trains was becoming urgent, to combat

road competition. A locomotive was needed that could pull a 50-wagon freight train at up to 60mph but which would be equally at home on express passenger trains, except for those in the front rank. In other words, a true mixed traffic locomotive with good route availability. Gresley was quite equal to the task and produced the cel-ebrated 'V2' class of 2-6-2s. With 6ft 2in driving wheels, they were fully a mixed traffic version of the 'A3' Pacifics, and with similar dimensions — three cylinders 18^{1}/$_{2}$in x 26in and boiler pressure of 220psi, giving a tractive effort of 33,730lb. The first one appeared in 1936 (another mile-stone!) — No 4771 *Green Arrow* — and the class ran to 184 engines by 1943. Gresley believed in producing engines that were masters of the job. He wasn't to know that within three years the 'V2s' would be performing heroic feats

Top: Probably the most famous locomotive in the world, No 4472 *Flying Scotsman* is polished up ready for display at the British Empire Exhibition, Wembley, in 1924. *W. J. Reynolds*

Above: In 1928 the LNER decided to run non-stop between King's Cross and Edinburgh, and modified some tenders to provide through corridor access from the train to the footplate so that crews could change over at the halfway point north of York. No 2580 shows off its corridor tender to the photographer. *F. Moore*

on the East Coast main line pulling huge trains. 184 'V2s' could not have been afforded or justified in peacetime, but in wartime they proved their worth many times over. They were a fitting tribute to Gresley's foresight.

Great men such as Gresley, who was in the limelight for 30 years, tend to attract a degree of criticism. His conjugated valve gear caused problems in wartime and postwar maintenance conditions, and his use of three cylinders instead of two for middle rank engines might be questioned. But he designed engines for prewar conditions and they did all that was required of them. He could not have foreseen wartime and postwar conditions, and criticism based on hindsight is unacceptable. Furthermore, he never rested on his laurels, but was always looking for ways of improving the steam locomotive. He is well fitted to stand with other giants in the Pantheon of great locomotive engineers.

Right: In his search for an improved Class A3 Pacific, Nigel Gresley carried out some trials on the East Coast main line in 1934. During these trials, No 2750 *Papyrus* achieved 108mph with a seven-coach train, a new speed record, and provided the justification for the Class A4 streamliners. *IAL*

Below: Sir Nigel Gresley, knighted in 1936, stands alongside his finest creation — the Class A4 streamlined Pacifics, one of which, No 4498, is named in his honour. *British Railways*

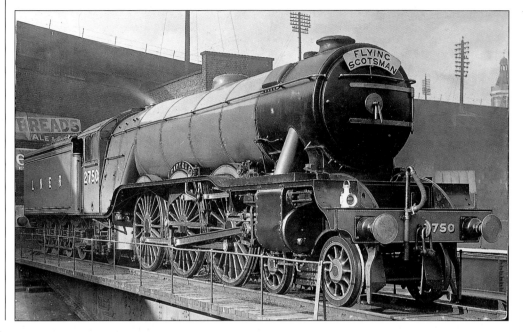

The 'Royal Scots' of the LMS

The LMS inherited quite a large fleet of 4-6-0s from the LNWR and the L&YR, including 130 'Claughtons' (discussed in Part 1) and 75 L&Y 'Dreadnoughts' (some of which were built after Grouping), but both classes had proved themselves to be incapable of the standard of performance that was needed on West Coast main line expresses. In February 1926, orders were approved for five four-cylinder compound Pacifics, and work on the boilers was put in hand. However, James Anderson, a former Midland man and Motive Power Superintendent of the LMS, favoured a Midland design of three-cylinder compound. The GWR 'Castles' had demonstrated on the LNER in 1925 what could be achieved by a 4-6-0, and Anderson, together with J. H. Follows, Chief General Superintendent of the LMS (Anderson's boss and another Midland man), arranged for a 'Castle', *Launceston Castle*, to take part in trials on the West Coast main line. Once more a 'Castle' effortlessly showed its superiority both in power and coal consumption.

At once all work on the compound Pacifics ceased, and it was decided to produce a 4-6-0 (Fowler, the CME, appears not to have been involved in the decision). Anderson, to his credit, specified three cylinders, a high-pressure boiler and adequate grate area for long non-stop running. Chambers, the Chief Locomotive Draughtsman, and E. S. Cox (of later fame)

supported long-travel, long-lap valves, which Anderson accepted. The operating department needed 50 locomotives for the 1927 summer service, and Swindon was approached for a set of drawings for 'Castle' class engines, but the request was refused. The LMS then turned to the Southern Railway, which had just built a powerful 4-6-0 *Lord Nelson*, and the request for drawings received more favourable treatment. The locomotive works of the LMS were fully occupied with current orders, and the company immediately placed a contract with the North British Locomotive Co of Glasgow. The 50 'Royal Scots' were turned out in time and proved to be a great success, for which the much maligned Anderson can surely take some credit.

Right: The finished product, and a tribute to the North British Locomotive Works. 'Royal Scot' Class No 6147 *The Northamptonshire Regiment* passes Kilburn with a down express. It was originally named *Courier* and was renamed in 1935. It is also fitted with a Stanier tender. *IAL*

Below: Stanier built two 'Princess Royal' Pacifics in 1933, then evaluated them for two years before building 10 more in 1935. One of these, No 46207 *Princess Arthur of Connaught,* rounds the curves near Thrimby Grange, south of Penrith, at the head of the 9.30am Glasgow to Euston on 11 June 1950. *E. D. Bruton*

For the beleaguered LMS the 'Royal Scots' were indeed a milestone. A further 20 were built at Derby in 1930. Under William Stanier they became even better, using the standards he introduced and developed.

William Arthur Stanier joins the LMS

The date 1 January 1932 was one of the major milestones in the history of the London, Midland & Scottish Railway. On that day William Stanier took charge as Chief Mechanical Engineer of the LMSR at the age of 55 years. The events leading up to that remarkable appointment are described in the Millstones Section. Here we are more concerned to relate the impact that Stanier had on LMS locomotive policy. His brief was to reduce the number of

locomotive classes on the LMS and to introduce a range of new classes that would equip the LMS with an adequate locomotive stock of modern design. The locomotives were to be economical in both fuel and maintenance and capable of working long through turns, leading to greater utilisation.

Not all of Stanier's designs were successful, and some of his initial ideas, such as Swindon's low-superheat, had to be modified, but he was quick to learn.

The Pacifics

The 4-6-0 'Royal Scots' were performing well on the West Coast main line, but a more powerful locomotive was required for the heaviest long-distance expresses, especially the Anglo-Scottish

services, and the railway world waited with eager anticipation to see what Stanier would produce. In June 1933 the answer was revealed. Engine No 6200 was wheeled out of the shops — a Pacific. By LMS standards it was a monster, but a monster with beautiful lines. Its measurements closely followed those of the GWR's 'King' class engines — four cylinders 16¹/₄in x 28in, 6ft 6in diameter driving wheels, 250psi boiler pressure and a tractive effort of 40,300lb, but externally it was a new design which immediately attracted admiration. Initially two engines were produced, with No 6201 following quickly. There was then a long period of trials, resulting in a number of modifications, including new boilers, before 10 more engines appeared in 1935, Nos 6203-6212. No 6200 was named *Princess Royal* and the other engines also received the names of princesses, or other members of the Royal Family. They were a great success, and the gripping story of the development of the 'Princess Royals' has been recounted by Roland Bond in his excellent book *A Lifetime with Locomotives*. He spoke with authority because he was there. Fortunately, two members of the class have been preserved and can still be seen in steam, Nos 6201 *Princess Elizabeth* and 6203 *Princess Margaret Rose*. It is still a thrilling sight, even after 70 years.

Stanier then turned his mind to other new classes, but it is convenient to continue the Pacific story. In 1936, the LMS authorities were considering the running of high-speed expresses between Euston and Glasgow Central in preparation for the Coronation of King George VI the following year, and it was known that the LNER had something up its sleeve. The 'Princess

Royals' were doing everything that was asked of them, but what was needed was a locomotive that could maintain high speeds for several hours.

The result was a class of Pacifics known as the 'Princess Coronation' class, although very quickly they were dubbed the 'Duchesses'. They had been very carefully designed not only to produce copious quantities of steam, but also to ensure that it was used in the most efficient manner. The results were dramatic, and the 'Duchesses' were a huge success, both mechanically and visually. Streamlining and air-smoothing was in vogue, and the LNER had introduced its streamlined Pacifics in 1934. The LMS therefore decided that the 'Duchesses' should also be streamlined, partly to reduce air-resistance at high speed, but also for the publicity value. They ensured that Stanier's name would join the list of great locomotive engineers and would go down in history.

The dimensions of the 'Duchesses' were simi-

Top: Stanier was planning an engine that could maintain high speeds for several hours, and it appeared in 1937, just in time for the coronation of King George VI. His streamliners were an instant success. No 6221 *Queen Elizabeth* gets into its stride with a down express including 'Coronation Scot' coaches, just south of Watford. *IAL*

Above: A batch of five Stanier Pacifics, Nos 6230-34, was built without streamlining. One of them, No 6231 *Duchess of Atholl,* coasts though Oxenholme with an up express. The tall LNWR co-acting signals were a feature of the junction at Oxenholme for many years. *IAL*

lar to the 'Princesses', but the cylinder diameters were increased by a quarter of an inch and the wheel diameters were increased to 6ft 9ins for higher speeds. However, in order to provide the extra steam capacity the boilers were provided with increased heating surfaces, resulting in the total heating area rising from 2,967sq ft in the 'Princesses' to 3,637sq ft in the 'Duchesses'. Success was guaranteed, and was demonstrated in spectacular fashion when No 6220 *Coronation* achieved 114mph approaching Crewe on a press trip on 29 June 1937, taking the speed record for British steam from the LNER.

Nos 6220 to 6229 were turned out in streamlined form from Crewe in 1937 and 1938, to be followed by five non-streamlined engines, Nos 6230 to 6234, also in 1938. Many regard the latter as the most powerful and massive-looking of any express passenger locomotive ever built in Britain. Crewe then reverted to more streamlined engines, which became the 'City' class. Nos 6235 to 6244 were built in 1938/39 and a small number were built during the war. After the war a few more were built, ending with No 6257. Appropriately, No 6256 was named *Sir William A. Stanier, FRS.* The last batch never had a streamlined casing, and it was removed from the others. Three have been preserved —

Nos 6229 (the original 6220), 6233 and 6235. No 6233 *Duchess of Sutherland* hauled the Royal Train with HRH The Prince of Wales over the Settle-Carlisle line as recently as 22 March 2005. The 67-year-old locomotive looked magnificent and behaved appropriately.

The 4-6-0 two-cylinder and three-cylinder locomotives

By the end of 1933, the LMS had a desperate need for modern locomotives for other than top-rank express passenger trains and for mixed traffic duties. It had nothing suitable for the former, other than the 52 'Patriots', Nos 5500 to 5551, and nothing suitable for the latter other than the Hughes 2-6-0s, Nos 2700 to 2944.

The two-cylinder 4-6-0s, known initially as Power Class 5P5F, were an instant success, indeed, one of the most successful engines ever designed. At home on almost any duty, they spread far and wide throughout the LMS system and enabled many obsolete engines to be withdrawn almost en masse. The first engine to appear was No 5020 in 1934, built by the Vulcan Foundry, and the whole of the first batch of 452 engines had been completed by 1937. Vulcan Foundry built 100 and Sir W. G. Armstrong Whitworth's built no fewer than 326, aided by the availability of government loans to alleviate unemployment. However, building did not stop there. Several more were built during the next few years; then, after the war, large scale building recommenced until the class numbered 842 engines, Nos 4658 to 5499. If Stanier had built nothing else he would be remembered and revered for his two-cylinder 4-6-0s.

The three-cylinder 4-6-0s, Power Class 5XP, were specially designed for second-rank express passenger duties, and a third of them went to the Midland Division, to enable accelerated services to be introduced. Both classes were a revelation to

the Midland, which had soldiered on for many years with little better than the compounds, good though they were, and the Class 3P 'Belpaire' 4-4-0s. The first batch of 'Jubilees', as the 5XPs came to be known, consisted of no fewer than 113 locomotives, and they were produced straight off the drawing board. Initially they were a disappointment and were indifferent steamers, requiring expensive modification before they became really satisfactory. But then they became fast-running and willing horses on medium-weight trains. The 'Jubilees' were often asked to take on loads in excess of those for which they were designed, and tackled them manfully, but the class would have been a greater success with another 3,000lb of tractive effort. Two of them, Nos 5735/6, were fitted with larger boilers during World War 2, which gave them the power they needed. Perhaps with

Above: The three-cylinder 'Jubilees' were among the most attractive of Stanier's designs, captured beautifully in this study of Holbeck's No 45569 *Tasmania* on York shed in early BR days. *Eric Treacy*

Left: 'Jubilee' class No 5742 *Connaught* was the last of the class and was fitted with a double chimney. It was shedded at Bushbury, which had a stud of them for working the Wolverhampton–London expresses, and here it is climbing Camden Bank with a down express. *Eric Treacy*

hindsight the second tranche of 'Jubilees' should have had larger boilers from the start. But the 'Jubilees' were a delight to generations of schoolboy trainspotters and it was a stroke of genius to give them all suitable names to mark the Silver Jubilee of King George V.

A comparison with the other companies reveals a disparity, based on the immediate prewar situation and using the post-1948 power classification:

LMS
Class 6P: 51 'Patriots' and 191 'Jubilees'
Class 7P: 71 'Royal Scots'
Class 8P: 38 Pacifics

LNER
Class 7P: 153 Class V2 2-6-2, 79 Class A1 and A3 Pacifics
Class 8P: 34 Class A4 Pacifics (streamliners)

GWR
Class 7P: 131 'Castle' class
Class 8P: 30 'Kings'

In summary, the LNER had 266 modern engines in power classes 7P and 8P, the Great Western had 161, whilst the LMS, the largest company, had a mere 109. In 1946 the LMS began to rebuild a few of the 'Patriots' with larger taper boilers, but concentrated on rebuilding the 'Royal Scots' with taper boilers.

The Class 8F 2-8-0s

The LMS sorely needed a modern heavy freight engine. Double-heading was still rife on the Midland Division, and the Beyer-Garratts, 33 of which had been built by 1930, had not been as successful as had been expected. Derby had interfered with the design, instead of leaving the contractor to produce a satisfactory machine, which he was perfectly capable of doing (this issue will be dealt with in more detail in the Millstones section). Stanier's answer was a 2-8-0, Class 8F, which was an immediate success and exactly what the LMS needed. Crewe began to build them in 1935, but only about a dozen were produced that year. However, Vulcan Foundry received a large order for 70, all of which came into traffic in 1936. Crewe continued to produce about a dozen each year right up to the outbreak of war, by which time the fleet numbered 126. Stanier's 8F masterpiece was then chosen as the standard heavy-freight wartime locomotive, and several hundred were built both by contractors (mainly the North British Locomotive Company) and all four main line companies. Many of them went overseas, especially to the Middle East. Eventually, when everything was sorted out after the war, the LMS (and British

Railways LM Region) became the possessors of a huge fleet of 666 excellent heavy freight engines.

In summary

Stanier caused a revolution on the LMS in a few short years, 1934-7. Almost all his ventures were rewarded with success, but his great achievements were the Pacifics, the two-cylinder 4-6-0 mixed traffics, the 2-8-0 heavy freight engines and the 2-6-4 tank engines, which numbered 186 of the two-cylinder version, and 37 of the three-cylinder version for the London, Tilbury & Southend Section. The 'Jubilees' had a bad start, and even after various modifications to improve steaming some commentators believe that they never quite delivered the performance they promised. On the other hand O. S. Nock regarded them when modified as extraordinary willing and hard slogging engines, as well as being very swift on favourable stretches of line. And A. J. Powell, in his *Living with London Midland Locomotives,* said that by and large they were grand machines for fast running with medium-weight trains or for heavy pounding on difficult routes. It is clear that the debate on the merits of the 'Jubilees' is far from over. Stanier's only failures were the 2-6-2 tanks which followed the equally sluggish Fowler design.

Perhaps the greatest tribute to his greatness was paid by his successors, who continued for years to build more of his established designs and build on the foundations he had laid. Nor did this cease with nationalisation in 1948; the lineage of two of BR's best designs can be traced back to the LMS in the mid-1930s — the Class 5 4-6-0 and the Class 4 2-6-4 tank. 1 January 1932 was indeed a major milestone for the LMS.

Millstones — Locomotives

Oliver Bulleid's 'Merchant Navy' class Pacific locomotives and the 'Leader' class

This is one of those cases that might well have fallen into the category of Milestones, because, when they were in good fettle, Bulleid's 'Merchant Navy' Pacifics were free steaming and fast running, masters of any job that the Southern Railway (and BR) could put them to.

Oliver Bulleid was born in 1882 and joined the Great Northern Railway in 1901 at Doncaster Works as a premium apprentice with the redoubtable H. A. Ivatt, the Locomotive Engineer. Apart from an early short spell, he was to remain at Doncaster for the next 36 years, 25 of them as assistant to Nigel Gresley, one of the most famous Chief Mechanical Engineers of all

Below: Newly built 'Merchant Navy' class No 21C2 *Union Castle* with a short train on 4 July 1941. *Southern Railway*

Bottom: BR decided to rebuild the 'Merchant Navies', producing a very powerful-looking machine that overcame what were regarded as its inherent defects. A preserved example, No 35028 *Clan Line,* is accompanied by a bowler-hatted inspector, and both he and the driver are looking out for the official photographer. *BRB*

time. Surprisingly little is known of his work at Doncaster, but when R. E. L. Maunsell retired as Chief Mechanical Engineer of the Southern Railway in 1937, Bulleid was appointed as his successor.

His *chef-d'oeuvre* was to be the 'Merchant Navy' class of Pacifics, the first five of which appeared in 1941. They had three cylinders and 6ft 2in diameter driving wheels, but it was not until April 1949 that the last of the class of 30 was built. Somehow he persuaded both his own management and the wartime Railway Executive Committee that their building was justified in wartime on the grounds that their moderate sized driving wheels allowed them to be classi-

fied as mixed traffic locomotives akin to the Class V2 2-6-2s on the LNER, although that was clearly not the builder's real intention.

Having achieved authority to build the engines he took the unwise step of producing five machines straight off, without any trials, which was surprising for a locomotive with so many novel and untried features, but particularly its unique chain-driven valve gear, enclosed in an oil sump, which was to be its Achilles' heel. No one would deny that they required skilled maintenance, but it was not always available in wartime, nor afterwards. Cecil J. Allen wrote that the oil-bath could not be kept oil-tight, resulting in leakage and excessive oil consumption. The inaccessibility of the motion required increased time at the sheds for maintenance. However, whilst the 'MNs', as they became known, were less than popular among the fitting staff, it was quite another matter with the enginemen. They had never had such powerful and speedy engines, and such comfortable cabs. The Merchant Navies' all-welded steel firebox and a boiler with excellent steam-raising capacity gave the drivers all the steam they needed for any job. So from that point of view they were a milestone, especially since the 'Lord Nelsons' which preceded them were generally regarded as less than 100% successful until Bulleid improved them.

Johnson and Long in their masterly book *British Railways Engineering 1948-80* relate how postwar conditions eventually persuaded the, by

now, nationalised railway to take action over the chain-driven valve gear and inside motion enclosed in an oil-bath. Bulleid had intended these novel features to reduce the extent and cost of maintenance, but they had had the opposite effect, resulting in unreliability and loss of availability. Repair costs per mile during 1950-2 were almost twice those of the LNER Class A1 pacifics and 50% higher than the LMS 'Duchesses'. Statistics of coal consumption and availability were equally unfavourable and a case was made for rebuilding the 'MNs' on more conventional lines. It was an entirely successful change but, by then, Bulleid had departed for Ireland. His completely laudable aim had been to attempt to improve the steam locomotive and he gave the Southern a more than adequate stock of express passenger locomotives that were fully masters of the job.

Bulleid took his desire to improve the steam engine several stages further with his highly unorthodox 'Leader' tank engine design. It had an 0-6-6-0 wheel arrangement and the whole locomotive body was mounted above a massive girder frame. It had cabs at both ends and a separate compartment in the centre for the fireman. Each bogie was equipped with a three-cylinder engine. When completed, it was found to be overweight and the temperature in the fireman's

Right: Bulleid's burning desire to improve the steam engine even further found expression in the optimistically named 'Leader' class, one of which, No 36001, ran trials with the dynamometer car between Eastleigh and Guildford in August 1950. *S. Townroe*

Above: The LMS acquired from the Midland Railway hundreds of elderly 0-6-0s. A Class 2F, No 3527, simmers at Willesden Junction on 21 June 1949. *C. C. B. Herbert*

Right: The Midland Railway Class 3F 0-6-0s were simple, sturdy machines and quite powerful. Most of them survived until the late 1950s/early 1960s. The class dated from 1885, but the locomotives were rebuilt by Fowler from 1920. No 3243 heads a raft of coal wagons near Derby in June 1941. *H. C. Casserley*

compartment was far too high to be acceptable. How Bulleid persuaded the Southern management to allow him to build 35 of these engines is a mystery, but in the event only two were actually completed, the first one appearing on 21 June 1949. The new Railway Executive was not so compliant and the project was cancelled. The two engines were broken up. But if Bulleid had come to the Southern at an earlier age, and if the war had not intervened, he might have achieved great success with more time for extended trials of his advanced designs. He had many achievements to his credit, and his boilers were particularly good.

The LMS locomotive policy in the 1920s

Much has been written about this, and about the ascendancy of former Midland men in the locomotive and operating departments of the LMS. Actually, the locomotive department was organised in two separate fields — those of the Chief Mechanical Engineer and the Superintendent of Motive Power — and it was the latter, under J. E. Anderson, which wielded most power. Anderson had previously been deputy CME of the Midland and works manager at Derby. It was his job to specify traffic demands so that the CME could build locomotives to meet them, but Anderson wielded undue influence. He reported directly to J. H. Follows, the Chief General Superintendent, who was himself a former Midland man and allowed Anderson to interfere in matters of locomotive design to a quite extraordinary extent. Such interference was obviously tolerated by the CME. George Hughes was the first CME of the LMS, having been CME of the L&YR, and CME of the merged LNWR/LYR in 1922. He was a forward looking locomotive man and made his HQ at Horwich, but he retired in September 1925, clearly having found working relationships uncongenial. Hughes was followed by the genial Sir Henry Fowler, who had been knighted for wartime service at the Ministry of Munitions. Fowler had been CME of the Midland since 1910, so it was a Midland takeover, with Anderson supreme.

The Midland had been wedded to the small

Below left: Belatedly, the LMS realised that it needed something stronger than the Class 4F 0-6-0s for heavy freight haulage, and the Class 7F 0-8-0s were the result. They were numbered 9500 to 9674 and the entire series was built at Crewe between 1929 and 1932. They suffered severely from hot axleboxes. No 9658 appears to be quite comfortable with its long load of mixed goods as it ambles along the up slow line somewhere south of Roade. *H. Gordon Tidey*

Below: Whilst the compounds were underpowered for working heavy express trains, they were fully at home on eight coaches. Ex-Midland engine No 1012 is in charge of such a train on its home ground north of Derby in the early 1930s. *IAL*

In the 1930s the Big Four sought to improve the efficiency and reduce the costs of their branch line and secondary passenger services. The Great Western was the most successful and introduced a fleet of diesel railcars, one of which formed the 4.20pm Shrewsbury to Kidderminster (the Severn Valley line) on 25 June 1960, a typical service. *M. Mensing*

Derby. However, the Midland Division needed a heavy goods engine and George Hughes had initiated discussions with Beyer Peacock for a Garratt-type locomotive. James Anderson managed to interfere with the design, specifying axles and axleboxes of a Class 4F 0-6-0 and short-travel valves. The result was little short of a disaster. Hot axleboxes were common and coal consumption was heavy. Three machines were produced in 1927, followed by 30, still with the same faults, in 1930. They were disliked, even hated, by locomen and shed staff alike. Then came the fiasco of the Class 7F 0-8-0s. This class of 175 engines was all built at Crewe, but Derby Class 4F axleboxes were specified. How the Crewe men must have winced. They appeared between 1929 and 1932. The '7Fs' were good performers but they spent too much of their time on shed being treated for hot axleboxes and were swept away in large numbers after World War 2 after quite a short life, when there were plenty of more modern heavy freight engines available. As a final indignity, the standard 0-8-0s were well-outlived by the elderly but reliable LNW 0-8-0s.

It was a sad period for locomotive affairs on the LMS and much of the blame may be put on the shoulders of James Anderson, but J. H. Follows and Sir Henry Fowler must also take their share of blame for allowing it to happen. Top management was also not blameless, but in 1930 the LMS Board took the first step towards improving matters. It realised that locomotive affairs needed a firmer hand on the tiller and moved Sir Henry, appointing him as Assistant to the Vice-President for Works, with special responsibility for Research and Development. He was succeeded *pro tem* by Ernest Lemon, the C&W Engineer, whilst the LMS sought a suitable candidate. Sir Josiah Stamp, the President and Chairman of the LMS, knew that if the rivalry between Crewe and Derby was ever to be solved, the new man would have to come from neither stable. The LMS looked with envy at the GWR with its fleet of highly capable 'Castles', and thoughts turned to approaching the GWR for one of its best men. Stanier was invited to lunch with Ernest Lemon and Sir Harold Hartley, following which official overtures were made. Stanier must have been both astonished and flattered, but he had been at Swindon for nearly 40 years and knew that the CME's post there would never be his. The prospect of moving to the largest company, the LMS, with virtually a free hand to produce a range of modern efficient locomotives, must have been irresistible. It was also a stroke of genius on the part of the LMS management.

engine policy, with double-heading resorted to whenever necessary. Its express passenger timetable was based on a frequent service of comparatively light trains, and it could be argued that to employ larger engines than was necessary was a financial extravagance. Small freight engines were cheap and lasted for half a century. And not all goods trains were too heavy for a single engine. This gave flexibility. The Midland's policy was quite evidently "Small is Good", but it was wrong to apply that policy to the whole of the LMS where conditions might be different. However, there was another factor in the reckoning. The LMS acquired nearly 400 different types of locomotive from its constituents, and, in order to achieve economy in spares, it was felt necessary to reduce that number. Many of those types had belonged to smaller companies with only a few engines of each type. It was therefore good policy to produce a standard type. The standard passenger types chosen were the Midland Class 2P 4-4-0 and the Midland Class 4P compound, and several hundred were built. For the freight business the Midland Class 4F was chosen, and 531 were built by 1928, almost all of them by contractors. The Midland 4F was a reasonable performer, but it was unsatisfactory mechanically.

There were three successes during this period. George Hughes designed a modern mixed traffic 2-6-0, of which 244 were built, and an equally good 2-6-4 tank engine. And the 'Royal Scots' were built, but fortunately not designed at

Milestones — Diesel trains and locomotives

Introduction

Even before World War 1, several railway companies had been examining ways and means of reducing the cost of working local passenger trains, especially on branch lines, and the idea of the push-pull train was born, in which the engine pulled its train of two or three carriages in one direction, and then pushed them in the reverse direction. The outer end of the last carriage had a compartment for the driver to use when the train was being propelled. Guards were not usually employed on such workings.

During the 1920s, the LNER introduced a number of steam-powered single carriage units, known as Sentinel steam railcars, but almost all had been withdrawn by World War 2. The Clayton company also built a few, and the other railway companies carried out trials, but the results were not encouraging. Thoughts then turned to diesel traction.

Diesel railcars

In the 1930s, several companies experimented with diesel railcars, but the most successful was the Great Western. The well-known AEC company discussed with the GWR the idea of a diesel railcar for branch lines and rural routes and the suggestion was adopted. The first railcar, in attractive streamlined form, was introduced into service, based on Southall depot, on 4 December 1933, a major milestone. In the next few years, up to the outbreak of World War 2, more diesel railcars were introduced, including a number for high speed secondary routes, until there were 38 in the fleet.

The other companies no doubt watched with interest, but took little or no pains to emulate the success of the GWR's enterprise. The LMS carried out a number of trials of railcars produced by various manufacturers. In 1933 the firm of Dick, Kerr of Preston produced an English Electric diesel-electric railcar which ran experimentally on a number of lines, but even though it appears to have been quite successful the LMS decided not to buy it.

Concurrently the Leyland Motor Company built three four-wheeled diesel-hydraulic railcars, which were taken into LMS stock in 1934 as Nos 29950-2. They worked in the Blackburn/Clitheroe area and also from Hamilton shed, but gradually their use declined. They were finally withdrawn in 1951. It is evident that the LMS did not judge them to be sufficiently successful to support further production.

The LMS continued to experiment with diesel-powered railcars of various types from a number of manufacturers, but none was adopted. The most promising candidate, however, was a three-car diesel-hydraulic unit of very modern appearance, powered by six 125hp Leyland engines. After extended trials it began operation on 5 September 1938 between Bletchley and Oxford, and after six months it was transferred to the Midland Division to run a semi-fast service between St Pancras and Nottingham via Leicester. Unhappily, this promising beginning was overshadowed by the approaching war and no further units were built. They were numbered 80000-2.

Finally, mention must be made of a unique road-rail Karrier bus that was built in 1931, incorporating rubber-tyred wheels for road use and conventional rail wheels, with a changeover device. On the road it resembled an ordinary bus. In concept, it would travel at speed between stations, then transfer to road to visit the town centre and return to the station to rejoin the railway. The idea was born as a means of combating bus competition, but also to serve the newly opened LMS Welcombe Hotel near Stratford on Avon which was some miles from the railway station. In practice it was never likely to be successful, and when the railway companies began investing heavily in bus companies, after acquiring parliamentary powers to do so in 1928, it ceased to be an attractive venture.

Diesel shunting locomotives

By 1930 the LMS was considering what economies might be achieved by using diesel power instead of conventional steam for shunting operations, and it was decided to rebuild an 0-6-0 steam shunting tank engine to provide the basis for an experimental design. An ex-Midland

An unorthodox approach to shunting. The LMS was looking for economies in the cost of manning shunting engines and turned to the Sentinel Waggon Co, which built some small 0-4-0 engines in 1929/30. No 7163, later renumbered 7183, spent at least some years at sub-sheds of Shrewsbury LMS shed. It survived until 1955. *IAL*

The LMS was the most progressive of the four main-line companies in the 1930s in the development of diesel shunting engines. No 7063 was delivered from Armstrong Whitworth's in September 1936 at Carlisle Kingmoor and was soon transferred to Willesden. It had a 350hp Armstrong-Sulzer diesel engine and Crompton Parkinson electrical transmission. Many of the LMS diesel shunters were requisitioned by the War Department during World War 2, and renumbered in the WD series. No 7063 was requisitioned in 1940 and sold to the War Department in 1944. *Modern Transport*

Class 1F engine, No 1831, was chosen to provide the frames and wheels. Davey Paxman & Co of Colchester provided a 400hp diesel engine and the firm of Haslam & Newton, of Derby, provided the hydraulic transmission.

On 18 November 1932, No 1831, in its reincarnation guise, emerged from Derby Works and a new era was born. It went through a lengthy process of modification, but the LMS was satisfied that the way ahead lay in diesel-powered shunting engines, and a number of contracts were given to various manufacturers. Nine engines were built during 1933-35 to eight different designs, all except one using mechanical transmission. They became LMS Nos 7050-58, No 7058 having electric transmission.

No 7058 was built by Sir W. G. Armstrong Whitworth and Co in 1934 and was considered to be superior to all the other designs. At about the same time the firm of R. & W. Hawthorn Leslie & Co had loaned a diesel-electric shunting engine to the LMS and the matter was settled. Electric transmission was to be the standard. This engine became No 7079.

In the meantime C. E. Fairburn had been appointed as Electrical Engineer in the CME's Department. He had previously worked for the English Electric Co and took a special interest in the development of diesel-electric shunting engines. On the basis of the trials two batches of 10 engines each were ordered in 1934. Nos 7059-68 were built by Armstrong Whitworth, using Armstrong-Sulzer diesel engines and Crompton Parkinson electrical transmission. They were delivered in 1936 and were employed on the Western Division at Willesden, Crewe and Carlisle. The second batch, Nos 7069-78, were built by Hawthorn Leslie, using English

Electric diesel engines and transmission. They were also taken into stock in 1936 and employed at Willesden and Crewe.

The employment of diesel shunting locomotives using 350hp diesel engines and electrical transmission proved to be so successful that the LMS decided to embark on volume production with an order of 40, to be built at Derby using English Electric diesel engines and transmission. The first one, No 7080, appeared just before the outbreak of World War 2 and established a standard which continued in British Railways days when many hundreds were built for the whole of BR. The LMS pioneered the development of the diesel shunting locomotive, but the other companies showed little interest prewar, although the Southern acquired three in 1938. This lack of interest is difficult to understand, as both the economics and the operating advantages of using diesel-electric shunting engines on a three-shift basis were considerable.

Diesel main line locomotives

Whilst the potential advantages of diesel shunting engines and diesel railcars were becoming evident in the 1930s, the picture was less clear regarding diesel main line locomotives. The technology was already well understood in the United States, and diesel main line locomotives were being built there on a large scale, but circumstances in the USA were quite different from those in the UK. There was a very large automotive building industry in the USA and General Motors had begun to produce diesel railway locomotives. Oil was plentiful and cheap. Rail distances were vast, and the availability of water for steam engines was a problem in desert areas. The advantages of diesel locomotives over steam were clear.

In Great Britain those conditions did not apply, in fact the reverse was the case. There was no major manufacturer ready to turn out a fleet of well-tried and tested diesel locomotives; water supplies were plentiful; good quality locomotive coal was readily available whereas oil had to be imported (and there could be no guarantee of long-term supplies); and there was no shortage of applicants for posts in the locomotive department, either as locomen or fitters.

But more significant was the attitude of Chief Mechanical Engineers. Both Gresley on the LNER and Stanier on the LMS were competing to see who could produce the best, most efficient and fastest express passenger steam locomotive. Gresley's 'A4' streamlined Pacifics and his Class V2 2-6-2s were near the ultimate in steam locomotive design, and Stanier's brief had been to equip the LMS with a modern fleet of

The first and only main line diesel locomotive placed into service before nationalisation was No 10000, built by the LMS at Derby and completed just a few weeks before the LMS ceased to exist. It was initially allocated to Derby shed so that it could be adjacent to the works for any modifications needed, and was often employed on St Pancras–Manchester services.
E. R. Wethersett

steam locomotives. There was certainly no time on the LMS for diverting attention and resources to designing and testing diesel main line locomotives. Indeed, both Gresley and Stanier were out-and-out steam men, and if they had had to consider any other form of traction it would have been electric haulage. In that context, it has to be pointed out that in the LNER's New Works Programme for 1935-40 there was provision for the electrification of the Manchester, Sheffield and Wath route via the Woodhead tunnel to overcome the problems of steam haulage of heavy coal trains up the steep gradient to Penistone.

However, there was on the LMS a certain Charles Edward Fairburn, who had been Chief Engineer in the traction department of the English Electric Company. He had originally been a pupil of Henry Fowler at Derby locomotive works, but then joined Siemens Dynamo Company and was closely involved with the North Eastern Railway's Shildon-Newport electrification. In 1919 he established the English Electric Company's electric traction department and became General Manager at its Preston and Stafford works. He joined the LMS in 1934 as Chief Electrical Engineer and became deputy to Stanier in 1937, with responsiblity for the large-scale introduction of diesel-electric shunting locomotives. He became CME of the LMS for a short time in 1944 but died prematurely in 1945 at the early age of 58. However, he had already laid plans for postwar 1,500hp diesel-electric main line locomotives, and those plans were followed up by his successor.

Diesel locomotives were seen to have many advantages, such as instant and greater availability, a cleaner working environment both for drivers and maintenance staff, and a more predictable and even performance. There were big savings to be made in the closure of steam sheds, together with all the facilities which had to be provided for servicing steam engines. On the debit side, diesel locomotives cost several times as much to build as comparable steam engines and the savings to be made had to match the increased initial cost of a diesel locomotive.

In the general euphoria that attended the end of hostilities in 1945, and oblivious of the incoming Labour government's declared intention to nationalise the railways, the LMS set about planning the construction of two prototype diesel locomotives. Discussions were held with the English Electric Company in May 1946 and it was agreed to build two 1,600hp diesel-electric locomotives capable of working either singly or coupled together in multiple. The race was on because it was now known that nationalisation was definite. On 5 December 1947, with just a few weeks to spare, the first locomotive of the pair emerged from Derby Works, proudly bearing the letters LMS in stainless steel on the sides of the loco, and the number 10000. It was indeed a proud moment, because it marked the beginning of the British railways' main line diesel-electric fleet, albeit after some years' delay.

There had been other experiments with main line diesel locomotives, but they were not successful. No 10000, and her sister, No 10001, were a triumph, and if nationalisation had not intervened it is quite probable that the LMS would have embarked on large-scale dieselisation. The LMS was the only company to build a successful main line diesel. It was a milestone.

A down Chessington train formed of a 4-Sub LB&SCR-type unit with a steel trailer approaches Clapham Junction on 8 November 1949.
C. C. B. Herbert

Milestones — Suburban electrification

The Southern Railway and its constituents

As we saw in Part 1, suburban electrification in the South London suburbs began before World War 1, and the completion of schemes continued until 1916. All three of the Southern Railway's constituents had developed such schemes, although the LB&SCR had adopted overhead electrification, whilst the SE&CR and the LSWR had adopted third rail. Electrification began again after World War 1 and continued throughout the 1920s, reaching into the outer London suburbs and as far out as Wimbledon and Bromley. However, it was still regarded as *suburban* electrification.

The big breakthrough came in the 1930s under the guidance of the redoubtable Sir Herbert Walker, the Southern Railway's General Manager. There were extensions and the infilling of existing lines, but what might be regarded as main line electrification, still using multiple-units and third rail, began in 1933 with the electrification of the lines to Brighton, Hove and Worthing. Waterloo to Portsmouth was electrified in 1937 and the North Kent towns in 1939. Much more was planned, but WW2 intervened, and 20 years were to elapse before the North Kent electrification was extended to Margate, Ramsgate and Dover in 1959, due to government restrictions on investment.

The Southern's suburban electrification policy was a considerable success, propelled forward as a rolling programme. It was a commercial success because the train service was based on clockface timetabling. It was a financial success because each individual scheme concentrated on the provision of trains, and the electric current to propel them. The carriages were often provided by modifying existing stock, and there was no attempt to modernise the stations and the signalling concurrently. Such modernisation *was* carried out, but as individual schemes that could be justified financially.

There is no doubt that Sir Herbert Walker ranks high in the Pantheon of great General Managers. The milestone was his appointment as General Manager of the Southern Railway in 1923, but he had previously been General Manager of the London & South Western Railway since just prior to World War 1. LMS steam locomotive enthusiasts may well have mused over the name of 'Patriot' class 4-6-0 No 5535 *Sir Herbert Walker KCB* and wondered who this eminent gentleman might be, and how a Southern Railway General Manager came to have his name on an LMS engine. In fact, Herbert Walker had been employed by the London & North Western between 1885 and 1912 and had become Outdoor Goods Manager of the Southern Division. One of the 'Claughtons' carried his name, hence its continuance on a 'Patriot' engine. He received his knighthood, as did so many other railwaymen, for his wartime services with the Railway Executive Committee. It was very unfortunate for both the LNWR and the LMS that they lost the services of such a capable railway manager.

On the LMSR

The first milestone of suburban electrification in the railways that later made up the LMS occurred in 1916, when the LNWR completed the suburban electrification of the Broad Street-Richmond line of the North London Railway, a prewar scheme approved in 1911 (the LNWR was two thirds owner of the NLR). The Euston-Watford line followed in 1922. Apart from these two schemes, the LNWR had showed little interest in suburban electrification.

Of all the constituents of the LMS, only the Lancashire & Yorkshire had been really active, and for several years the LMS showed little interest in further electrification. However, in 1931 the 8¾-mile long Manchester, South Junction & Altrincham line was electrified, jointly with the LNER, on the 1,500-volt dc overhead system.

The financial performance of the LMS made it difficult to raise funds for investment, but in 1935 the government — in an apparent act of generosity, but actually to relieve unemployment and stimulate the economy generally — provided finance at low rates of interest (shipbuilding and industry similarly benefited). Through a Railway Finance Corporation, £30 million was made available to the four main line companies for a five-year New Works Programme, and the LMS decided to electrify the Wirral lines, which

it had taken over at Grouping. In 1938 electric services began on the lines from Birkenhead Park to West Kirby and New Brighton.

Some commentators believe that the LMS could, and should, have carried out more suburban electrification, especially if it had followed Sir Herbert Walker's example on the Southern. The London, Tilbury & Southend line from Fenchurch Street cried out for modernisation, and Stanier had responded in 1934 by introducing a fleet of three-cylinder 2-6-4 taper-boilered tank engines in order to improve the service. The LT&S had to wait until 1962 for electrification.

On the LNER
The LNER's suburban lines from King's Cross and Liverpool Street were obvious candidates for electrification, but it did not happen for two reasons.

First, the LNER's financial performance ruled it out after 1929, but it could have been done on a limited scale in the 1920s if there had been sufficient determination. But neither the GNR nor the Great Eastern had showed any interest in electrification; therefore there was no groundswell of opinion which might have generated interest, despite the example south of the Thames.

Second, Gresley, the CME, was a dedicated steam man who believed that the steam locomotive had not yet reached the limits of its potential. He proved his point with his 'A4' streamliners, but that was of little help to the London suburban services. However, the commuters did get some new coaches, the articulated 'quad-arts' and 'quin-arts'. The former remained in use on the GN services until the 1960s.

It was not until 1935 that some relief
occurred, when the government made funds
available at a low rate of interest (see 'On the
LMSR', above). The LNER therefore set out its
plans for suburban electrification from
Liverpool Street to Shenfield, and for main line
electrification from Sheffield and Wath to
Manchester, but World War 2 intervened and
the schemes were delayed until after nationalisation. Long-suffering commuters on the GN had
to wait until the 1970s for their electrification.

However, the LNER did have two successes. It
worked with the LMS to electrify the Manchester,
South Junction & Altrincham suburban line in
1931 and it electrified the South Tyneside line
from Newcastle to South Shields in 1938.

Signal and telecommunications engineering

Chapter 7

Milestones

The multiple-aspect colour-light signal

For many years up to World War 1, lineside railway signals had been of the semaphore type, with two indications — arm horizontal, meaning 'danger'; and arm inclined downwards at about 45 degrees, meaning 'clear'. However, thoughts then turned to the use of semaphore, three-indication signals, moving in an upper quadrant and conveying three different messages to drivers — danger, caution and clear. At that time, the night indication to drivers for 'caution' was a red light, the same as the indication for a danger signal; therefore it was necessary to select a different colour to represent 'caution'. Yellow was chosen.

Concurrently with these developments, a practical design emerged for an electrically lit colour-light signal without semaphore arms and the Ministry of Transport appointed a committee in 1921 to investigate and report. The committee reported favourably in October that year, setting out the main advantages of the colour-light signal over the semaphore signal:

- The same indications by day and by night, instead of an arm by day and a light by night as was the case with semaphore signals;
- A more penetrating light during darkness and bad weather.

The use of colour-light signals enabled the employment of fogsignalmen to be discontinued and reduced the delays to trains during bad weather.

One of the first applications of three-aspect colour-light signals was between Marylebone and Neasden on the former GCR in 1923. This was a milestone, and eventually colour-light signals became the normal form of signalling.

The newly formed Southern Railway was carrying out major resignalling schemes on the approaches to its London termini and was installing power signalling with colour-light signals. In order to maintain the closest practical spacing of trains and keep them moving at the highest possible speed it was considering adapting the signals to give a fourth indication, meaning preliminary caution, when the next signal

Typical three-aspect colour-light signals in use at Skipton. The three lenses at the top are green, yellow and red in descending order. The lower signals are for route indicating and shunting etc purposes.
Author

ahead was at caution. In 1924 a committee of the Institution of Railway Signal Engineers reported on this question and confirmed the need for a fourth aspect in such situations, recommending the simultaneous display of two yellow lights, which became known as a 'double yellow'. This system came into operation on the Southern Railway in the London area in 1926 and has since become widespread.

Although this book deals with Britain's main line railways, it ought to be mentioned that the Liverpool Overhead Railway, which ran on an elevated structure along the docks, installed colour-light signals in 1921. This was the first such installation in Britain.

The interior of the signalbox at Woking in 1937, showing electrical operation of points and signals using miniature levers. The Southern Railway was very progressive in modernising its signalling to improve the working of its heavy suburban electrified services. *Southern Railway*

Developments in the control of points and colour-light signals

The power operation of points and signals had developed rapidly in the years preceding World War 1, but such changes came more or less to a halt in 1914. Progress was not resumed for several years after the war ended, as the railway companies struggled to return to prewar standards in dramatically changed economic conditions. They also had to face the immense distraction of being grouped into four main line companies following the Railways Act of 1921.

However, the Great Western was little affected by the Grouping and in 1922 it experimented at Winchester Chesil with a system of route-setting levers, in which the operation of a route lever not only set the points but also cleared the signal if everything was in order. In 1927 the same principle was adopted in two signalboxes at Newport (Monmouthshire). This interesting development was not taken further by the GWR, but the concept of route setting ultimately

formed the basis of all railway signalling. In most new power signalling installations of the time, separate miniature levers worked points and signals.

The most significant development of the inter-war period was probably the route-relay, route-setting signalbox at Thirsk, opened in 1933, controlling several miles of the East Coast main line. The signal engineer concerned was A. E. Tattersall, formerly Signal Superintendent of the Great Northern Railway and now Signal Engineer of the LNER. He created a completely new generation of signalboxes, incorporating the following:

- The interlocking between points and signals was performed by electrical relays;
- Routes were set by using thumb switches;
- The track layout, including all points and signals, was represented on a large illuminated diagram;
- Continuous track circuiting and automatic signals controlled by the passage of trains were provided.

The Thirsk installation was a great success and a milestone in signal engineering. It was followed by similar installations at Hull and Northallerton. They were known as 'One Control Switch' (OCS) systems. The OCS system was widely adopted by British Railways in its signalling modernisation schemes in the late 1940s and 1950s.

The benefits of these large new installations might be stated as:

- Colour-light signals are preferable from the driver's point of view;
- Safety of train operation is enhanced by the use of continuous track circuiting;
- Those elements of safety which are the signalman's responsibility in traditional signalboxes are largely absorbed by the signalbox equipment. Safety is therefore enhanced;
- The signalman's larger overview of an area, coupled with his ability to set routes quickly, improves train regulation considerably.

Another development of the period ought to be mentioned, because in its way it was a milestone and was widely adopted in the 1960s. In 1937, a unique control system was introduced in Brunswick signalbox, near Liverpool Central, on the Cheshire Lines company. It became known as the 'Entrance/Exit' system, NX for short. In this system, a route was set and signals cleared by turning a switch located on the signalling panel at the start of the route and then pressing a button at a position representing the end of the route. The switch was the 'entrance' and the button the 'exit' of the route. As soon as the 'exit' button was pressed, the equipment automatically performed all the functions necessary to set the route, clear the appropriate signals and then protect the route from any conflicting setting. This system formed the basis of BR standard NX installations from the 1960s onwards.

Automatic Train Control (ATC)

In Part 1, we took the story of Automatic Train Control as far as the outbreak of World War 1, and it will be remembered that several companies were active in developing various systems. These developments ceased on the outbreak of war, and the upheaval of the Grouping in 1923 caused them all to be abandoned, except one — the Great Western. By 1939 the GWR had equipped 3,250 engines and 2,850 miles of track. The reasons for the reluctance of the other companies to install ATC will be examined in the Millstone section.

However, in 1931 a new system came to notice. It had been invented by a Mr Hudd, who was an employee of the Strowger firm, and it became known as the Strowger-Hudd system. The Southern Railway was persuaded to give the necessary facilities for trial working at Byfleet. The system was designed on the magnetic induction principle, with no physical contact between the track equipment and the locomotive. The track equipment was associated with the Distant signal and consisted of a permanent magnet and an electromagnet laid between the rails. When the Distant signal was clear, the electromagnet was energised. When the signal was at caution, the electromagnet was not energised, causing the brakes to be applied and a horn to be sounded on the footplate. The LMS held perfunctory trials of the system at Millers Dale in Derbyshire but took no further action for the time being.

However, the prevalence of fog on the former London, Tilbury & Southend line, together with its heavy and frequent suburban service, caused the LMS to have second thoughts in 1935, when it decided to equip the line with the Strowger-Hudd system. By the outbreak of war in 1939, the experimental work was approaching completion, but the system was still not in full use. It was finally approved by the Ministry of Transport in 1947, and was a milestone because it laid the foundations for the system developed by British Railways after nationalisation the following year.

The LNER also decided to install the Strowger-Hudd system between Edinburgh and Glasgow following a very serious collision between two express passenger trains at Castlecary in 1937, but all work ceased during World War 2.

Millstone

The failure of most companies to install ATC

The pages of railway history are littered with examples of fatal accidents caused by drivers wrongly passing signals at danger, and we have already seen that many companies pre-World War 1 were developing technical systems to guard against such errors. One can only guess what the outcome might have been if there had been no war, but the effect of that conflict was to halt all development. In the succeeding years, the attention of railway managers was distracted by the pressing needs of postwar reconstruction and renewal, and the major organisational changes presaged by the Grouping.

Several constituent companies of the LNER had been experimenting with forms of ATC, including the Great Eastern, the Great Central and the North Eastern, but the Great Northern, under Nigel Gresley as Locomotive Engineer, had not done so. Gresley was not really in favour of ATC because he felt that any equipment which might have the effect of reducing the driver's concentration was undesirable. It was therefore inevitable that when Gresley became CME of the newly formed LNER, the develop-

The result of the accident at Castlecary (LNER) in December 1937 when an Edinburgh to Glasgow Queen Street express ran into the rear of a stationary passenger train from Dundee to Glasgow. The weather was snowy and the signals had not been cleared for the train from Edinburgh. There were over 300 passengers in the two trains and no fewer than 35 of them were killed. It was the worst peacetime accident on Britain's railways up to that time (excepting the Tay Bridge disaster).
Hulton-Deutsch Collection

ment of ATC would not be high on the agenda. In any case, Grouping itself brought many other problems to be dealt with, of greater or lesser urgency. By the time those problems had been dealt with, the LNER's financial situation had worsened. And Gresley could point to the very good safety record of the LNER in the 1920s so far as fatal accidents caused by drivers passing signals at danger were concerned.

Confirming Gresley's view, Colonel Pringle, the Chief Inspecting Officer of Railways, in his Annual Reports for 1925, 1926 and 1927, commented that in view of the generally good safety record, the case for the adoption of ATC was less urgent. It did not appear, he said, that the expenditure that would be incurred could justifiably be called for at the present time. Nonetheless, he was anxious to achieve some progress before he retired and he organised another ATC Committee in 1928/29 'to review the recommendations made by the 1922 ATC Committee'. It was a very high-powered committee, counting among its members Collett, CME of the GWR; Gresley, CME of the LNER; an Operating Superintendent; two Civil Engineers; and two Signalling Engineers. Pringle was chairman, and its deliberations were brought into sharp focus by the Charfield accident (LMSR) on 13 October 1928, a few days after the first meeting of the committee. That accident was deemed to have been caused by a driver passing a signal at danger and colliding with a goods train, causing 15 fatalities. Less than three months later there was a similar accident at Ashchurch (LMSR) with four fatalities. The Committee's report, published in 1930, made a firm recommendation in favour of the GWR's fixed ramp system at Distant signals.

As mentioned before, the LNER, by now in serious financial difficulties, had no money to spare for ATC and saw no justification for it, at least until the serious accident at Castlecary in 1937 (see above). By then it was too late — World War 2 was imminent. However, the LMS did not have such a good record in the interwar years, but none of its constituents had made much progress with ATC. The LMS had a number of serious accidents caused by drivers wrongly passing signals at danger, but it also had some which were caused by signalmen's errors, and it devoted its financial resources to dealing with those and to the replacement of semaphore distant signals with colour light distants. The Pringle Committee had recommended such an alternative policy.

The failure to adopt ATC *was* a millstone, but the reasons were valid in the circumstances. And there was no great outcry from the public who generally considered the railways to be very safe, which indeed they were compared with over 7,000 deaths on the road each year in the later 1930s.

1947 was a bad year for accidents. The up main line south of Goswick LNER was blocked for Sunday engineering work and all trains were being diverted onto the adjoining independent line, requiring a reduction of speed to 15-20mph. The 11.15am express from Edinburgh to King's Cross was derailed whilst traversing the facing points at about 50mph. ATC warning apparatus at the distant signal would have warned the driver of the need to slow down. *NRM*

Freight and general

Chapter 8

Freight

During the 1920s and particularly during the 1930s the railway companies were faced with an unprecedented rise in road competition. The catalyst was one of the consequences of World War 1. The army had ordered large numbers of lorries for military use, and had trained large numbers of men as drivers and mechanics. At the end of the war, surplus lorries were put on the market at low prices, to be snapped up by those same drivers and mechanics and paid for by their demobilisation gratuity. There were virtually no restrictions on the use of those lorries — the owners could pick and choose their traffics and customers, and go where they pleased, charging whatever they could negotiate. The railway companies had no such freedom, because they were bound by restrictions imposed when they had a virtual monopoly of inland freight transport. That was a huge millstone for the railways until long after World War 2.

A new road haulage industry was born, based on small, often one-man, firms, and immediately the attack began on the railway's merchandise traffic, which carried the highest railway rates. The government took no steps to ease the restrictions to enable the railway companies to respond to the new competition, and tacitly encouraged the growth of the road haulage industry for political reasons. Railway strikes and threats of strikes were a recurring problem for the government, and a healthy, non-unionised road haulage industry was a useful counterpoint. In 1920 there were only 101,000 motor lorries, but by 1935 this had risen to 435,000.

Here are some of the measures which the railways took to meet the competition:

Reducing costs
One of the objects of the formation of the 'Big Four' in 1923 was to achieve economies, and the railway companies made substantial strides. Between 1923 and 1937, staff numbers were reduced from 651,000 to 575,000, whilst passenger numbers and freight net ton miles declined by only 3%. On the LMS the number of locomotives was reduced from over 10,000 to below 8,000 by greater efficiency, including scrap and build.

Modernisation
There were a number of milestones, such as the introduction of containers in the mid-1920s, whose stock had risen to 13,800 by 1937. They generally had a capacity of four tons (similar to typical lorries of the day) and were craned to and from road trailers and specially constructed 'Conflat' wagons. There were various types of

The age of containerisation had arrived. These are LMS four-ton insulated containers on vacuum-braked wagons. *LMS*

container, including refrigerated and insulated containers, and ones which were specially adapted for the conveyance of clothing on hangers, and of bicycles. By 1947 there were nearly 20,000 containers in use. Special shock-absorbing wagons were built for traffics that were susceptible to breakage. The LNER was particularly active in developing express freight services using wagons equipped with the vacuum brake, in order to speed up the overnight merchandise services.

Marshalling yards were modernised and mechanised. Whitemoor on the LNER was the first, where the Up yard was opened in 1928 — a milestone — followed by the Down yard in 1933. New Inward yard at Hull was opened in 1935. The LMS opened the mechanised Toton Down yard in 1939. Major improvements were also made to many other marshalling yards. Much more would have been done, but the railway companies did not have the money.

The mechanical horse — a milestone

The railway companies had many large goods depots, almost all of which had been built in the 19th century. Traffic was collected and delivered by horse and cart, and the whole process of loading, unloading and transfer of goods traffic in the depots was very labour intensive. The depots had been designed for use by horses and

carts, which required little space for manoeuvring, but were in many cases unsuitable for use by lorries. Hence the mechanical horse, a brainwave which enabled trailers to be moved about in the restricted space available. They were ideal for use in towns, where their limited speed was adequate. They had another advantage over the normal lorry: dozens of trailers could be backed up to the goods platform for continuous loading for specific delivery areas, with a mechanical horse coupling up when the trailer was full. It would have been uneconomic to use lorries in this way. However, the cheap and trusty four-legged horse continued to be very suitable for town deliveries close to the goods depot.

The problem of road haulage competition
The railway companies would no doubt have done more to improve the efficiency and economics of their freight services, in order to compete more effectively with road haulage, if they had had the money to do it — but they hadn't. And whilst the government provided some funds at low rates of interest which enabled some improvements to be made, it was done with the purpose of reducing unemployment and reviving the economy rather than helping the railway companies. What the companies needed to be able to compete more effectively was freedom from the 19th century shackles on rates and conditions of carriage in order to improve their competitive position by placing them on an

equal footing with road haulage. This was the real millstone. Hence, the 'Square Deal' campaign, which was launched in the late 1930s and was a lobby to try to persuade the government to abolish all restrictions on railway charges and remove the railways' 'common carrier' status, on the basis that the railways were no longer a monopoly and should be allowed to compete freely with road haulage on an equal footing.

In November 1938 the chairmen of the Big Four railway companies wrote to the Minister of Transport and sent a copy of the letter to *The Times* newspaper, setting out the problem and seeking to persuade an unresponsive, and indeed hostile, government of the justice of their demands. To paraphrase, it said that the railway industry employed 600,000 men and women and had a capital of £1,200,000,000. It gave a service to industry that was more efficient than ever before, but circumstances were reducing it to a point where it would be impossible to maintain that measure of efficiency in peace time, and where it would be quite impossible for it to give the enlarged service in wartime which would certainly be demanded of it (in the event, such impossibility did not occur).

It went on to point out that the principal cause of the steady decline in the industry was road competition, and particularly in the carriage of freight. The railways had no complaint about competition, and expressed the view that traders were free to choose which mode of transport

The LNER Class V2 2-6-2s had been built in 1936 specifically for hauling high-speed merchandise trains and No 4771 is seen on such a duty. They were so successful as general purpose machines that the LNER went on to build 184 of them up to 1943. *IAL*

Above: Despite the LNER's straitened circumstances, its East Coast main line services continued to achieve a high standard in the 1930s. Class A3 Pacific No 2559 *The Tetrarch* in splendid condition heads a King's Cross to Harrogate train. *F. R. Hebron*

Right: The railways exploited the excursion business to a high degree and took every opportunity of earning every penny they could. Ex-Midland Class 4F 0-6-0 No 3963, allocated to Normanton shed, takes a Morecambe excursion train past Marley Junction signalbox. *Eric Treacy*

they wished to employ. They sought no preferential position; on the contrary, the chairmen stressed that the scales were heavily and unjustly weighted against the railway industry. Other forms of goods transport were free to decide for themselves, or to agree with their customers, what charges they should make for the services that they rendered. The railways had no such freedom. They were hampered and bound by a whole series of statutory restrictions and regulations which clogged the operation of the machine, causing expense, irritation and unnecessary delays.

The letter explained that the restrictions may have been necessary when the railways possessed a large measure of transport monopoly, but that there was no justification now when road competition extended to every class of commodity and every corner of the country. The railway industry urged the government to withdraw those restrictions and place the railways in exactly the same condition of freedom as other and competing forms of transport.

The Times ran a leader the same day supporting the railways' case, but still the government took no positive action. It indicated that it would do so, but World War 2 intervened before it did and the question became academic. In any case, cynics doubt whether the government really intended to help. It remains a mystery as to why the government consistently failed to act over the years, but that failure was a huge millstone for the railway industry to bear. It was clear that there were certain elements within government who disliked the railways for whatever reason, but any sensible, efficient government could not have failed to accept the logic of the railways' case and take action to remove the grievance.

However, the discussions between rail and road which began at the time of the Square Deal campaign in 1939 were resumed in May 1945, helped by the work of the Road/Rail Conference during the war. The discussions took place between the general managers of the four main line railway companies and the Road Haulage Association, the latter body having been formed by an amalgamation of the six principal road haulage associations. The Minister of War Transport, Lord Leathers, lent his support, as did his successor, Alfred Barnes.

Agreement was reached that road and rail should be organised so that traders were provided with adequate alternative facilities with competition on fair terms, and that road and rail transport should have the same public service obligations including:

• providing reasonable and regular services in the districts they purport to serve;
• accepting any traffic offered which they hold out to carry and which is within their capacity;
• conforming to approved standard conditions of carriage, classification of merchandise and national rate structures.

One of the most important issues was that of rates, and both parties were already engaged on the preparation of their respective rates structures. A second important issue concerned the statutory restrictions upon the railways and it was agreed that these should be relaxed.

A memorandum entitled 'Co-ordination of Road and Rail Freight Transport' was presented to the Minister of Transport in July 1946, signed by the Chairman of the Railway General Managers' Conference and the Chairman of the Road Haulage Association. However, it was too late. The Labour government was already developing its plans to nationalise transport and the memorandum was stillborn. It was an oddity of the period that the railway companies continued to make plans as though the threat of nationalisation did not exist.

But in all this rail versus lorry debate it has to be borne in mind that the lorry had some innate advantages over rail, which would still have existed if the rates issues and statutory restrictions on the railways were resolved. The lorry provided door-to-door transport. It was flexible and gave personal service. It was adaptable. In many cases the lorry was bound to win.

The problem of the small wagon — a millstone

In the mid-1920s the railway companies owned 721,000 wagons for public traffic, and in addition traders owned 600,000, nearly all of them for the coal trade. The great majority were small two-axle wagons of limited carrying capacity, commonly 10 or 12 tons, and relatively few had any form of brake other than a handbrake. The companies were frequently criticised for not building higher capacity wagons, but opportunities for employing them were limited by the demands of traders. The average size of merchandise consignments in the 1920s was between 5cwt and 6cwt, and the average wagon load was about 3 tons. The scope for larger merchandise wagons was therefore limited.

Most coal traffic, except in the North East and in South Wales, was conveyed in privately owned wagons, and small wagons suited the trade, both at the colliery and in the station coal yard. The average wagon load was about 9 tons.

An interesting example of the small coal wagon problem, as LMS Class 4F 0-6-0 No 4128 takes a long rake of them through the Calder Valley. These 13-ton-capacity wooden-bodied wagons would then need shunting and delivering to their individual owners. *E. R. Wethersett*

The use of larger wagons, which would have enabled substantial economies to be made by the railway companies, was difficult to achieve. And traders would have demanded a share of the economies, especially if they incurred substantial costs themselves. This was a subject of considerable complexity. In a more stable economy than existed in the 1920s and 1930s it is possible that the railway companies and traders could have worked together to achieve the use of larger wagons, but it was not to be. Little progress was made until after World War 2, when the coal industry, the electricity generating industry and the railways were all nationalised.

The passenger business and road passenger transport

The bus appeared as a serious competitor for short distance traffic about 1924, and rapidly gained a very strong foothold, severely denting the railway companies' short distance passenger receipts, which had already been eaten into by tramcar competition. The railway companies could not match the low fares charged by the bus companies, owing to the high terminal and track costs which road transport did not have to bear. The companies decided to tackle this, not by going into competition and operating their own fleets of buses, for which they lacked the legal powers, but by buying an interest in the existing bus companies. For this purpose they applied for parliamentary powers, and these were granted under the (various railway companies') Road Transport Acts, 1928. This was a milestone. The companies then invested considerable sums in established bus companies, up to 49% or 51% of the holdings. They were also the joint owners of bus services with four municipal corporations — Sheffield, Halifax, Huddersfield and Todmorden.

The railway companies regarded these investments as a separate business, and made little attempt to co-ordinate bus and rail services or facilities, but despite that, a number of loss-making branch line passenger services were withdrawn in 1930. By 1933 the railways had invested over £9 million in bus companies and were receiving earnings of nearly £1/2 million per annum.

Arguments have raged over the years as to whether this money was well spent, and whether

it might have been better to have invested it in railway modernisation and improved facilities. However, the railway companies were commercial concerns and had to have regard to their future financial prospects. Diversification was one of the means available for doing this. To a much smaller extent they also invested in road haulage and air transport.

One important milestone of the 1930s was the introduction of the Monthly Return fare, at the rate of single fare and a third, thus equating to a penny a mile, a spectacular advertising feature. It rapidly became the normal return fare, especially during World War 2 when cheap return fares of various types were withdrawn.

The railways and air services

The railway companies were determined to become involved in the provision of air services within the British Isles at an early stage in order to counteract the possible emergence of a powerful competitor for their long distance passenger traffic. They needed parliamentary powers to do this, because they could only undertake such activities as were authorised by the Railways Act of 1921, and they obtained the necessary powers in 1929 under the [various companies'] Railway (Air Transport) Act (each company had its own act). This was a milestone.

The LNER had little involvement, but the other companies saw possibilities in over-water links such as the Channel Islands and the Isle of Wight, and on routes where the railway journey was circuitous, such as Plymouth to Cardiff. In 1934 the railways jointly formed a subsidiary operating company, known as Railway Air Services, in which the Imperial Airways Company participated. Among the services operated were Liverpool-Birmingham-Bristol-Southampton-Ryde, Liverpool-Birmingham-Cardiff-Plymouth, London-Belfast-Glasgow, and across the Channel to France and Jersey/Guernsey.

In the 1930s there was very little internal competition from airlines, but it was sensible for the railway companies to became established before such competition grew. It was a small-scale business and generally unprofitable. However, at the end of World War 2, the railways were busily planning a wide expansion of their air services in view of the huge improvement in air-

One for the bus enthusiasts. A West Yorkshire Bristol K-type double-decker built in 1939 and subsequently rebuilt. Here, it was on hire to the Yorkshire Woollen District Bus Co in Dewsbury in June 1969, hence the destination 'Thornhill'. By 1934 over 50% of the ordinary shares in the West Yorkshire Road Car Co were held by the LNER and the LMSR. *M. J. Fenton*

A de Havilland DH86 aircraft belonging to Railway Air Services stands on the apron at Speke Airport. *IAL*

services in view of the huge improvement in aircraft technology which had occurred during the war. Those hopes did not last long. The incoming Labour government quickly nationalised air transport and Railway Air Services was swallowed up. Another opportunity for diversification was lost.

The railway companies' post-World War 2 plans

Towards the end of the war, the railway companies began to develop their plans for postwar reconstruction and modernisation. Nationalisation was not then on the agenda and there were no grounds for supposing that a Labour government would be returned with a working majority at the general election to be held as soon as the war ended.

Despite that, the LNER issued an ambitious programme in 1946 when nationalisation was a certainty. It stated that there was a trust fund of £40 million accumulated during the war to cover arrears of maintenance and that £50 million would be needed for its new works programme. Some of the items on the list are familiar, but were not achieved for many years:

King's Cross — alterations and improvements to the station, including a new station frontage and concourse;
Additional four-tracking between Hadley Wood and Sandy;
Peterborough — new central station, new centralised goods depot, new marshalling yards;

Leeds Central — reconstruction of the station;
York — new locomotive depot and marshalling yard;
Colour-light signalling between Newcastle and Edinburgh;
Edinburgh — new marshalling yard, station improvements;
Electrification between Liverpool Street and Shenfield;
Main line electrification between Sheffield/Wath and Manchester.

In addition there were extensive plans for new locomotives and carriages, and for a host of smaller schemes. It was almost as though the LNER, realising that it was soon to be swallowed up in a greater British Railways, was making sure of getting in first with its bids.

However, the first priority was to restore the railways to their prewar condition. War-damaged buildings had to be restored, and destroyed ones rebuilt. Tracks had to be relaid and rolling stock repaired and replaced. New locomotives had to be built. The railways quite rightly expected that the enormous profits that they had earned during the war, which were still in the government's hands, would be used for those purposes, but the government had other ideas. It was as duplicitous as ever, and control of the railways was never relinquished. No one foresaw the difficulties that would arise in obtaining materials, nor how long the restoration process would take. All the postwar emphasis was, inescapably, on exports. Railways would have to wait and soldier on. They were not on the government's list of priorities.

Government intervention

Chapter 9

Control in World War 1 leads to Grouping and the Big Four

On the outbreak of World War 1, the government, under the powers of the Regulation of the Forces Act 1871, took possession of the whole of the undertakings of the main line companies, and instructed each general manager to 'carry on' under the direction of the Railway Executive Committee set up to work the railways as one for war purposes. The committee consisted of the general managers of the leading companies. This arrangement continued until the passing of the Ministry of Transport Act of 1919, when the Minister took control and retained it until 15 August 1921.

However, the government seriously mishandled the financial affairs of the companies during the control period. It took charge of all railway revenues, and in return it paid the companies an amount equal to their profits in 1913, but it did not allow freight rates to be increased until 1920 despite the considerable increase in the costs of labour and materials. And it paid nothing at all for the conveyance of the vast quantities of government traffic of men and materials. No other private business was treated in such cavalier fashion, and it was not until 1921 that some equilibrium was reached. Sir Felix Pole, General Manager of the GWR, wrote bitterly that 'seven years of government control had reduced the railways from relatively prosperous commercial concerns to a precarious financial position'. During those seven years, wages costs had increased under government direction by 268%. Whether or not those costs increases were justified is immaterial; the government was seriously in default in not arranging for the railways' income to increase commensurately.

One of the LNER's postwar ambitions was the building of a new marshalling yard at Edinburgh, and this was achieved under the 1955 Modernisation Plan. The new Millerhill Yard occupied a huge area a few miles out of Edinburgh astride the Waverley line to Carlisle, as seen in this 1963 photograph. *BR*

The LNER's postwar programme also included the resumption of work on the Sheffield and Wath to Manchester electrification, which was finally opened in 1954. At Wentworth Silkstone Junction two Class 76 electric locomotives haul a long rake of coal empties. These are all 16-ton capacity steel-bodied wagons all belonging to one owner — BR (cf the earlier photograph of No 4128).
Dr L. A. Nixon

However, the dividends paid on ordinary stocks during the 1913 to 1920 period make interesting reading. The LNWR paid between 6 and 7^1/$_2$%, the Midland between 6^1/$_2$ and 7^1/$_4$%, the Great Western between 5^3/$_4$ and 7^1/$_4$% and the North Eastern between 6^1/$_2$ and 7^1/$_2$%. At the other end of the scale, the Great Northern paid just over 4%, the Great Eastern between 2 and 3% and the Great Central nothing. The modest financial position of the three 'Greats' boded ill for the infant LNER, encumbered as it was with its Scottish partners also paying around 4%. How did the companies manage to pay such dividends in view of their worsening financial position? The answer is that shareholders were paid at the face value of their shares. It was a novel situation.

The Grouping and the Big Four — milestone or millstone?

In the early days of railways, amalgamations of companies were commonplace, leading to the formation of such undertakings as the LNWR, the Midland, the North Eastern and the Great Eastern. However, as long ago as 1852 there were more ambitious proposals for amalgamations, such as the LSWR with the LB&SCR, and the LNWR with the North Staffs and the Midland. The government took fright and set up a parliamentary select committee, which opposed the principle of amalgamation.

The question resurfaced in 1872, concerning the LNWR, the Midland, the L&Y and the Glasgow & South Western. Another Parliamentary Committee was set up. It said no.

Thereafter, relationships between companies took the form of working agreements and the pooling of receipts for certain traffics and routes in order to simplify operations and reduce wasteful competition. In 1904 the LNWR and the L&Y (long time friends) entered into pooling and working agreements, and in 1908 the LNWR and the Midland did the same. In 1909 the Great Northern, the Great Eastern and the Great Central promoted a bill for a working union, having found that their common interests pointed to a closer union than could be founded on a working agreement. The Board of Trade set up another committee — on Railway Agreements and Amalgamations. Nothing conclusive occurred before the outbreak of World War 1, but the seeds of grouping had been sown.

The spur towards greater co-operation stemmed from the increased costs that the companies were having to bear, not only through increased labour and materials costs, especially coal, but also the running of heavier, faster and more comfortable passenger trains with increased facilities, such as dining, sleeping and corridor accommodation. These factors reduced their profits.

The experience gained by the railway companies in the close co-operative working of the railway system as a whole formed a valuable preparation for the grouping that was to follow. It became clear to the government also that the changes that had resulted from the war, especially in the economic basis of the railway industry, made it impossible for the railways to revert to prewar conditions. A select committee was

therefore established to consider the future of the railway industry. Its recommendations led to the formation of the Ministry of Transport and the Railways Act of 1921, which led in turn to the grouping and the creation of the Big Four — the LMSR, the LNER, the GWR and the Southern.

Grouping was achieved quickly and easily by sensibly merging the large companies in accordance with their prewar aspirations. The LNWR, the Midland, the L&Y, the North Staffs and some other smaller companies formed the English portion of the new London, Midland & Scottish Railway Company Limited, although initially a separate Midland/GCR group was considered. It could have been a success too, but it was feared that the Midland would swallow up the GCR and close quite a lot of it. There was certainly scope for rationalisation. The Midland could have closed its expensive Hope Valley route and made a connection from its Sheffield station to the Woodhead route. And a merger with the G&SW, as was envisaged in the 1870s, would have given the new Midland group a through Anglo-Scottish route.

The three 'Greats' — the GNR, the GER and the GCR — together with the North Eastern, formed the London & North Eastern Railway. The three companies south of the Thames — the LSWR, the LB&SCR and the SECR — formed the Southern Railway, and the GWR stood by itself, apart from absorbing some small companies in Wales. There was no logical company with which it could have merged. It had been intended to have a separate Scottish

Railway, or perhaps two — one for each side of Scotland, but the Scottish railways were not especially profitable and it was felt that they would find it hard to survive economically on their own. So they were tagged on to the LMS and the LNER, thus weakening both those companies. In 1913 the Caledonian was paying just over 3% on its ordinary stock, the North British 4^1/$_4$% and the Highland 2^1/$_2$%.

The Stock Exchange view of the financial status of the Scottish Railways can be judged by the rate of exchange of the pre-Grouping ordinary stock with stock in the new companies:

£100 Caledonian Preferred Ordinary
= £50 LMS Preference Ordinary
£100 Caledonian Deferred Ordinary
= £10 LMS Ordinary

£100 North British Preferred Ordinary
= £60 LNER Preferred Ordinary
£100 North British Deferred Ordinary
= £40 LNER Deferred Ordinary

£100 Highland Ordinary
= £32 LMS Ordinary

It must be admitted that even some of the larger English companies had their ordinary stock marked down. But some of the small English companies were slaughtered in this respect. Perhaps the smaller companies should have been excluded from the Grouping and made to stand or fall on their own merits. Their attachment to the larger companies was a millstone for the latter.

The LNWR would have liked to amalgamate with both the L&YR and the Midland in the period 1900-14 but knew that Parliament would not agree. It therefore entered into working agreements and the pooling of receipts. Ironically, it would be *compelled* to amalgamate after World War 1. An LNWR express passes Pinner on a Liverpool Boat Express, headed by 'Claughton' class 4-6-0 No 42 *Princess Louise*. *F. R. Hebron*

The principal architect of Grouping was Sir Eric Geddes. Here was a man gifted with a quick brain, who could instantly grasp the essentials of any issue. He was also gifted with great ability, energy and self-confidence, tremendous drive and determination. He joined the North Eastern Railway in 1904 at the age of 29 and rapidly made his mark in management techniques and statistical analysis, becoming Deputy General Manager in 1914. His remarkable abilities did not go unnoticed in government, and he was co-opted into the country's service during World War 1, dealing successive-ly with the supply of munitions, the organisation of military transport in France (for which he was appointed a Major-General), and naval supply. He was appointed Director-General of Military Railways in 1916, and so impressed Lloyd George that he was created First Lord of the Admiralty in December 1916 and made an Honorary Vice-Admiral. An astonishing record.

After the war, Geddes, now Sir Eric, was appointed by Lloyd George in the coalition government to be Minister of Transport in the newly formed ministry. He set about his plans for reorganising the railways, based on bringing all the railways together under one umbrella with himself at the head, but it was not to be. He had to be content with masterminding the Grouping. He had hoped to become General Manager of the newly formed LNER, but he had made enemies and the directors would not accept him. He left the ministry and became chairman of the Dunlop Rubber Company in 1922. But for the war he would undoubtedly have become General Manager of the North Eastern Railway.

But what is the judgement on the question of the 1923 Grouping? With certain reservations it was a successful milestone.

The railway companies' financial structure

The capital structure of the railways was unusual, and generally consisted of debentures, guaranteed stock, preference stock and ordinary stock. Debenture stocks were really certificates entitling the owners to receive x per cent in perpetuity on their face value. In the event of default, the holders could appoint a receiver to work the line for their benefit until all arrears had been paid off. Such an event never occurred during the lifetime of the Big Four, because debentures had first call on profits and their interest was always paid.

As examples of capital structure, the North Eastern railway in 1922 had the following:

Debentures	£28 million
Guaranteed stock	£8 million
Preference stock	£19 million
Ordinary shares	£34 million

The LNWR's capital structure was:

Debentures	£61 million
Guaranteed stock	£18 million
Preference stock	£12 million
Ordinary stock	£57 million

The capital structure of the LMSR was:

Debentures	£85 million
Guaranteed stock	£32 million
Preference stock	£134 million
Ordinary stock	£88 million

Debentures, guaranteed and most preference stock bore a fixed rate of interest which was generally paid in the years between the wars, although in the worst years of the depression in the early 1930s some of the junior preference stocks received little or even nothing. The LNER was particularly badly hit, owing to its dependence on heavy industry. It was the ordinary shareholders who reaped the benefits in good years but took the risk in bad ones. Unfortunately, there were more of the latter. The price of LMS ordinary stock fell from £103 per £100 share in 1923 to £25 in 1934, but improved somewhat up to 1937. The LNER preferred ordinary shares fell from £76 to £21. The GWR fared better by dipping into its reserves to preserve its trustee status, its shares falling from £109 to £54. The Southern did best, being mainly a passenger railway. Calamitous falls such as these made it almost impossible, at least for the two largest companies, to raise investment funds on the Stock Market. This was the millstone that the railway companies had to bear. The Great Depression was not of their making.

However, it must not be concluded that the railways were largely bankrupt before World War 2, as some politicians would have had us believe. They were all paying their way, although the ordinary shareholders were receiving little or nothing. But it is the nature of things that ordinary shareholders take the risk.

Railway Passenger Duty

The history of this tax was dealt with in Part 1, and for many years the railway companies had pressed the government to abolish it, as there was no similar imposition on passenger traffic by road. It was levied on fares above a penny per mile. In 1929, with unemployment rising alarmingly, the government sought ways to create jobs, and offered to abolish the tax if the railways would use an equivalent amount on modernisation projects which would not otherwise be undertaken. On 1 April 1929 the Chancellor stated that the Railway Passenger Duty receipts for 1928/29 were £366,967, which if capitalised would amount to £6.5 million.

The tax was repealed in the 1929 Finance Act, and passenger duty works of £7.34 million were authorised, involving the four main line companies and the Metropolitan Railway. By March 1930 work had begun costing £6.6 million. The Southern Railway extended electrification to Brighton and Worthing, whilst the other railway companies built locomotives, yards and relief lines, and modernised rolling stock, stations and coal-shipping appliances. The railways were, of course, using their own money. But it was a millstone removed.

Municipal rates

As we saw in Part 1, rates had been imposed on the railway companies throughout their history, but in 1929, the government, seeking to ease unemployment, found an ingenious way to do so. In 1929 the Local Government Act relieved the railways of 75% of local rates payable 'on hereditaments used wholly for transport purposes', with the savings being paid to freight users of the railway by means of rebates on the carriage charges of prescribed traffics in the coal, iron and steel industries, and agriculture. The Railway Clearing House administered the fund. Those industries gained in two ways — they also were given relief from municipal rates, and secondly their freight charges were reduced by the railways. The railways' financial position was unchanged — they gained no relief.

World War 2 and government control

Preparations

In 1937, when few people had started to think seriously about the prospect of another European war, the government had formed a Railway Technical Committee to report on measures that should be taken to protect the railway system and keep traffic moving if Britain should become exposed to the risk of bombing. This committee included members of the Big Four and the London Passenger Transport Board (LPTB), together with the Home Office and the Ministry of Transport. It was clear that if war came, the railways would once again come under government control.

This committee reported in June 1938 under five headings:

> Protection of staff
> Protection of administrative centres and other vital points
> Provision of stocks of material for emergency repairs
> Provision of additional equipment
> Lighting restrictions

The total cost of these recommendations was over £5 million. The government paid £4 million, leaving the companies to find the rest from their own fairly slender resources. 1938 had not been a good financial year for the railways, as industry was working off its stocks. And in Europe, matters were reaching crisis point. Austria was annexed by Germany and

The evacuation of children from the larger cities had been carefully planned and was put into operation immediately on the outbreak of war. Children and their accompanying adults wait for their special train at East Ham whilst a friendly bobby paces gently up and down.
Syndication International

Czechoslovakia was threatened. War now appeared imminent, and in 1938 the government appointed a Railway Executive Committee as an advisory body to ensure that the railways were run in the interest of public safety, and to maintain essential supplies.

Railway preparations covered many separate issues, but the main ones were:

The removal of the main administrative offices from London, to large country houses about 20 miles from the capital.

The protection of signalboxes, and the construction of a number of specially fortified ones, such as Crewe North and South.

The duplication of telephone facilities.

The duplication of control offices, often in heavily fortified buildings.

Emergency lighting, and the arrangements for working trains, yards and depots during the blackout.

The evacuation of children from cities — a milestone

A scheme for evacuation of children from cities had been prepared in September 1938 when war had appeared imminent, and in the months before war actually broke out in September 1939 the plans had been finalised. Evacuation started on Friday, 1 September and continued for four days. During that period, 1,577 special trains were run from London, carrying 617,480 passengers. Evacuation also took place from other major centres. 382 trains left Merseyside with 161,879 passengers; 302 trains left Manchester with 115,779 passengers; and 322 trains left the Glasgow area with 123,639 passengers. Large-scale evacuation also occurred from Birmingham, Edinburgh, Hull, Portsmouth/Southampton and Tyneside. No one could have foreseen that such haste was unnecessary, but at least the nation was prepared. It was an example of the ability of the railways to respond to an emergency.

The state of the railways in 1939

Although the railways had been unable to make satisfactory profits in the 1930s, and had been unable to attract investment on a large scale, they entered the war with their assets in remarkably good shape. Track and signalling had been maintained to a very high standard, and the railways had an adequate amount of rolling stock. Only a few branch lines had lost their passenger train service in the 1930s, and there had been almost no closures of lines. Admittedly, some engines were elderly and some rolling stock had seen many years of service, but all were fit for further use. During the 1930s the companies had engaged in the construction of a large fleet of modern powerful locomotives, aided to some extent by government loans at a low rate of interest provided purely to ease unemployment. Stanier had provided the LMS with an extensive fleet of both passenger and freight engines; Gresley had built large numbers of Pacifics and 'Green Arrow' 2-6-2s, as well as rebuilding many heavy freight engines. The Great Western had consistently had an excellent stud of locomotives, as had the Southern.

The railways were well prepared in this respect. They concentrated on maintenance, so that the number of locomotives out of traffic awaiting overhaul or repair could be kept to the minimum. The workshops were also heavily engaged during the war in the production of guns, tanks, aircraft parts, etc. However, the LMS continued to turn out a new 'City' class locomotive every few months throughout the war and also built about 40 more Class 4F 0-6-0s. The LNER continued building the splendid Class V2 2-6-2, equally at home on enormous East Coast expresses and heavy fast freights. The GWR continued to produce 'Castles' and 'Halls', both well-tried and excellent designs.

The evacuation of the British Expeditionary Force from France — a milestone

The 'Phoney War' came to an abrupt end on 9 April 1940 when Germany invaded both Denmark and Norway. Then on 10 May 1940 the German armed forces launched their 'Blitzkrieg', sweeping through Holland and Belgium and on into Northern France. Within little more than a fortnight, most of the British Expeditionary Force was driven into a small pocket of land around the port of Dunkirk, and a desperate venture was launched to evacuate them by sea.

Hundreds of ships and boats, large and small, were gathered to undertake a desperate rescue and bring the BEF back to Britain. They were landed at a variety of South Coast ports, but mainly at Dover owing to its superior dock facilities. So far as the railways were concerned, they were suddenly faced with an urgent demand to provide hundreds of trains, including ambulance trains, to move the BEF away from the ports as quickly as possible owing to the threat of air attack.

Fortunately, the railways were well equipped to respond, and their control organisation was equal to the task. And it was a huge task, requiring minute by minute control and decision, depending on the ever-changing number of men being landed at many different ports at all hours

of the day and night. There was no forward planning; everything had to be improvised. And it was one thing to provide the empty trains at the ports; it was another to take the crowded trains away to destinations nominated by the military authorities. Between 20 May and 4 June 1940, 620 special troop trains left the South Coast ports, conveying 319,056 officers and men. The whole railway operation was a great success and might be regarded as one of the railways' finest hours. Railwaymen had every reason to be proud of their part in it.

Traffic levels — a milestone

Neither the railway companies nor the government foresaw at the beginning of the war that Britain would become what was referred to as 'a floating aircraft carrier' for the immense amount of war material that would flood into the country from 1942 onwards when the USA joined the war against Germany. The daylight bombing campaign carried out by the US Army Air Force required a large number of airfields to be built at a great rate, and thereafter supplied with trainloads of bombs and petrol. At the same time, the Royal Air Force was stepping up its night bombing campaign. Each 1,000 bomber raid required 28 trainloads of petrol and 10 trainloads of bombs.

Secondly, Britain became a base for the invasion of Europe, requiring the concentration of war material of all types in the south of England, both produced from our own factories and brought over by sea from the USA to West Coast ports.

Thirdly, the course of the war caused large-scale diversions of coastwise shipping traffic to the railways, especially along the East Coast and particularly of coal.

The amount of goods traffic conveyed, excluding coal and minerals, measured in ton-miles, had almost doubled by 1943 compared with prewar. This might indicate that the railways had a degree of surplus capacity prewar, but centralised control of the system helped, with resources being allocated to the best advantage, irrespective of company ownership.

Financial arrangements — a millstone

One might have expected that the railways would have received some sort of payment for all the extra work they performed. After all, they were private undertakings. But the government neatly circumvented this obstacle by taking control of the railways (as they had done in World War 1) and dictating all the financial arrangements.

There was nothing new in this: the government had been interfering in the railways' commercial practices and freedom since the 19th century, and when the Big Four were formed in 1923, their freight rates were fixed by the Railway Rates Tribunal (a sort of government quango but also a court of law) at a level that was intended to remunerate them at something akin to their 1913 profits of £52 million. The tribunal was blind to the effects of road competition and made no allowance for inflation since 1914. In the event, the trade depression of the early 1930s ensured that the railways were unable to achieve profits of £52 million.

In the end, after much wrangling, the government decided that it would provide the railways with an annual sum of £43 million out of the railways' own revenue, based on their profit in the prewar years, but it took no account of the extra work being performed by the railways on government account. Whilst before the fall of France in 1940 no one could have foreseen the enormous increase in the workload from 1942 onwards, the £43 million was never increased, which was grossly unfair, and parallels the shabby treatment meted out to the railways during World War 1.

The actual profits of the railways increased from £43 million in 1940 as follows:

1941	£65 million
1942	£89 million
1943	£106 million
1944	£90 million
1945	£62 million

The surplus amounted to £176 million, of which the railways received not a penny. It was daylight robbery and the shareholders had a genuine grievance. Ordinary shareholders had received poor or even non-existent dividends before, and even during, the war, because the companies felt they were under an obligation to maintain their assets in good condition, which left less for the ordinary shareholder. The government and the country benefited in 1939-45, but neither the railways nor the shareholders received any thanks. One might have felt that the government would have been grateful to the railways for this, but if it was, its gratitude was never expressed in a tangible form. In financial matters it treated the railways in a quite disgraceful manner. In the period 1941-1944, the railways received £174 million; the government took £176 million. In effect, as in World War 1, government traffic was carried free of charge. No industry was expected to provide war materials free of charge.

But it was all academic because the railways remained under government control until 1948, when they were nationalised. It is interesting to note that throughout their history the railway companies have never had the normal freedoms of other commercial concerns — a unique millstone.

The safety of operation of passenger trains

In the five years 1940-4, 133 passengers lost their lives in train accidents, which was somewhat fewer than in the next five years. Yet, far more passengers were carried during the war and train operation during the blackout was intrinsically more difficult and potentially dangerous. Mist and fog added their own dangers. Drivers running through a darkened landscape lost their normal landmarks and could easily have missed the flickering oil lamp of a signal at caution or danger.

The railway hardware, tracks, signals, engines, coaches and wagons were used more intensively than ever before, but not maintained to the high standards of prewar years. Repairs and maintenance were deferred, building up trouble for the postwar railway. New building was restricted to essential wartime use.

A coach of the 4.52pm train from Salisbury to Bristol after it had been struck by a bomb at the mouth of Fox's Wood tunnel, near Bristol, on 6 December 1940. *GWR*

The Chief Inspector of Railways, Ministry of War Transport, Lt-Col Sir Alan Mount, wrote in July 1945 in the Annual Report on Railway Safety for 1944 the following eulogy:

'There can be no doubt that the services rendered by the railways contributed in no small measure to the success of the country's war effort. Besides normal transport activities connected with industry, vast movements of men and materials for the services were involved both before and during the build-up after the landing of the Allied Forces in France on 6 June. Compared with prewar, passenger miles increased by 68% and freight ton-miles by 47%. These unprecedented demands on the railways were met with depleted staffs and impaired equipment; their record is an eloquent tribute to their efficiency, standard of maintenance, and the high factor of safety attained, all of which reflect the greatest credit on every Railway man and woman for the part they played in this historic year.'

It was a milestone.

The nationalisation of the railways — milestone or millstone?

The return of a Labour government with a huge majority in July 1945 was not expected, and rather took the railways by surprise. They were busily planning their postwar activities and seemed to take some time to adjust to the real threat of nationalisation, although it was obvious that railways would be near the top of the list for being taken into public ownership, along with the coal industry. The well-known Clause 4 of the Labour Party Constitution read: 'To secure for the producers by hand or by brain the full fruits of their industry, and the most equitable distribution thereof that may be possible, upon the basis of the common ownership of the means of production, distribution and exchange, and the best obtainable system of popular administration and control of each industry and service.' The nationalisation of the railways had been railway trade union policy since the 1890s, and in 1945 the railway trade unions were very powerful within the Labour Party.

Just as experience of government control of the railways during World War 1 had led to the Grouping in 1923, the similar experience during World War 2 led once more to thoughts about the appropriateness of the current railway organisation. As early as 1942, when the out-come of the war was by no means settled, both the railways and the Ministry of War Transport started to consider the railways' postwar control. The chairmen of the companies, meeting in the Railway Companies Association, established a committee for this purpose, whilst the Director General of the Ministry of War Transport, Sir Cyril Hurcomb, initiated a review within the department. The railway companies envisaged closer working arrangements and a fruitful agreement with the road haulage industry, implementing the prewar agreement with the Road Haulage Association regarding the 'Square Deal'. A booklet entitled *A National Transport Programme — The approach to a long-term plan* was published by the *Railway Gazette* in 1943, with a foreword by Sir James Milne, Chairman of the Railway General Managers' Conference.

But senior civil servants took a different view, just as they had done in World War 1. They thought that the views of the railway companies 'would not be satisfactory'. Hurcomb believed that some form of public control board would be needed, and some of his colleagues argued for outright nationalisation, just as they had done during World War 1. The railways' enemies were plotting. Lord Leathers, the Minister, argued in a speech in the House of Lords in 1943 that the 'Square Deal' was dead and that a more radical solution must be found. The plotters therefore started to consider various forms of organisations incorporating public control boards, including all forms of transport, so that when Alfred Barnes, the new Labour Minister of Transport, set to work on the remit to nationalise transport, he found that much of the groundwork had already been done.

The government announced its intention, in November 1945, to bring transport services under public ownership and control, and the bill was introduced into parliament in November 1946. There had been little contact between the civil servants drafting the bill and the railway companies. No attempt was made to seek the railway companies' views on organisation. No attempt was made to draw upon a century's experience of running railways. It was as though the ministry people preferred to live in their ivory tower, insulated against the reality of the outside world in case some of their beliefs turned out to be flawed. Which indeed they were.

When the bill was published, there was widespread scepticism about the concept of a huge state transport corporation, and the Railway Companies Association mounted an ill-fated campaign against the bill, citing the railway

The streamlined casing of Stanier's 'Princess Coronation' class Pacifics was eventually removed after the war, but the former streamlined engines could be identified by the slightly flattened top of the smokebox door, as seen here on No 6223 *Princess Alice* taking the up 'Royal Scot' past Thrimby Grange, just south of Penrith, in about 1947.
Eric Treacy

companies' achievements in war and peace since 1923. They issued a rebuttal of criticisms of the railways which had been made in parliamentary debates and in the press. But if they expected any sympathy for their prodigious wartime achievements, they were doomed to disappointment. The public was not interested — they were more concerned about surviving the hardships and shortages of the winter of 1946/47, one of the coldest on record. They might even have thought that the railways would be improved under public ownership. Why should profits go to line the pockets of wealthy shareholders rather than being invested in modern stations and electrified suburban railways? But the ordinary shareholders might have felt that if the assets were to be confiscated by the government, less should have been spent on maintenance and renewals between July 1945 and December 1947 so that the extra profit could be paid as dividend. And who could have blamed them? They owed no duty to the government.

We will consider the provisions of the act in Chapter 10, but it is interesting to consider what the future of the railways might have been if a Conservative administration had been returned in 1945. Perhaps the railways would have achieved equality of rates and conditions with road haulage. Probably they would have increased their diversification, especially in air services. There would have been greater co-operation with road haulage companies. There would have been a Beeching-type study of the viability of branch line and stopping services, and the poor performers would have been withdrawn. The companies might ruthlessly have exploited their immense property holdings. But the relentless increase in car usage and road haulage would eventually have made their financial position difficult, and assistance would have had to be sought from the government, pre-empting the 1968 Transport Act and the establishment of Passenger Transport Authorities, including grants for passenger services. But the railways could not have expected their 19th and early 20th century pre-eminence to last for ever.

And what happened to the shareholders? The stock of the four main line companies was exchanged for British Transport Stock, based on the nominal value of the existing securities on several days in November 1946. Debentures and guaranteed stock was exchanged approximately at par. The exchange rate for other stocks is given below, per £100 of nominal value:

London, Midland & Scottish Railway Company
4% Preference stock — slightly below par
Ordinary stock — £29.10.0

London & North Eastern Railway Company
4% First Preference stock — £58.5.0
4% Second Preference stock — £29.5.0
5% Preferred Ordinary stock — £7.6.3
Deferred Ordinary stock — £3.12.6

Great Western Railway Company
5% Preference stock — at par
Consolidated Ordinary stock — £59.1.3

Southern Railway Company
5% Preference stock — at par
Preferred Ordinary stock — £77.12.6
Deferred Ordinary stock — £24.0.0

The Stock Exchange view of the prosperity of the Big Four is clearly evident from the above ranking.

So, was nationalisation a milestone or a millstone? We shall have to wait for Chapter 10 to answer that.

Personality

Sir Josiah Charles Stamp

Even before the railways were grouped in 1923, the future chairman of the LMS, Sir Guy Granet, was dissatisfied with the quality of management talent at the top level of the constituent companies of the LMS and he had approached Sir Herbert Walker of the LSWR with a view to his becoming a future general manager of the LMS. Walker, although a former LNWR officer, turned down the offer. He probably thought that the post of General Manager of the Southern Railway would provide more job satisfaction than the bear pit which the LMS was likely to be. The history of the LMS might have been quite different if he had accepted, but the new Southern Railway might have regretted its loss.

Sir Guy Granet realised that the only way to achieve a cohesive board, and put an end to the in-fighting and intrigue that was handicapping the LMS, was to look for a figure from outside the industry. He found a director of ICI who was an ex-civil servant and a brilliant writer and lecturer on economics. His name was Sir Josiah Stamp (later Baron Stamp of Shortlands), and in 1926 Granet offered him the job of chairman. Stamp accepted.

Stamp (1880-1941) was unimpressed with the top-level organisation of the LMS and redesigned it on American lines, with himself as president of the executive and, a year later, chairman of the company. He then assembled an executive committee of vice-presidents, who were mostly railwaymen, including William V. Wood, an accountant who provided Stamp with the statistical analyses that Stamp wanted.

Under Stamp, the LMS developed a sense of direction and economic efficiency which had not always been present before, and he guided it through all the travails of the 1930s. His great prestige, his quickness of mind and power of expression made him a formidable champion, especially when dealing with government ministers and their civil servants. Had he lived it is very likely that he would have been chosen to be chairman of either the British Transport Commission or the Railway Executive, when the first few years of British Railways might have been more firmly guided. But it was not to be. Lord Stamp was killed in an air raid in his home in 1941 and the railways lost a formidable champion.

PART 3
1948 to 1970

Chapter 10

The nationalised railway

The new dawn

On 1 January 1948, the Big Four railway companies, the LMSR, the LNER, the GWR and the SR, were absorbed into the new British Railways. For the man in the street, the passengers and the staff, life went on as before. Only a few posters proclaimed the new dawn.

However, the change was one of immense significance. The former railway companies had been governed by their boards of directors and administered by headquarters officers. Prior to World War 2 they had been independent, subject only to the laws and regulatory bodies governing their activities. They received no government subsidy and were owned by their shareholders. In effect they largely determined their own destiny.

After nationalisation, the shareholders received British Transport Stock in exchange for their railway company shares, at a value which reflected the Stock Exchange rating. BT stock paid a guaranteed dividend, but most

ordinary shareholders received much less for their shares than their face value. That situation represented the Stock Exchange's view of the likely degree of prosperity of the railway companies if they had not been nationalised. It was not an optimistic view.

The boards of directors were immediately redundant, and their role was partly taken over by the British Transport Commission (BTC), under which body were all the executive bodies responsible for the various forms of transport. The Railway Executive in effect performed the role of general manager of the railways. The former companies became Regions, with a separate North Eastern Region and a Scottish Region. Subject to British Transport Commission policy, the Railway Executive was responsible for running the railways, and the Regions were regarded as being responsible for the day-to-day railway. The Railway Executive (known henceforth as the RE) saw its main task to be establishing common standards throughout the railway sys-

The shape of things to come. BR's first two main line diesel locomotives, Nos 10001 and 10000 (built by the LMS), pass Camden Goods Station with the up 'Royal Scot' in 1951. *F. R. Hebron*

tem in traction, rolling stock, engineering, accountancy, coach liveries, uniforms, house style, etc. Professor Gilbert Walker said that the 1948 BTC organisation was the least promising form of business organisation yet devised by man. But it wasn't intended to be a business organisation. It was intended to be bureaucratic, because that is all that civil servants understood.

Fortunately, the RE was formed almost exclusively from former chief officers of the railway companies, so at least they knew what they were doing. The chairman was Sir Eustace Missenden, formerly the General Manager of the Southern Railway. The first choice had been Sir James Milne, the highly respected General Manager of the Great Western since 1929, but he was 65 and in any case he heartily disliked the prospect of nationalisation. Missenden was a good administrator, but he was not happy in government circles and was suspicious of both politicians and civil servants. It was not a good start! However, temperamentally he was balanced by his Deputy Chairman, General Sir William Slim — friendly, outgoing and with a quick grasp of essentials, but unfortunately for the RE he left in less than a year to become Chief of the Imperial General Staff and a Field-Marshal. It was a great loss. His replacement

was another military man, General Sir Daril Watson, who was very capable but lacked Slim's charisma. There were other members of the RE, appointed by the Minister of Transport, one for each departmental function — commercial, operating, civil engineering, and mechanical & electrical engineering. Those four members consisted of one from each company, which avoided any resentment or allegations of favouritism.

W. P. Allen, formerly the General Secretary of the trade union ASLEF, was put in charge of staff matters. It was a political move clearly intended to prove the government's socialist principles in putting a worker on the board, but whilst the move didn't impress the railway trade unions, Bill Allen was a popular appointment with both sides. He was a genial, outgoing personality and had the distinction of having a locomotive named after him — LNER Class A1 Pacific No 60114.

Sir Cyril Hurcomb was appointed Chairman of the British Transport Commission. Sir John Elliot, who had been General Manager of the Southern Railway and would have been a much more effective chairman, wrote that Hurcomb was out of his depth where business experience was concerned. Another commentator was less polite, saying that Hurcomb was a safe, bureau-

W. P. Allen was appointed to the Railway Executive to be responsible for staff matters. He had previously been General Secretary of the Associated Society of Locomotive Engineers and Firemen. Former LNER Class A1 Pacific No 60114 carried his name and symbolically emerges from the tunnel into the sunshine in early BR days. *C. C. B. Herbert*

A Class A2/3 Ex-LNER Pacific No 60512 *Steady Aim* runs slowly into Peterborough North with an up express on 22 April 1951. The LNER had for a long time entertained plans to improve the layout at Peterborough and eradicate the slow approach, but it was to be another 20 years before it was achieved. *P. H. Wells*

cratic mediocrity whose entrepreneurial experience and engineering knowledge were nil.

Hurcomb wrote to Missenden, saying:

'The primary task is to unify the four railways in a real and operative sense, and at the same time to do so in such a way as to avoid excessive centralisation and to provide a suitable distribution of authority . . .'

It was easier said than done! It was to lead to endless arguments as people struggled to obtain what they saw as their share of that authority. The staff who reported for duty in HQ offices on Thursday, 1 January 1948 were identical to those who had gone home the previous evening, but they soon realised that they had been downgraded. Important policy decisions were taken elsewhere.

Staff out on the line, and passengers, saw very little change for several months, even years, although the words 'British Railways' began to appear on engine tenders, and four-figure engine numbers had another figure added to the beginning to denote former company ownership (except for the GWR — owing to its cast numberplates, its locomotives were sensibly allowed to retain their original numbers). Headed notepaper began to appear, lettered variously The Railway Executive, British Railways, London Midland Region, etc.

The government wanted a homogeneous railway system. It had worked well during the war, but the RE wanted standardisation, which went a lot further. With hindsight, the RE should have abolished the Regional HQs and taken over all their responsibilities direct, using them as outbased units of the RE, but it was considered too difficult and complicated. Railwaymen just wanted to get on and restore prewar standards, and a massive reorganisation would have been a tremendous distraction.

But above all this sat the imperious British Transport Commission, which also wanted a finger in the pie, and had a railway section, along with sections dealing with London Transport, docks, canals, hotels, buses and long-distance road haulage. So far as the railways were concerned, they lost their docks (except the packet ports), including major ones such as Hull, Grimsby and Immingham, and the South Wales docks. They also lost their hotels and catering, and their interests in buses and road haulage. Some of these interests had been an integral part of their business, and they soon treated themselves as independent concerns, to the detriment of integrated working. Civil servants regarded this as mere tidying up, to create a neater organisation on paper and one which they had more chance of understanding. Whether it improved efficiency overall (which it didn't) seemed not to matter.

It must be agreed that there was scope for a properly integrated transport system for both passengers and goods, but it was a major task, and ultimately impossible, because only a portion of the bus and road haulage industry, and of the docks, was acquired. The powers were available, but not the time. It would have taken many years to sort things out, and events conspired to defeat the proud, and perhaps desirable, objective. The return of a Conservative government in 1951, to whom all nationalisation was anathema, was the downfall of the dream. The Conservatives rapidly denationalised road haulage and buses (although some lorry fleets remained unsold), but left the railways untouched for the time being to face, ultimately, unbridled road competition. But in any case, even if the railways ran at a loss, they could not go bankrupt and would have to be supported by public funds, and that is precisely what happened in due course. So, in a manner of speaking, the railways were in a very comfortable position, protected from the harsh winds of the market. And yet, the market is a very effective discipline, and without that discipline management can become complacent. It becomes too easy to waste money, to produce schemes which haven't been properly thought through. And eventually, the Treasury has to call a halt, or try to. How successfully it did so, we shall see.

So was nationalisation a millstone or a milestone? Without it the railways would have had to ruthlessly prune their system Beeching-fashion and make every economy. They would have had to diversify as far as they could, and exploit their huge property ownings. But changes in industry and the development of road transport, aided by the construction of motorways, would eventually have compelled them to seek government aid, because they would have reached a financial position in which they could not raise capital (as happened prewar). Nationalisation, even with its clumsy and excessive management structure designed by civil servants, was preferable, and ensured the survival of a reasonable railway network. So, sad as one might be to see the demise of the much-loved Big Four, it has reluctantly to be considered a milestone and not a millstone.

October 1951 — The Conservative Party regains power

Nationalisation was anathema to the Conservative Party, but it was reluctant to attempt to sell the railways back to private shareholders. Who would have bought them, especially as they were denuded of their ancillary interests? However, the new government was also opposed to the centralisation of the British Transport Commission which it considered excessive, so it decided instead to abolish the hapless Railway Executive and decentralise administration. it also had a quaint idea of encouraging healthy rivalry between the railway Regions, although how this was to be achieved was not specified. Since the beginning of the century and even earlier, the privately owned railway companies had been working towards co-operation in their mutual interests.

There had always been friction between the BTC and the RE, and between the RE and the Regions. It was an organisation devised by civil servants who did not consult senior and experienced railway managers, and it did not work. The government's answer was to abolish the RE, effective from 1 October 1953, with many of its functions being directly undertaken by a section within the BTC. This was Hurcomb's revenge for being repeatedly snubbed and ignored by the RE. Statutory area boards were set up to manage the Regions under the overall authority of the BTC on 1 January 1955.

At the same time, Hurcomb (now Lord Hurcomb) retired. There was a very capable candidate available in the shape of John Elliot, chairman of the RE, and he should have headed the BTC, but that didn't suit the government. Instead it chose General Sir Brian Robertson, an excellent administrator, but unlikely to rock the boat. He allowed the Regional railway boards a fair degree of latitude, which was sometimes misplaced. John Elliot was shunted off to head London Transport, but received a knighthood as recompense. His loss was keenly felt by the railways.

The 16-ton all-steel mineral wagon with end and side doors, adopted as standard by BR. Handbrake only and three-link coupling.
Modern Transport

Did the 1953 act achieve anything so far as the railways were concerned? The answer is — very little. It removed a running sore in the shape of the RE, which caused friction both upwards to the BTC and downwards to the Regions. But a new running sore developed between the Regions and the BTC. The Regions felt themselves to be perfectly capable of managing their own affairs, as they had always done, without interference from the BTC. The BTC felt that it was not getting proper co-operation from the Regions. The ordinary railwayman just soldiered on, appropriately under a General. It was neither milestone nor millstone, except that the act deregulated road haulage and sold off many of the Road Haulage Executive's lorries, leading to increased competition and giving a considerable boost to the expansion of privately owned road haulage.

Each Railway Act begets the next one
The 1953 Act did very little to deal with the railway's financial position, which was soon to deteriorate. The 1955 strike by locomen did permanent damage to the railways' merchandise traffic, and by 1956 working expenses began to outstrip gross receipts. The deficit that year was £16.5 million, but the position continued to worsen. In 1957 the deficit reached £27.2 million and in 1958, £48.1 million. The government took fright, despite the fact that it had been told, and common sense indicated, that the fruits of the 1955 Modernisation Plan would take several years to emerge. The first main-line

diesel did not appear until 1958, with the first faint glimmerings of main-line electrification the same year. The BTC also pointed out, quite rightly, that many passenger services were being provided unprofitably in what was seen as the public interest of a publicly owned railway. It was a conflict of policy which was to dominate thinking in the next decade, but the railways had not been idle. Many unremunerative passenger services had been withdrawn throughout the 1950s and the number of passenger stations had been reduced from 6,785 to 5,264 during the 10 years since nationalisation.

The government failed to understand the intricacies of the situation. It did not trust the BTC, even under the redoubtable General Sir Brian Robertson, and resorted as usual to more reviews. In 1958 the government had asked the BTC to reappraise the 1955 Modernisation Plan, then the parliamentary select committee on nationalised industries independently investigated railways and reported in July 1960. Its main finding was that:

'There was no doubt that a large-scale British railway system could be profitable, but what size and shape should British railways be?'

And pigs can fly. By 1960 there was no way in which the British railway system could be profitable. Too much freight traffic was being lost, not through any railway shortcomings, but through the growing efficiency of the road haulage industry and the new network of motorways being created. And there was a limit to the extent to which freight charges and passenger fares could be increased to pay for the annual increases in salaries and wages. In view of this, the Minister of Transport, one Ernest Marples, appointed a small, shadowy special advisory group to tell him what to do. The group was chaired by an industrialist, Sir Ivan Stedeford, and worked in private. Its reports were not made public, but it was understood that it painted a less flattering picture of the railway's prospects than the select committee and was strongly critical of the BTC's organisation and its policies, and of the government's involvement. The group thought that the railway should shed its 'public service' mentality (that would have closed most suburban lines and all branches). It also felt that Sir Brian Robertson was not a suitable chairman owing to his training and background. It went on to say that the unwieldy BTC should be abolished and the railways should be put under a board directly responsible to a Minister (good thinking!). Two out of three wasn't bad going.

Lord Beeching (right) is introduced to Harry Whitehouse, the Yard Master of Tinsley new marshalling yard, whilst J. R. Hammond, the General Manager of the Eastern Region, looks on. *Modern Transport*

The Transport Act 1962 tidies things up. But was it too late?

The government took note, abolished the BTC, created the British Railways Board responsible directly to the Minister, and appointed Dr Richard Beeching (a member of the Stedeford Committee) as its chairman. These various changes required legislative action, and this was achieved in the Transport Act 1962. It was a considerable milestone, made even better by the government deciding that the railways should be freed from all statutory control over all their charges, except for passenger fares in the London area. This is what the railways had lobbied for in the 1930s. Now the prize was theirs. But it was too late to repair the damage.

By now, the railway's capital liabilities stood at £1,600 million, some of which was borrowings to cover losses. The government recognised that there was no prospect of these losses ever being recovered, and in an act of unparalleled generosity (with the taxpayers' money, of course) it proposed to write off or suspend most of them. £400 million was written off, and £800 million was placed in a suspense account carrying neither fixed interest nor fixed repayment obligations. This left only £400 million on which interest should be paid, representing the investment in modernisation since 1955. It gave the new British Railways Board a good start, and its borrowing powers were increased to tide it over until all the benefits of the Modernisation Plan had been achieved.

Visually, the railways were changing rapidly. 80% of passenger trains were now either diesel or electrically-hauled (but only 26% of freight trains). Passenger carryings, judged by the number of passenger journeys, were almost exactly the same as in 1948. But merchandise carryings had declined to 36 million tons, compared with 56 million in 1948. That was the nub. Freight had always provided much of the railway's profits, and it continued to decline.

Dr Beeching promptly got down to work, supported (and guided, it must be said) by most senior railwaymen. Major policy changes rapidly emerged, in a three-pronged attack on the financial losses:

- The withdrawal of unremunerative branch line and other stopping passenger services and the closure of stations (continuing the present policy, but accelerating it).
- A review of trunk routes to see which should be chosen for investment, and identify those which were no longer justified and should be closed or downgraded.

- The development of one-company freight trains, liner and container trains and merry-go-round coal trains.

The problem caused by the 'public service' ethos of carrying passengers at a loss had at long last been resolved. The BRB, when putting forward proposals to withdraw passenger services, did not now have, nor was it required to have, regard to the 'service to the public' argument. That was for the government to decide. It was for the government to judge the balancing act between the hardship to passengers against the losses incurred in providing the service. And that was a very proper allocation of responsibility. BR's public service ethos was no longer sustainable. It did not have the financial strength to continue to cross-subsidise loss-making lines. It could only have done so if the government had been willing to underwrite those losses, which it was not. But it did have the unhappy effect of some closure proposals being submitted which were only marginal loss-makers.

The passenger business

The railways examined the whole of their business in detail, and their studies confirmed what they had long suspected — that branch line passenger trains and stopping passenger services on main lines were making a thumping loss. However, it was astonishing to learn that a third of the total route mileage carried only one per cent of the total passenger miles on BR, and that half of the total route mileage carried only 4% of the total passenger miles. Even worse for the future of the small station was the revelation that half of all the stations produced only 2% of the total passenger receipts. The answer was glaringly obvious — the day of the small station was over. They had been built in the 19th century when the only competition was the horse-drawn vehicle. Now buses, coaches and the private car were providing fierce competition that the railways could not possibly match.

The Railways Board therefore published its proposals, which shocked everyone by their magnitude. Even hardened railwaymen, who knew that something pretty drastic had to be done, were taken aback. It was proposed to close no fewer that 2,100 stations (1,400 in England, 500 in Scotland and 200 in Wales) in addition to the 520 proposed closures already in the pipeline. Many branch lines would close altogether, and most small stations on main lines would be closed. But it should not be overlooked that the withdrawal of passenger services was a policy that had been vigorously followed ever since 1948. The Beeching Report merely

Hardly a profitable business? In a very nostalgic scene BR Standard Class 2 2-6-0 waits at Kelso with a one-coach train forming the 11.52am to St Boswells on 20 July 1963. Services such as this were killed off by buses and the private car. *IAL*

accelerated the process, but most of the obvious candidates for closure had already been dealt with. Some of the ones listed for closure now were very marginal.

The British public reacted predictably with outraged horror. They loved their branch line and local station with its pretty gardens, but most of them never, or hardly ever, used the trains and they were living in cloud-cuckoo land. On the other hand, there were some marginal cases which, with hindsight, ought not to have been progressed. But even if they were marginal in 1963, trends were not favourable and it could be expected that their financial state would worsen year by year. In the event, not all the proposals were carried out, but although the Labour Opposition argued furiously against the proposals, they were quite happy to put most of them quietly into effect when they came into power the following year. There were big savings to be made. In 1961 receipts from stopping

passenger services were £30.8 million, whilst the direct costs were £56.9 million, plus indirect costs of £29.8 million. What was missing was any recognition of the role of railways as a social service. That was a tragedy, rectified in 1968, but too late to affect the closures. The effect of the closures was as follows:

• Between 1964 and 1970 the route mileage open to passengers declined by 3,490 miles to 9,095.
• By 1967 the annual loss in providing stopping passenger services had reduced by £14 million, but revenue had declined by only £3 million.
• The total savings from closures from 1963 to 1970 produced £16.3 million per annum by 1970.

The savings might be considered relatively insignificant against the annual loss, which by

1968 had climbed to well over £100 million. It indicates that the more marginal cases ought not to have been progressed, but there were hawks within BR as well as within government circles. However, it is wrong and misguided to vilify Lord Beeching. He had been appointed by the government to carry out a policy. Any quarrels about that policy should be directed at the government. And it should be remembered that almost 3,000 miles open to passengers had been closed between 1948 and 1963 without any outcry.

The freight business

There were some very positive proposals, such as the building of new, mechanised, goods depots to take in traffic from a wide area, with road collection and delivery. This concentration of forwarded traffic would enable wagons to individual destinations to carry more traffic, and intermediate marshalling and tripping would be reduced.

Discussions were in hand with the National Coal Board, aimed at more coal being forwarded in block train loads, with the ultimate aim of coal for major users, especially electricity generating stations, being conveyed into overhead bunkers at collieries so that complete trains of empty wagons could be run beneath the bunkers and loaded quickly without the wagons being detached at all. Substantial progress was made, especially where new power stations could be designed to unload trains on the move. The 'merry-go-round' concept was born.

The Liner Train concept of containers on flat wagons was also being progressed, which ultimately led to a network of depots being constructed, connected by liner trains running to fixed schedules, and completely avoiding marshalling yards. The concept became known as Freightliner and initially was very successful. One effect was the abrupt and belated end of plans for more new marshalling yards.

The problem of the duplicate trunk routes

Railway development in the 19th century had left a legacy of duplicate trunk routes between many main centres, and the BRB decided to examine the situation in order to decide which routes should be selected for investment and which should be closed or relegated in importance. Detailed studies were made of passenger and freight flows and there were considerable discussions with industry. Concentration of traffic on fewer routes would produce big savings and make the remaining routes more profitable.

The routes concerned were:

Between London and Edinburgh/Glasgow
(three routes)
Between London and Manchester/Liverpool
(three routes)
Between London and Birmingham
(two routes)
Between London and Exeter/Plymouth
(two routes)
Between Birmingham and Bristol
(two routes)
Trans-Pennine (five routes)

In the 1960s contracts were made with the oil companies to carry their products in trainloads. This train is conveying naphtha for the VIP Petroleum Co from West Thurrock to Tipton (Staffs) gasworks on 28 September 1966. The wagons are 45-ton gross laden weight and are fitted with roller bearings. *BR*

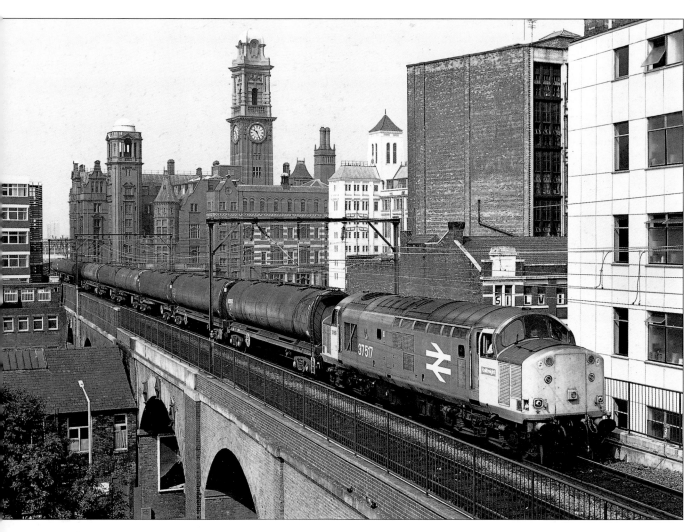

Above: The 100-ton gross laden weight bogie oil tankers made their appearance in the later 1960s, and over 20 years later they are still in use, as English Electric Class 37 (formerly type 3) diesel No 37517 runs along the viaduct between Oxford Road and Manchester Piccadilly with train No 6E20, the 08.46 from Glazebrook to Haverton Hill, on 19 July 1990. *Paul D. Shannon*

Right: The block train working revolution really got under way in the 1960s. Brush Type 2 diesel No D5518 heads a trainload of new motor cars from the Ford Company's works at Dagenham to a distribution depot at Bathgate on the first day of operation, 4 May 1964. *BR*

Complete closure was proposed for the following routes:

Perth to Aberdeen via Forfar
The Waverley route between Carlisle and Edinburgh
The Settle-Carlisle line
The Great Central route from south of Sheffield to Marylebone
The Midland Peak Forest route between Derby and Manchester
The GWR Honeybourne route between Birmingham and Bristol

The following routes were to be retained to serve intermediate stations, with possible singling of track:

The G&SW route between Carlisle and Glasgow via Kilmarnock
Newcastle to Edinburgh
Leicester to St Pancras
Basingstoke to Exeter

In order to improve the financial return from the West Coast electrification, Midland expresses to St Pancras were to be diverted through new chord lines over part of the GC between Leicester and Rugby and thence to Euston. And in order to bolster the case for the extension of electrification from Weaver Junction to Glasgow, all the East Coast Scottish traffic was to be diverted to Euston. Astonishing as it may seem now, these ideas were being examined, based on traffic forecasts. Fortunately they were not progressed. The Basingstoke-Exeter singling might be seen as the Great Western's revenge as it now lay within the Western Region, whose HQ was at Paddington. It would have been better to have developed the former LSWR route via Salisbury and downgraded the GWR line from Reading to Taunton via Westbury (the Berks & Hants).

The closure of the Peak Forest route was more questionable, because it resulted in trains between the North West and East Anglia having to travel on the more circuitous route via the Hope Valley and Sheffield, but on the other hand it improved Sheffield's services. That became more important when the Woodhead route closed.

The verdict
The 1962 Transport Act initially placed the railways' finances on a firm footing. That was a milestone.

The abolition of the British Transport Commission and the creation of the British Railways Board was also a milestone.

The closure of many small stations was merely the continuation of previous policy. It went a little too far because it became a bandwagon, and it was a tactical error to produce a huge 'shopping list' that was bound to cause a furore. The same result could have been achieved over a somewhat longer timescale by dealing with schemes on an individual basis, as had been done previously, and leaving the most marginal

A post-nationalisation Ivatt Class 4 2-6-0, No 43117, arrives at Ilkley with a local train from Leeds to Skipton in July 1955. This picture is of particular interest because it shows the wide expanse of running lines and sidings which served this small West Riding town before the line beyond Ilkley to Skipton was closed in 1964.
F. W. Smith/Transport Treasury

Clash of giants with BRB Chairman Stanley Raymond (left) graphically describing some development to George Smith, the tough Station Manager at Birmingham New Street, not long after the inauguration of the West Coast main line electrification via Birmingham in 1967. *BR*

cases until last, by which time the future may have been clearer. There was little wrong with the policy, which was inevitable, but the way in which it was presented was a tactical error and became a millstone. The exercise didn't produce huge savings. They came from the ongoing changeover from steam to diesel and electric traction and the consequent closure of engine sheds.

The trunk routes policy produced large savings and, based on forecasts of traffic levels, seemed in some cases a sensible rationalisation at the time, much as we might regret the demise of well-loved lines and the singling of others. But the plans for the diversion of Midland expresses into Euston, and East Coast Scottish expresses via Carlisle, were clearly born in an overheated think-tank. On the other hand, no one could possibly have foreseen the upsurge in traffic that would come 30 years later, and plans can only be laid on the basis of the best information available at the time.

The freight proposals of liner trains, merry-go-round coal trains, company trains, etc was a very considerable milestone.

So the verdict appears to be that the Beeching Era was by no means a millstone. Most of it was sound management policy and inevitable.

How did it all work out?

The 1962 Transport Act was expected to put the railway's finances on a firm footing, with all the changes it introduced, and with the full benefits of the 1955 Modernisation Plan being achieved. It did not, nor could it. Many loss-making pas-senger services which could not politically have been withdrawn were retained, but without any financial support from the government. Wages and other costs rose faster than realistic increases in passenger fares and freight charges and, despite the freedom which had been given to the railways in the 1962 Act, the government intervened to delay such increases by invoking the Prices & Incomes Act for purely political reasons. As a result, losses began to mount in the next few years. But help was on the way.

1964 — Labour returns to power

After 13 years in opposition, a Labour administration gained power under Harold Wilson, the new Prime Minister, in October 1964, and within seven months the newly ennobled Lord Beeching was back at ICI. Surprisingly, Labour had no firm plans for transport, and the first Minister of Transport, Tom Fraser, was described unflatteringly by the *Economist* as 'a very nice man'. He was ineffective, and nothing changed. The railway trade unions were not impressed; this was not what they had expected from a Labour government.

Fraser's tenure was short lived. He was out in December 1965, to be replaced by the fiery and effective Barbara Castle. History shows that this was a real milestone. By now, Stanley Raymond was Chairman of the BRB. He was also a tough character and he and Barbara Castle fought many battles for the next couple of years.

Many tales are told of Raymond's determination to bring the Western Region to heel when he was its General Manager. For whatever reasons, the BTC had looked benevolently upon the Western Region's independent stance, and the Region considered itself to be the inheritor of the Great Western Railway's proud and well-deserved traditions as a Gentleman's Railway. It regarded Raymond as an uncouth upstart, but he had the last laugh.

Barbara Castle appointed Lord Hinton, former chairman of the Central Electricity Generating Board, as a special adviser on transport planning and asked him to produce a plan for the co-ordination of transport (shades of 1948!). However, to her dismay, Hinton said in his report that there was no case for co-ordination, but that an entirely new nationalised organisation should be set up for collection and delivery services, anticipating to some extent the National Freight Corporation which appeared a few years later.

Raymond and Castle together produced a volatile and potentially explosive cocktail. Their meetings were tense affairs with little agreement on policy, but the idea eventually emerged of a

Joint Steering Group (JSG) that would examine the railway's financial problems yet again. Raymond wanted the BRB to be in charge. Castle took the opposite view. She wanted to be in charge. She won.

The Joint Steering Group was a powerful body. Its chairman was John Morris MP, Joint Parliamentary Secretary, Ministry of Transport, and its members were drawn from very senior people in the BRB (4), the ministries (4), industry (2) and others (2). The unions too wanted a seat at the table, but Barbara Castle vetoed this on the rather provocative grounds that a union man would take too narrow a view. She must have had considerable persuasive powers.

Very positive and far-reaching recommendations were to emerge, the main ones being:

Finance — Write down the capital debt to a reasonable level, scale down the valuation of assets, abolish the provision for deficit grants.
Grants for unremunerative passenger services — Grants should be given for those passenger services which are loss-making, but which the government wishes to be retained for social and/or economic purposes. The grants should cover all costs of providing those services which cannot be recovered from fares (this had been recommended by a select committee several years earlier).
Standby and surplus capacity — Under this scheme, a grant would be paid for the elimi-nation of surplus capacity and the rationalisa-tion of the system. Changes in freight traffic and methods of operation had led to many goods lines, yards and sidings etc seeing declining use, and the government decided that, wherever practicable, they should be taken out of use to save the costs of mainte-nance (which in fact were quite small). It was a time of major change, and any idea of keep-ing some running lines and sidings 'just in case' was firmly vetoed. Based on traffic fore-casts, it was a sensible measure, and no one could possibly have foreseen the changes that might take place 30 years later, much as we might regret the loss of such facilities today.

The 1968 Transport Act

The JSG reported to Barbara Castle in September 1967 and its recommendations formed part of a Railway Policy blue paper which she presented to parliament in November 1967 and which were expressed in the 1968 Transport Act, receiving the Royal Assent on 25 October 1968. It was an enormous milestone.

The Transport Act 1968 was a voluminous and meaty document of 281 pages, containing 166 sections and 18 schedules. It introduced fundamental changes designed to help the rail-ways not only to become more prosperous, but also to capture more freight traffic. It is quite clear that Castle wanted to help the railways, but she faced considerable opposition both from

That incomparable railwayman Gerry Fiennes (centre), when General Manager of the Western Region, presiding at the unveiling of the name plate of another genius, George Jackson Churchward, carried by a Class 47 diesel-electric. *BR*

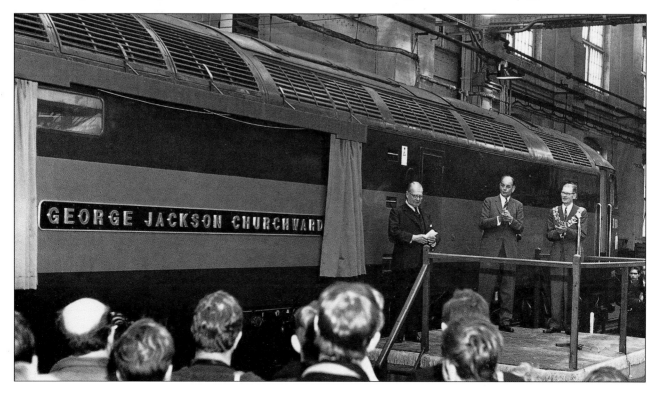

113

An English Electric diesel, No D413, takes the Glasgow to King's Cross York Way freightliner through Leyland on 18 July 1968. The Transport Act that year transferred Freightliner to the newly created National Freight Corporation. *Leslie Riley*

road interests (including trade unions) and from within her own department, which has never been renowned for wanting to help railways, before or since. In any event, the unexpected return of a Conservative administration in 1970, before some of the act's provisions had been put into effect, put paid to some of her hopes. But, short-lived though her reign was, she was probably the most effective Minister of Transport we have ever had and many of the provisions of the act have stood the test of time.

Part 1 of the act created the National Freight Corporation (NFC), a public body whose duties were:

1. To provide properly integrated services for the carriage of goods by rail or road (shades of 1948).
2. To secure that goods are carried by rail whenever it is economic and efficient to do so (an astonishing development).

The NFC acquired a wide range of road haulage interests including British Road Services, plus the following transferred from British Rail — Freightliners, the Sundries division (small consignments by freight train), and Collection & Delivery (C&D) vehicles. BR strongly resented losing Freightliners, which it had created and nurtured, and it wanted to retain those C&D vehicles used in the Parcels business, but it was glad to get rid of the heavy loss-making Sundries business.

Part 2 of the act created Passenger Transport Areas in the major conurbations, a measure of immense and lasting importance. They were to be headed by Passenger Transport Authorities

(PTAs), appointed by the minister and run by Passenger Transport Executives (PTEs). It had the effect of BR having to hand over to the PTA policy decisions on the provision of passenger train services in their areas — an unprecedented but wise measure. It was an exciting time for railwaymen — the loss of independence of policy was balanced by the prospect of a revitalised local passenger service and the full-scale involvement of the local authorities, who had historically shown little interest in rail, and not a little animosity towards it. And surprisingly the bus men in the PTEs showed themselves to be remarkably pro-rail. The PTAs now not only controlled all bus services within their areas, but also local rail services, and could co-ordinate them to the best advantage together with the local authorities' planning policies. It was hugely successful and has remained so, despite the Conservative administration's damaging deregulation of bus services in the 1980s at the behest of the Treasury. It was a very important milestone.

Part 3 of the act established the National Bus Company, which acquired 65 separate bus companies, including many famous names.

Part 5 of the act introduced what became known as quality licensing and quantity licensing. Quality licensing was aimed at improving standards in the road haulage industry and was unexceptionable. Quantity licensing was a major change, designed to increase the amount of goods traffic carried by rail and to boost the carryings of the Freightliner services. It was a complex and complicated part of the act, but it never really became established because the Conservative government that regained power in 1970, acting according to type, refused to put it into operation. It is impossible to estimate what the effect of the measure might have been, but it was certainly designed to reduce the number of heavy lorries on the roads.

The 1968 Transport Act was the last major alteration to the railway industry until privatisation. The Beeching era was quietly buried, and it was decided that the railway network in the future should remain at about the current level, apart from those closures already in the pipeline. A measure of stability was about to fall upon the railway industry for the first time for many years.

The Hixon level crossing accident — a millstone

On 6 January 1968, a massive road transporter lorry carrying a 120-ton transformer was proceeding very cautiously over an automatic half barrier (AHB) level crossing at Hixon, Staffordshire, when the red lights started to flash and the barriers to descend. The lorry was moving so slowly that it was unable to get clear before the train, a Manchester to London express passenger train, which had caused the barriers to lower, arrived at the level crossing, travelling at about 75mph. The electric locomotive struck the transformer and hurled it aside, becoming derailed in the process. Several coaches were also derailed. The train was conveying 12 carriages, carrying about 300 passengers. Eight passengers were killed, together with three railwaymen in the driving cab. British Rail should have been informed beforehand of the movement of the transporter lorry over the level crossing, so that it could have taken special precautions, but no such prior notice was received. In addition, both the lorry driver and the escorting police should have telephoned the signalman before travelling over the crossing, in accordance with a notice clearly displayed at the crossing.

The British public had always been suspicious of AHB level crossings and loved the old fashioned gated crossings. The Hixon accident — even though it was a million to one chance unlikely to be repeated for many, many years — confirmed their prejudices, despite widespread evidence from the rest of Europe of the safety of AHB crossings, and from Britain of the dangers of manned level crossings with gates. By this time German Federal Railways had over 800 AHBs whilst the French Railways had over 2,000. Nevertheless, the bizarre nature of the accident attracted tremendous public attention, and the government decided that a more formal inquiry should be held under the provisions of Section 7 of the 1871 Regulation of Railways

Act. Accordingly, it appointed Mr E. B. Gibbens QC to hold the inquiry, rather than one of the usual Inspecting Officers, because it was felt that as the Railway Inspectorate had been so closely involved in formulating proposals for AHBs, and as the accident had involved non-railway people, the inspectorate's independence may have been open to question. In the circumstances it has to be considered a correct decision, even though it was the first time such a course of action had been taken for almost a century, from the Tay Bridge disaster of 1879.

The remit to Mr Gibbens from the Minister of Transport was to inquire into the causes and the circumstances of the accident, and additionally 'to inquire generally into the safety of the system of protection of railway level crossings by automatic half barriers and to make recommendations'. So far, so good. The outcome was a confirmation of the policy of automating level crossings, but with additional, and in some cases unnecessary, irrelevant and expensive, safeguards. This had the unfortunate effect of defeating the policy of automation because the extra costs made it uneconomic. The programme for the automation of level crossings came to a sudden stop, and there was to be little or no progress for the next 10 years or so, during which time thousands of level crossings were automated in Western Europe. Unfortunately, Mr Gibbens, eminent though he may have been in his own field, overlooked the need to judge the value of his recommendations against their cost and practicality. And this despite the fact that he acknowledged the need, when assessing the degree of safety desired:

'. . . to put into the balance, on the one side, the magnitude of the danger to be eliminated and, on the other, the sacrifice in money, time, convenience, material resources (and the neglect of other pressing safety needs elsewhere) involved in eliminating that danger. There is no such thing as unbounded resources for every desirable reform.'

Wise words indeed. What a pity that they were not followed in his recommendations, the cost of which killed off all progress in level crossing automation until the recommendations were reviewed 10 years later. Failure to do a cost-benefit analysis of recommendations appears to be endemic among eminent legal persons holding railway inquiries and continues to be a major millstone. It might be added that BR was supinely at fault for not questioning the value of some of the recommendations, as per Mr Gibbens' quote above. They were not mandatory.

Chapter 11

Steam, diesel and electric traction

Riddles' locomotive policy

Each of the four main line companies had its own engineering workshops for building locomotives, and traditions and pride were nowhere more strongly entrenched than in the locomotive department. The problems that faced the newly formed Railway Executive were many, but the principal ones were:

- Should the former companies' designs continue to be built until a firm and practicable modernisation policy became available?
- Should the best of the former companies' designs be built and spread throughout British Railways?
- Should new standard designs be built incorporating the best of standard practice?
- Ought the new policy to embrace an immediate shift to diesel and electric traction, with new building of steam locomotives being limited to the extent necessary to cover the interim period?

The team

The new member of the Railway Executive responsible for mechanical engineering was R. A. Riddles, formerly a vice-president of the LMS and previously Principal Assistant to the Chief Mechanical Engineer of the LMS. He had joined the LNWR in 1909 and was a man of considerable ability, having spent his working life with steam locomotives and workshops. He chose as his assistants R. C. Bond, to be Chief Officer (Locomotive Construction and Maintenance), and E. S. Cox, to be Executive Officer (Design). Both men had held very senior posts in the LMS locomotive department, and all three had worked together, an essential feature of a new team. It was an LMS takeover, but the LMS had been in the forefront of design incorporating new technology.

The plan

Riddles believed that electrification must be the ultimate aim, but it was also a long-term aim. He foresaw that there would be considerable problems in acquiring the necessary capital investment and that alternative forms of traction would be needed in the meantime. And in any case there would be many lines that would not qualify for electrification. He considered that diesel locomotives would not be suitable to cover the interim period because he was concerned that it might delay electrification. There was also the question of the availability of fuel oil, all of which had to be imported and paid for in scarce dollars, whilst supplies of locomotive coal were readily available and home-produced. Finally, diesel locomotives were more expensive to build than their steam equivalents and would have to work in multiple to equal the power output of the best steam locomotives.

All four main line companies had been considering the use of diesel power and the LMS and the Southern had produced prototype designs. The GWR had experimented with gas-turbine engines, and the LNER had produced a plan just prior to nationalisation for a fleet of diesel locomotives for use on the East Coast main line. It would have been sensible for Riddles to continue those experiments, in order to produce efficient designs for subsequent volume production when finance became available, but in the event, nothing was done until the Modernisation Plan of 1955 embraced diesel traction on a large scale. Seven years were wasted, and the urgency of the transition from steam to diesel which then arose produced some unhappy results. Riddles ought to have been considering his long-term traction policy for the replacement of steam on those lines which could not financially support electrification.

However, Riddles had other plans. He decided that a fleet of standard BR locomotives would be produced, and the drawing offices began their task of producing detail drawings for 12 new standard types of steam locomotive. It has always been a contentious decision. In the former company days, he would have had to persuade a board of directors to agree to the expenditure. On the nationalised railway there was no such effective system of checks and balances. The BTC was, naturally, interested, but Riddles kept it at arm's length by various subterfuges until the end of 1951, when it was too late to reverse the policy.

No doubt Riddles was anxious to avoid a repeat of the provocative policy in early LMS days, of which he would have been fully aware, of flooding the system with ex-Midland types of doubtful quality. Although most BR designs had obvious LMS parentage, they could be passed off as new designs to forestall too much resentment. A lot of design work was carried out in the drawing offices of other Regions and the new designs were built in their workshops.

In the meantime

At nationalisation, the four main line companies had been in the midst of building locomotives to their own designs, as though nationalisation was just a bad dream that could happily be ignored. In fact, it was essential for this to continue until the standard designs were available, and 1,518 steam locomotives of former company types were built between 1948 and 1956, outnumbering the BR standard fleet of 999. The BR fleet might almost be regarded as a sideshow. The only completely new BR designs were the 'Britannia' Pacifics and the Class 9F 2-10-0s. Almost all the others were derivatives of perfectly good LMS designs.

Of the company designs built after nationalisation, the LMS built 620, including 100 Class 5 4-6-0s, 159 Class 4 2-6-0s, 147 Class 4 2-6-4 tanks, 138 Class 2 2-6-0s and 70 Class 2 2-6-2 tanks. To some extent, the LMS had forestalled Riddles by establishing its own postwar steam locomotive building policy, which included a number of design features incorporating ease of

servicing and maintenance. All four of the Class 4 and Class 2 designs mentioned above were used fairly extensively on the lines of the other former companies, often being built in the workshops of those companies. For example, Brighton Works built 41 LMS 2-6-4 tank engines.

The LNER built 396 locomotives, including 63 more Pacifics, 136 Class B1 4-6-0s, 70 Class K1 2-6-0s (the entire class) and 99 Class L1 2-6-4 tanks. The LNER's 63 additional Pacifics formed a greater number than the entire Pacific fleet of the LMS, and in retrospect the former LMS lines would have benefited from an influx of LNER Pacifics. The 'Jubilees' were of only relatively moderate power and it is not clear why the LMS and Riddles did not rebuild more of them with a larger boiler following the successful conversion of Nos 5735 and 5736 in 1942. The 'Jubilees' were not really sufficiently powerful for many tasks that they were called upon to perform in the postwar world, on the hilly routes of the Midland Division of the LMS.

The 1948 Inter-Regional dynamometer car trials

Dynamometer car trials took place between April and September 1948, and encompassed three separate groups of locomotives — express passenger, mixed traffic and freight. Group 1 consisted of LMS 'Duchesses', LMS 'Rebuilt

The LMS reboilered many of the 'Patriot' class after the war, and in early BR days No 45535 Sir Herbert Walker KCB *stands proudly in apparent ex-works condition. The name dates back to LNWR days when Walker was employed by the LNWR and was carried on one of the 'Claughtons'. Sir Herbert Walker was knighted in 1917 for his wartime services, and moved to the LSWR as General Manager and then to the Southern. He was one of the finest railwaymen of all time.* IAL

Right: The first batch of 'Britannias' mainly went to the Great Eastern Section when new in 1951 to accelerate the Liverpool Street–Norwich expresses. No 70012 *John of Gaunt* makes light work of a heavy train. *IAL*

Below: The BR Standard Class 5 4-6-0s were a derivation of the LMS Class 5s and were very successful, 172 being built. But wouldn't a similar number of LMS Class 5s, LNER 'B1s' and GWR 'Halls' have been just as effective? No 73001 is on shed at Cardiff Canton locomotive depot on 5 January 1962. *R. J. Henly*

Scots', LNER 'A4s', GWR 'Kings' and SR 'Merchant Navies', working over the main lines of the East Coast, the West Coast, the GWR and the former LSWR. Group 2 consisted of LMS Class 5s, LNER 'B1s', GWR 'Halls' and SR 'West Countries', working over the Marylebone to Manchester, St Pancras to Manchester and Bristol to Plymouth main lines. It was a marvellous publicity operation, but whether it had any real value is questionable. It made no difference to Riddles' plans, but at least gave the impression that the best locomotives of each former company were receiving careful consideration.

The new standard engines
The first engine to appear was a 'Britannia' class Pacific No 70000, which emerged from Crewe workshops on 2 January 1951, to be named *Britannia* by the Minister of Transport, Alfred Barnes, on 30 January. It was a handsome, powerful-looking engine and must have pleased Riddles and his team immensely. Many of the 'Britannias' were set to work on the Great Eastern main line to Norwich, where they were

little short of a revolution, but every Region had to have some, except the North Eastern. The London Midland Region was no doubt glad to receive 11, whilst the Scottish Region had five at Polmadie. It can be imagined that the Western Region was perfectly satisfied with its 'Kings' and 'Castles', but it had to accept no fewer than 13 'Britannias', which the drivers might have regarded as an insult. The LMR would have welcomed them. Even the Southern had to accept a couple to work the 'Golden Arrow', despite being awash with Pacifics.

The new designs were:

4-6-2 Class 8 No 71000 *Duke of Gloucester*. Built at Crewe in 1954 and really an extravagance when plans were already being made for a fleet of main-line diesels.

4-6-2 Class 7 'Britannias' Nos 70000 to 70054. They were built at Crewe between January 1951 and September 1954. After teething troubles had been sorted out they were a very successful class.

The BR Standard 2-6-4 tanks were equally successful and 155 were built. But was the building of a separate class justified, at a time when LMS 2-6-4 tanks were distributed around most of the BR system? No 80026 waits for its next duty at Glasgow Central. *IAL*

A BR Standard Class 9F 2-10-0 on express passenger duty north of Peterborough on 25 July 1959. The '9Fs' were essentially heavy freight engines and cleaning tended to be sporadic. *D. C. Overden*

4-6-2 Class 6 ('Clan' class) Nos 72000 to 72009. They were built at Crewe between December 1951 and March 1952. They were shared between Scotland and Carlisle Kingmoor. There was no justification for such a small class and it served no purpose.

4-6-0 Class 5, Nos 73000 to 73171. They were built between April 1951 and May 1957. Derby built 130 and Doncaster built 42. They were a very successful development of the LMS Class 5.

4-6-0 Class 4, Nos 75000 to 75079. They were built between May 1951 and January 1956, all at Swindon. It was hard to justify this class, except as part of a long-term plan.

2-6-0 Class 4, Nos 76000 to 76114. They were built between December 1952 and October 1957. 70 were built at Doncaster and 45 at Horwich. This was a useful development of the LMS Class 4 2-6-0.

2-6-0 Class 3, Nos 77000 to 77019. They were built at Swindon between February and December 1954. There was no justification for such a small class, except as part of a long-term plan.

2-6-0 Class 2, Nos 78000 to 78064. They were all built at Darlington between December 1952 and November 1956. The class was a development of the LMS Class 2 2-6-0.

2-6-4 tank Class 4, Nos 80000 to 80154. They were built between September 1952 and March 1957. Brighton built 130, Derby built 15 and Doncaster built 10. The class was a development of the very successful LMS Stanier 2-6-4 tank.

2-6-2 tank Class 3, Nos 82000 to 82039. They were built between April 1952 and August 1955, all at Swindon. Nearly all of them went to the Southern and Western Regions which had presumably indicated a need for them.

2-6-2 tank Class 2, Nos 84000 to 84029. They were built between June 1953 and June 1957. Crewe built 20 and Darlington built 10. The design was based on the LMS Class 2 2-6-2 tank. This is another class that was difficult to justify in the circumstances.

2-10-0 Class 9F, Nos 92000 to 92250. These were built between January 1954 and December 1958. Crewe built 208 and Swindon built 43. They were outstanding performers.

Most of the classes performed perfectly well, and except for 71000 they were two-cylinder machines with outside Walschaerts valve gear. They had been designed with ease of maintenance in mind, as appropriate in postwar conditions. But it is questionable whether the RE should have continued to build steam locomotives beyond the end of 1956, bearing in mind that large-scale dieselisation had been decided upon, and that many passenger services were being taken over by diesel multiple-units.

The main success of the fleet was undoubtedly the Class 9 2-10-0, because it filled a niche and was regarded as the finest heavy freight engine ever built. It was designed to accelerate the running of heavy freight trains and succeeded admirably. The 2-10-0s were the last steam engines to be built by British Railways, when No 92220, the aptly named *Evening Star*, emerged from Swindon workshops resplendent in Great Western livery in March 1960. It is a tragedy that these fine engines had such short lives and arguments will rage for a long time as to whether they should have been retained in service for longer on selected routes. The real culprit was the mad dash for dieselisation imposed upon the railways by the government, which wanted to see quicker financial returns from the Modernisation Plan.

The 1955 Modernisation Plan — a major milestone

For probably the first time in railway history, a comprehensive plan was developed, published and accepted by the government for modernising and re-equipping the whole of Britain's railway system. The 1955 Modernisation Plan set out to overcome the arrears of the previous 25 years and produce a modern railway system. It was costed at approximately £1,200 million, but the BTC pointed out that at least half that amount would be needed in any case for the normal maintenance and renewal of railway services and infrastructure on their present basis. The BTC went on to state that no one could seriously contemplate such a restricted objective; the only possible course, if the railways were to continue in being, was to bring them properly up to date. The Conservative government of the day warmly welcomed the plan, which had been produced in response to their asking the BTC how it intended to improve the financial situation. The government said that:

'The national interest requires that the future of the railways should be assured . . . the rail-

ways are essential and will continue to be so for as long as can be foreseen. It will take time to overtake decades of under-investment . . . The Government consider that on the basis of the BTC's proposals there are good prospects that the railways will not only be able to pay their way but also to earn an adequate surplus.'

A brave hope, but it never happened. However, it was almost unknown for the government to support the railways so handsomely.

Track and signalling

Track and signalling were to be improved to make higher speeds possible over trunk routes. There would be extended use of colour-light signalling, track circuiting and automatic train control, with more power-operated signalboxes and the installation of centralised traffic control where conditions were suitable. The use of modern telecommunication services would be extended. Estimated cost — £210 million.

All of this was necessary with the exception of centralised traffic control. This was an idea based on North American practice over long single lines, but its cost could not possibly be justified on such lines in Britain. It was not proceeded with, but some equipment was ordered and actually delivered on site on the Craven Arms to Swansea line.

Automatic train control was renamed the Automatic Warning System (AWS). It had been

The new colour-light signalling signalbox at Chislehurst Junction, using the 'one-control switch' (OCS) system of operation in 1959. *BR*

General Sir Brian Robertson (in raincoat) listens to Freddie Margetts' explanation of the working of the 'OCS' system at Cowlairs in May 1957. Margetts was General Manager of the Scottish Region. *BR*

needed for many years but the pre-nationalisation companies could hardly afford it. However, development work had started soon after nationalisation.

Traction

The report said:

'Steam must be replaced as a form of motive power, electric or diesel traction being rapidly introduced as may be most suitable in the light of the development of the plan over the years; this will involve the electrification of large mileages of route, and the introduction of several thousand electric or diesel locomotives.

'No express passenger or suburban steam locomotives are to be built after the 1956 programme and the building of all steam locomotives will cease within a few years. There are a number of reasons which make this change imperative. There is a growing shortage of suitable large coal for locomotives, and there are demands for a reduction in air pollution by steam locomotives and for greater cleanliness in trains and on stations. The manual labour involved with the operation and servicing of steam locomotives is unattractive and recruitment difficult. Shunting and trip working by steam locomotives is expected to cease within 15 years.

'Suburban electrification is planned for the LT&S line, on the lines from Liverpool Street, from Kings Cross to Letchworth, the Glasgow suburban lines, and the Southern Region lines in Kent.

'Main line electrification is planned from Kings Cross to Leeds (and possibly York) and from Euston to Birmingham, Liverpool and Manchester.'

The estimated cost was £345 million.

In the event, the West Coast electrification absorbed all the available resources and the East Coast had to wait for many years. Hence the GN suburban electrification was not dealt with until the late 1970s.

Passenger train services

The plan foresaw the large-scale introduction of diesel and electric multiple-units and the modernisation of passenger carriages, also considerable expenditure on passenger stations and parcels depots. Estimated cost — £285 million.

Diesel multiple-units had already started to appear in West Yorkshire and Cumberland. Station reconstruction had already been authorised at Peterborough, Plymouth, Banbury and Cannon Street.

Freight services

This was the most contentious part of the report. There was a need to speed up the operation of freight trains, and to reduce the amount of trip working and delays in old and inefficient marshalling yards. 19th century goods depots needed modernising and mechanising.

Left: The BR Standard Mark 1 carriages had a long reign, but started to be displaced by the Mark 2 version in the late 1960s. The interior seating arrangement shows that the system of table bays matching the window spacing was still *de rigueur. IAL*

Below: The modernised goods depot at Liverpool Huskisson, showing the conveyor belt in use. *BTC*

It was intended to fit continuous brakes to all freight wagons to enable faster trains to run. Whilst this was a laudable aim so far as merchandise wagons were concerned, and was carried out, there were considerable problems in applying the principle to coal and mineral wagons, both at the loading end and at the receiving end. Facilities in some places were unsuitable for wagons fitted with continuous brakes, and there was the added problem of the time taken, and the labour required, for coupling and uncoupling vehicles and brake pipes. In fact, little progress was made for many years, although a number of 16-ton mineral wagons were fitted with the continuous brake, which became very useful when diesel haulage replaced steam.

The greatest problem concerned marshalling yards. The plan provided for the construction or reconstruction of some 55 marshalling yards, resulting in the closure or partial closure of about 150 existing yards. Modern marshalling yards required huge areas of land and were very expensive. They were fine as sausage machines for processing wagons efficiently, but high quality merchandise traffic required different and far quicker treatment. However, there was optimism in the plan that all the improvements intended would provide such an attractive ser-

Above: This remarkable aerial photograph clearly shows the track layout at Carlisle Kingmoor marshalling yard, opened in 1963. It occupied a huge area of land but unforeseen changes in the railway's freight business soon rendered it largely redundant. What an awful waste. *BR*

Right: Tinsley (Sheffield) was one of the last new marshalling yards to be built in the 1960s. Its vast size is apparent. *BR*

vice that traders would flock to send their goods by rail. It was based on past knowledge and experience, but the plan quickly foundered on the capture by road haulage of increasing amounts of traffic before the benefits of the plans were achieved, and ultimately by the development of the trainload concept, avoiding marshalling yards altogether.

Work on new marshalling yards commenced at once, and in the next few years they were opened at such places as Ripple Lane (Barking), Carlisle, Perth, Millerhill, Temple Mills and Tinsley (Sheffield). Many more were planned at such places as New England (Peterborough) and Stourton (Leeds) and preliminary work had already started when it was suddenly stopped in 1960, after the plan had been reappraised on a more realistic basis. In a relatively few years these vast new yards on which such hopes had been pinned became sad deserts, and millstones.

Summary

The BTC assumed that the plan would achieve an annual return of at least £85 million, but that sum was swallowed up by cost increases and loss of freight traffic. The BTC also assumed that the benefits of modernisation would allow it

to achieve a balance on its revenue account by 1961/62, leading thereafter as modernisation progressed to an increasing surplus. In fact, the annual loss continued to increase in the second half of the 1950s, which caused the government to intervene as described in the previous chapter. It also caused the government to look far more carefully at financial forecasts than had been the case with the Modernisation Plan. But apart from that, the plan provided the capital for a whole range of benefits.

The diesel locomotive policy

The Modernisation Plan reported that orders had been placed for 174 main line diesel locomotives at a cost of £11.4 million and that delivery was expected towards the end of 1957. It was intended to put them into intensive operation, the subject of a thorough and selective trial. Essential data would then be obtained to enable orders to be placed for large numbers of standard types which could then be depended on to give the service required. Until those trials had been completed, further orders would be restricted to comparatively small numbers.

The 174 locomotives were of the following types:

Type	Class	hp	Mechanical parts/Engine/Transmission	No ordered	Fleet Nos
Diesel Electric					
1	15	800	Clayton/Paxman/BTH	10	D8200
1	16	800	NBL/Paxman/GEC	10	D8400
1	20	1000	English Electric	20	D8000
2	21	1000	NBL/MAN/GEC	10	D6100
2	23	1100	English Electric	10	D5900
2	24	1160	BR/Sulzer/BTH	20	D5000
2	26	1160	Birmingham RC&W/Sulzer/Crompton Parkinson	20	D5300
2	28	1200	Metro-Vickers/Crossley/Metro-Vickers	20	D5700
2	30	1250	Brush/Mirlees/Brush	20	D5500
4	40	2000	English Electric	10	D200
4	44	2300	BR/Sulzer/Crompton Parkinson	10	D1
Diesel Hydraulic (at Western Region insistence)					
2	22	1000	NBL/MAN/Voith	6	D6300
4	41	2200	NBL/MAN/Voith	5	D600
4	42	2200	BR/Maybach/Mekydro	3	D800

(Note — the Class numbers were introduced subsequently, with variations, eg the later Class 30s became Class 31)

The first ones to be delivered were D8000 in June 1957, D5500 in October 1957, D8200 in November 1957, D600 in January 1958 and D200 in March 1958. They all aroused great interest and initially went to Stratford (shed code 30A) except D600, which went to Swindon (82C).

Even whilst they were being delivered, the BTC was coming under pressure from the government to reduce its financial losses by speeding up the pay-off from the modernisation investment. The BTC recognised that accelerating the replacement of steam locomotives by diesels on an area basis would provide the biggest savings and they therefore went ahead by placing volume orders for diesels, despite the fact that there had been insufficient experience of the trial batch and there had been no time to sort out the inevitable teething troubles. Thus were the seeds sown of future maintenance and reliability problems.

The volume orders were as follows:

Class 15	D8200 series	34 units
Class 20	D8000 series	108 units
Class 21	D6100 series	48 units
Class 22	D6300 series	52 units
Class 24	D5000 series	155 units
Class 26	D5300 series	27 units
Class 30	D5500 series	243 units
Class 40	D200 series	190 units
Class 42	D800 series	35 units
Class 45	D10 series	127 units

These were the initial volume orders, numbering no fewer than 1,019 machines. The BTC should not have allowed itself to be panicked into such unwise action, but within a couple of years further volume orders were being placed for locomotives in Class 20, and for variants of Classes 24, 26, 42 and 45. The Class 21, built by NBL, were unreliable and the volume order should not have been placed. There may have been political pressures to assist NBL. No further orders were placed for Classes 16, 23, 28 and 41 which had proved unreliable, or duplicated a similar class.

There was an obvious gap in the programme for mid-power-range locomotives, Type 3, and volume orders were placed straight off the drawing board for the following machines:

Class 33	1550hp, BRCW/Sulzer/Crompton Parkinson	98 units	D6500
Class 35	1700hp, Beyer Peacock/Maybach/Mekydro	101 units	D7000
Class 37	1750hp, English Electric	309 units	D6700

Fortunately, the English Electric machines were reliable.

The headlong rush into dieselisation continued unabated. In 1961 more new classes were ordered:

Class 17	900hp, Clayton BP/Paxman/CEC.CP	117 units	D8500
Class 47	2750hp, BR/Sulzer/Brush	512 units	D1500
Class 52	2700hp, BR/Maybach/Voith	74 units	D1000
Class 55	3300hp, English Electric	22 units	D9000

Of these later units, Class 17 was generally regarded as a disaster, being very unreliable, and volume production should not have been ordered. Class 52 was a further Western Region venture into hydraulic transmission, and was known as the 'Western' class. The BTC should have vetoed this design, but the chairman, Sir Brian Robertson, was still reluctant to interfere with Regional preferences. The Western Region cunningly gave them all names with the prefix 'Western', which made them very popular with enthusiasts. The Class 55 locomotives were the famous 'Deltics', which revolutionised the East Coast main line until the High Speed Trains (HSTs) appeared in the 1970s (see below). The highly regarded Gerry Fiennes had famously said that 23 (sic) 'Deltics' would enable him to withdraw 55 Pacifics. But the star of the show was undoubtedly the Brush Class 47, which spread throughout the system and became one of the longest-lived classes. They were not perfect, but they were good enough.

By 1963, BR had 2,813 diesel locomotives at work or on order. Some had short lives, both from reliability problems and from the unexpected reduction in the volume of merchandise traffic. Type 4 locomotives, which had been intended for express passenger work, began to be redundant from the electrification of the West Coast main line and the introduction of HSTs in the Eastern and Western regions in the 1970s.

Above: A Brush Type 2 diesel heads north with a suburban train from King's Cross and passes one of King's Cross Top Shed's beautifully clean 'A4' Pacifics, No 60013 *Dominion of New Zealand,* gently backing down into the terminus. *IAL*

Left: The BR/Sulzer Type 4 Diesels were a common sight on the Midland Section from late 1961 onwards. No D150 gets a 'green' at a location on the Southern Region. It entered service during the last weeks of 1961 and was allocated to Derby. *IAL*

Below left: The English Electric Type 4s were among the first main line diesels to appear. No D200 was delivered in March 1958. They were not frequent visitors to the Settle–Carlisle line and No 40138 provided unusual power for the 15.37 Leeds to Carlisle on 18 August 1982. The signalbox at Horton-in-Ribblesdale has since been removed. *B. J. Beer*

Top right: An English Electric Class 3 diesel-electric locomotive, No D6723, takes a parcels train on the GE Section near Brentwood on 17 March 1971. This design has been one of the most successful of all the Modernisation Plan diesels. *J. Rickard*

Right: One of the early Brush/Sulzer Type 4 diesel-electrics, No D1512, heads the 'Master Cutler' Pullman train out of King's Cross and past the well-known but misnamed Belle Isle signalbox. It was a Belle Isle only to railway enthusiasts. *IAL*

Some types of diesel were spread among all the Regions, but the Regions tended to have their own specialities: for example, all the diesel-hydraulics were on the Western Region (they had short lives, partly from reliability problems but also because they were not common-user types), most of Classes 21/26 and 27 were in Scotland, most of Class 30/31 and Class 15 were on the Eastern Region, and the Class 33s were on the Southern. This was a deliberate policy as it concentrated driving knowledge and maintenance skills (and spares) in one Region.

Classes 20, 37 and 47 have been the big successes and fortunately were among the largest classes. Survivors can still be seen at work in the 21st century.

The headlong rush into dieselisation was in some ways a millstone, but it was precipitated by government pressure to reduce costs (and to help industry) which the BTC should have resisted. As a result, the railways had too many types of locomotives, some of which would not

have been ordered if dieselisation could have proceeded at a slower pace, giving more time for evaluation. But overall, dieselisation was a milestone and the headlong rush had the benefit of allowing the changeover from all-steam to all-diesel (and electric) to be accomplished within little more than 10 years. It was a hectic period.

Diesel railcars — a milestone

The LMS and the LNER had carried out small-scale experiments with diesel railcars in the 1930s but the Great Western had gone further and had successfully developed a fleet of 38 railcars by 1939. After the war, no further progress was made by the companies before nationalisation, and it was two or three years before the Railway Executive began to seriously consider the large-scale introduction of diesel railcars, or multiple-units (DMUs).

However, in 1952 approval was given by the BTC for the introduction of diesel multiple-units on an area-by-area basis. The West Riding of Yorkshire, Cumberland and Lincolnshire were the first areas selected, and on 29 April 1954 there was a demonstration run of a Derby-built DMU between Marylebone and Beaconsfield. It was the beginning of a revolution and pre-dated the Modernisation Plan. Many DMUs were built by BR at Derby and Swindon, but tenders were also submitted by a number of private builders, among them being Metropolitan-Cammell (who built the majority), Cravens, Gloucester, Pressed Steel and BRCW. The Modernisation Plan provided for 4,600 DMU vehicles to be built, but subsequent withdrawals of passenger services reduced the number required, and at the end of the Modernisation Plan period in 1970 there were 3,621 diesel multiple-unit vehicles in service.

Apart from DMUs for suburban, local and branch line work, a number of cross-country sets were built for such services as Hull to Liverpool via Leeds, and Birmingham to Cardiff via Honeybourne, and a fleet of Rolls-Royce engined DMUs was built for the Bedford-St Pancras suburban service.

It was hoped that the introduction of DMUs would improve the economics of branch lines to such an extent that many would remain open that might otherwise have closed. Train working costs would be reduced, and it was expected that cleaner, faster trains would attract more passengers. In 1952 most branch lines and local services were worked by elderly tank engines hauling two or three equally elderly coaches.

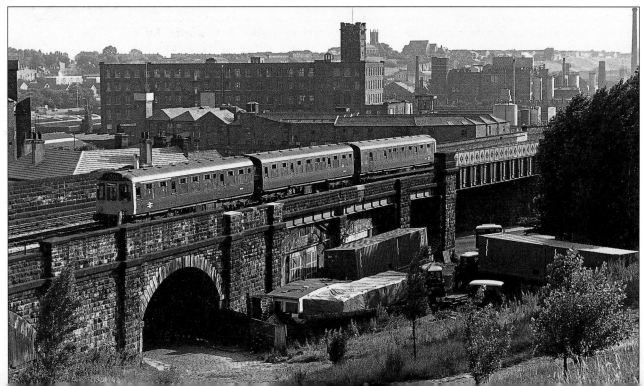

Above: The English Electric 'Deltics' became an everyday sight on the East Coast main line during the 1960s and 1970s, until displaced by the High-Speed trains (HSTs). No D9005 *The Prince of Wales's Own Regiment of Yorkshire* moves out of the platform at Kings Cross after working an up express in May 1973. *Peter J. Robinson*

But to really improve the economics of branch line and local services it would have been necessary to unstaff stations and issue tickets on the trains, and to reduce signalling costs. Many branch lines also had several public level crossings which had to be manned whilst the line was open. The concept of unstaffing stations and issuing tickets on trains was strongly resisted by the trade unions, and the automation of level crossings had not yet been embarked on. It would also have required a change in the law and substantial capital investment. So whilst the introduction of DMUs improved the economics of branch lines it was often insufficient to save them from closure, especially in the Beeching era.

The Class 55 'Deltics'
The story of the 'Deltics' goes back to the mid-1950s, when English Electric recognised a need for a diesel locomotive that was more powerful than those proposed in the Modernisation Plan, which were 2,300hp at most. English Electric proposed to use two 'Deltic' engines to provide a very powerful and lightweight locomotive of 3,300hp.

It was a private venture by English Electric, and the prototype was introduced in November 1955 when it began trials on the West Coast main line. In view of planned electrification, the London Midland Region saw no long-term use for such a machine, but over on the Eastern Region the renowned Line Traffic Manager, G. F. (Gerry) Fiennes, following the big-engine tradition of the line, quickly realised that the 'Deltics' were exactly what he had been looking for, following the abandonment of the plan to electrify the line from King's Cross to Leeds and possibly York. With nothing larger expected than a 2,000hp engine, large-scale accelerations were not possible, and Fiennes realised that traffic would be lost if the services were not speeded up. He therefore produced a scheme for 23 'Deltics' to give a much improved service and allow 55 steam locomotives to be displaced.

Surprisingly, the Eastern Region management was lukewarm at first, but Sir George Nelson, who was chairman of English Electric, approached Sir Brian Robertson personally, and the BTC authorised the building of 22 'Deltics'. They were all delivered between March 1961 and April 1962 and allowed the train service to be accelerated in September. Gerry had stolen a march on the West Coast people. Their train services were mired in the engineering work for electrification of the West Coast line for another four years.

For almost 20 years, the 'Deltics' were the pride of the East Coast main line and enabled Gerry Fiennes' dream to be realised. Gerry was a railwayman to his fingertips. All the locomotives were named and several are still running in preservation.

Seen throughout the length and breadth of the country, the 350hp diesel-electric shunting engine was a success story for the original LMS/English Electric prewar design. Well over a thousand were built and a few can still be seen. No D3489 shunts at Felixstowe. *IAL*

The 350hp diesel-electric shunter — another milestone

From the sublime to the mundane — from the glamorous 'Deltic' to the unsung hero of the marshalling yards — the 350hp diesel shunter, with that ever-so-familiar throb of its diesel engine as it wended its way around the sidings. As related in Part 2, diesel shunting engines date back to the 1930s, mainly on the LMS, and after the war building quickly restarted. The LM Region continued to build them until 1952, when the design became adopted as the BR standard shunting engine. The LMS engines were numbered in the series 12000 to 12138, and apart from the first three they all dated from 1939 to December 1952. Darlington built the last batch, Nos 12103 to 12138, and those were all allocated to the Eastern and North Eastern Regions.

The BR standard series, with some locomotives being uprated from 350hp to 400hp, began in October 1952 and production continued for 10 years, mainly at Darlington and Derby, until the series numbered from 13000 to D4192. It was by far the largest class on BR and speaks volumes about the excellence of the original design, a joint LMS/English Electric venture. English Electric products were almost always reliable. It was a great success story, and there are still a few to be seen.

Main-line electrification

Manchester-Sheffield-Wath

It will be recalled from Part 2 that this scheme was authorised before World War 2, and work had already started before the outbreak of war caused its suspension. Work was resumed in 1946, but progress was slow and was further delayed when it was discovered that it would be necessary to abandon the old single-bore Woodhead tunnels, which were slightly over three miles long, and construct a new double-line tunnel. Work on the new tunnel started in February 1949 and took four years to complete. It was 3 miles 66yd long. The first electrically hauled passenger train ran from Sheffield to Manchester on 14 September 1954.

The cost of the electrification scheme was based on improving the economics of moving large quantities of coal traffic from Wath marshalling yard, which was currently being done by steam engines. The line climbed steeply from Wath to Penistone and trains required banking assistance, for which the LNER had built a large Garratt locomotive, No 2395, in 1925. It had a 2-8-8-2 wheel arrangement and a tractive effort of 72,940 tons(b)The lines passed through the Thurgoland tunnel and the Woodhead single bores, and conditions for the footplate staff in

those foul, smoky tunnels were becoming unacceptable. And in any event, the old Woodhead tunnels were life-expired and could only have been retained in use by frequent and lengthy closures to enable repairs to be done. Such closures of the line could not have been allowed.

Motive power for the line was provided by 58 electric locomotives of Bo-Bo wheel arrangement, numbered in the series 26000 and 26057, for hauling the freight traffic both from Wath and from Rotherwood Exchange sidings near Sheffield. Seven Co-Co electric locomotives, Nos 27000 to 27006, were built for hauling express passenger trains between Sheffield Victoria and Manchester London Road.

This was Britain's first main line electrification scheme on a mixed traffic line — a milestone — and for many years the route was very busy with the constant passage of coal trains from east to west, with corresponding trains returning with empty wagons. However, by 1980 coal traffic over the route, the main reason for its existence, had declined considerably, partly due to the concentration of electricity generation in major new power stations in Yorkshire and Nottinghamshire, supplying the national grid. Eventually it was decided that there was no longer sufficient justification to retain the route in use and it was closed the following year. It was, and still is for some people, a controversial

decision, but the passage of time and the further decline in coal traffic appears to have justified the closure. However, if the Woodhead route had remained open, with electrification removed, it would have provided an alternative through cross-country route, although rather circuitous and 16 miles longer, for passenger traffic from East Anglia and the East Midlands to Manchester via Sheffield, Barnsley, Penistone, Hadfield and Guide Bridge. It would have put Barnsley firmly on the railway map. And only 16 miles separates Penistone from Hadfield.

The Manchester end of the line is still in use for the suburban electric passenger service between Manchester Piccadilly, Glossop and Hadfield.

London to Liverpool, Manchester and Birmingham — a milestone

This scheme was included in the 1955 Modernisation Plan together with a rival scheme to electrify from King's Cross to Leeds and (possibly) York. The LM Region had been lukewarm at first about main line electrification, whereas the East Coast Regions had been quite keen, and their scheme had initially been given first priority. However, the West Coast was preferred, owing to the greater traffic potential.

The West Coast scheme had a somewhat rocky beginning. The line from Manchester to

A pair of Class 76 electric locomotives, Nos 76015 and 76022, head a merry-go-round train from Darton colliery (Barnsley) to Wigan power station, past Huddersfield Junction (Penistone) on 31 May 1974. *F. R. Kerr*

Crewe was electrified first, and operation began in September 1960, to be followed by work on the Liverpool to Crewe section, opened two years later. This piecemeal process irritated the Ministry of Transport, who felt that they were being pushed into a huge scheme without knowing the full picture, and for a short while there was a possibility that electrification south of Crewe would not have gone ahead. This was the period when the railways' finances were under close and rather hostile examination by the Stedeford committee.

However, in the end the Minister gave his approval for the full scheme, and work began on the 158-mile section between Crewe and London Euston. It was completed in April 1966, with the route via Birmingham being completed in March 1967. It was a huge scheme, because in addition to the electrification itself at 25kV, track had to be renewed; bridges raised; signalling modernised throughout, with several new modern power signalboxes; and several stations rebuilt, including Euston, Coventry, Birmingham New Street, Wolverhampton and Manchester London Road (renamed Piccadilly). Then there were the new trains. A whole new fleet of carriages was built, known as Mk2.

Motive power was provided by several manufacturers, and all locomotives were of Bo-Bo wheel arrangement with 100 mph capability. They were in the following classes:

When the new services were introduced, it was not surprising to find that the cleaner, faster, more frequent and more comfortable trains generated more revenue. In the first year of operation from Euston to Liverpool and Manchester, revenue increased by 50% and the number of passengers by 65%, which was even better than expected. The 'sparks effect' of attracting passengers had been born, a card that was played heavily to gain approval of the extension to Glasgow in 1974.

In addition to the new express services, suburban services were also electrified throughout the line, using electric multiple-units in classes later know as '304' for local work and '310' for intermediate work.

Whilst the electrified service was undoubtedly a great success, there were disadvantages. Through services to stations off the line of route were jeopardised, and money could not be extracted from the government for the electrification of short sections of line or branches to give flexibility, such as Nuneaton to Birmingham, Kidsgrove to Crewe, Manchester to Euxton Junction, Preston to Blackpool and Oxenholme to Windermere. It was a short-sighted policy, but the government could not have been expected to understand the finer points of railway operating and certainly didn't trust the railways. But experience, and the emergence of the High Speed Train (HST) and more reliable, higher-powered diesel locomotives, rather took the bloom off further electrification. The East Coast, with its fleet of 125mph HSTs, certainly stole a march on Euston, and brings into question the justification of East Coast electrification. If privatisation had occurred a little sooner, would GNER, the new train operator, have bothered with electrification, or would it have gone all-out for a Mk2 HST replacement? We will study the HST saga in Part 4.

Class	hp	No of locomotives	Builder/electrical equipment	Fleet Nos
81	3200	25	BRCW/BTH	E3001-3023; E3096/7
82	3300	10	Beyer Peacock/MV	E3046-3055
83	2950	15	Vulcan/English Electric	E3024-3035
				E3098-3100
84	3000	10	NBL/GEC	E3036-3045
85	3200	40	BR/BTH	E3056-3095
86/0	3600	39	BR/AEI	E3101-3200
86/1	4600	3		
86/2	4040	58		

Double-deck car-carriers came into use to increase the capacity of motorail trains. *BR*

Freight services, which often started and/or finished at locations off the electrified route were a particular problem. Initially Euston HQ decreed that no diesels should run 'under the wires', but the fallacy of this policy was soon evident in the number of engine changes required, and the increase in traincrew costs. Under pressure from the government, BR also considered diverting Midland line St Pancras expresses into Euston via Nuneaton or by using the GC route over chord lines between the Leicester-Nuneaton line and Rugby. One can only be grateful that it did not happen.

It was all very well to practically rebuild a line from Euston to Liverpool, Manchester, Birmingham and Glasgow, together with new trains, but it was likely that a time would come when substantial expenditure would be required on renewal and replacements. That time arrived in the late 1980s, but the government was not interested. No money was provided and crisis point approached. BR and the government were saved from acute embarrassment by privatisation, when the problem was handed over to Railtrack, the new owners of the infrastructure.

Innovative services

Starlight Specials — a milestone, but short-lived

In the early 1950s, summer holiday traffic at weekends between Scotland and London was suffering increasingly from road competition by long-distance coaches. In order to combat this, a series of trains known as 'Starlight Specials' was introduced from selected stations in Scotland to London at a fare of 70 shillings return. The trains ran overnight and refreshments were available. Various routes were used, including the Midland and the GC into Marylebone, owing to the large number of trains involved. Starlight Specials were initially a great success, using stock and engines that would have been standing overnight, but the number of passengers gradually declined owing to increased car ownership, coach competition on improved roads and the growth of air travel.

The Starlight Specials were very profitable, because no additional coaches or engines had to be built and the tracks were already there, but the accountants decreed that fares would have to be raised as traffic fell. It was a policy guaranteed to kill the business, and it did.

Motorail — another success story

The carriage of motor cars by rail dates back to before WW1, but very little was done to expand the business between the wars, although the LNER conveyed small numbers of cars from King's Cross to Scotland during the summer. The idea was resurrected in 1955 when a twice-weekly overnight service was introduced between King's Cross and Perth, with the passengers being conveyed in sleeping cars. A daytime Motorail service was introduced in 1960 between London (Holloway) and Edinburgh.

Suddenly, Motorail become very popular, and a whole range of services developed, not only from London but also from provincial centres such as York, Sutton Coldfield (Birmingham) and Newton le Willows. Both daytime and overnight services were provided. Trains ran not only to Scotland, serving Stirling, Perth and Inverness, but also to St Austell and Fishguard. For several years Motorail flourished, but BR increased the prices because the accountants told them that the traffic was being carried at a loss. So the traffic withered away. What the accountants didn't say was how much money would be saved if the trains didn't run. The coaches and car-carrying vehicles were already there. The terminals were there. The track was there. Were any staff disposed of? It seems to have been a very short-sighted policy, which could have been reviewed when major capital investment was needed.

But there is surely room on today's privatised railway for an entrepreneur to revive the concept? There are far more cars on the road, and traffic jams at weekends and holiday times lessen the pleasure of motoring long distances.

PART 4
1971 to 2005

Chapter 12

The business concept and privatisation

After all the trials and tribulations and turbulence of the previous 60 years, the 1970s for the railways were almost a haven of peace by comparison, buffeted only by external events and political upheavals. Following the 1968 Transport Act, BR had shed its heavy loss-making Sundries business, together with all the freight depots that dealt with 'less than wagon load traffic', and as a result a long-standing and growing problem had been removed. BR retained only those depots dealing with full wagon load traffic.

The establishment of Passenger Transport Authorities (PTAs) had transferred to those authorities all policy issues regarding suburban passenger services within their areas. The PTAs were responsible for deciding which routes to support, the train services which were to be operated and their frequency, the types of trains to be used and the specifications of new trains, and the fares to be charged. BR was now in the situation of being the service provider. No more financial worries. BR did what was required of it, and was paid accordingly. Most services were still operated at a loss, and the deficit was paid from central government to the PTA, who passed it on to BR. It must have seemed like heaven to hard-pressed railway managers. What is more, the PTAs and their executive arm, the Passenger Transport Executives (PTEs), were in expansive mode, keen to improve and expand local train services within their areas. For railway managers, it was a very unusual period, but

a very satisfying one, and credit must go to Barbara Castle, the Minister of Transport responsible for introducing the concept. It has been one of the great and enduring successes in the long history of public passenger transport.

BR had lost the Freightliner business but continued to operate the trains. It had been transferred to the National Freight Corporation in the somewhat starry-eyed and naïve belief that the NFC, a freight haulage company, would encourage the use of the Freightliner service. The business was eventually returned to BR in 1974.

These changes meant that BR was now able to concentrate more on its express passenger business, and these developments will be reviewed in the Trains and Traction section (Chapter 13).

BR's finances had been put on a more stable footing in the 1968 Transport Act, and the 1970s were therefore a period of some stability. Annual deficits still occurred, but they did not increase year by year as had happened ever since nationalisation. The financial support for passenger services did not just apply to the PTA areas, but to all passenger services. Initially each service had been separately funded, but arising from a European Community directive, a block grant was given for all passenger services. By contrast with previous decades, the 1970s were happy and confident years.

But there was also considerable frustration. The big arguments were over investment and the deficit. Richard Marsh was the BRB chairman until 1976, an extrovert and relaxed, but sometimes impatient, personality. He had followed Barbara Castle as Minister of Transport in the Labour government, and was appointed Chairman of the BRB by the Conservative government in 1971. His frustrations over his dealings with the ministry, and the endless arguments over investment, became quite apparent, and he was replaced by Peter Parker. Parker was an intensely likeable chairman, another extrovert and a tireless champion of the railway cause. He was rather more tactful in his dealings with the government, but his frustrations were the same as Marsh's, and he will ever be remembered for his famous phrase about 'the crumbling edge of quality' caused by the lack of investment.

Peter Parker was followed by Robert Reid in 1983. Later known as Bob Reid I, because he

The creation of Passenger Transport Authorities was an act of genius by Barbara Castle, the then Minister of Transport. The West Midlands PTA has been particularly active in promoting new and improved services, and opening new stations, such as this one to serve Birmingham University. *BRB*

was followed by another Bob Reid, he reigned
from 1983 to 1990. He was a career railwayman, tall, reserved and almost austere, and he
knew that one of the railway's major problems
was its management and organisation, which
was costly and a barrier to efficiency. By then
the railway was undoubtedly top-heavy, and he
simplified the structure, sweeping away the lay-
ers without a murmur, and introducing the
'Business' concept for InterCity, Regional
Railways, freight, etc. The creation of Network
SouthEast was a stroke of genius, compounded
by the appointment of Chris Green as its director, who led it from a loss-maker into a surplus.
InterCity also became profitable.

Bob Reid believed that operators and engineers exercised too much power, and did not
have a sufficiently well-developed business
sense. That was a half-truth, but the business
concept prospered and led both to new
economies and to improvements in the businesses. He also followed a policy of ruthless
economy, reducing the deficit as a result, and
his undoubted success eased the passage of government approval for investment. But the government's negative and hostile approach to the
railways during the Thatcher era was a real millstone. And the government felt in its innocence
that privatisation could reduce the deficit even
further. Even Margaret Thatcher, an arch priva-
tiser, felt that the privatisation of the railways
would be a step too far. And from a financial
point of view so it has proved to be.

Privatisation — milestone or millstone?

John Major became Prime Minister in 1992, and almost at once privatisation of the railways appeared on the agenda. The method was devised by the Treasury and its advisers as a means of reducing the financial support needed by the railways, in the mistaken belief that handing over everything to private enterprise would reduce costs and improve efficiency. Entrepreneurial flair would increase business. In the event, costs have risen dramatically, whilst improvements in efficiency are questionable.

The opportunity created by privatisation for the exercise of entrepreneurial flair has been demonstrated by several of the train operating companies. On the other hand, the Treasury's calculations showing a reduction in the financial support needed by the railways have been proved to be wildly over-optimistic, and how anyone could make such huge errors beggars belief. The support needed now is three times greater than in the much-maligned pre-privatisation era, and we are talking billions.

Above: One of BR's finest and most successful managers, Chris Green (right), observes with justifiable pride a symbolic moment in the Ayrshire electrification at Largs on 1 June 1985. *T. H. Noble*

Right: Chris Green went on to become the director of Network SouthEast and took it from a loss-maker into a surplus. If he could perform such wizardry today it would make a sizeable dent in the current losses. *Chris Wilson*

The 1993 Railways Act

Legislation in 1993 enacted a major revision of the railway's ownership and organisation and received the Royal Assent on 5 November. One might have expected that in such a complex and far-reaching, not to say revolutionary, measure, the authors would have consulted far and wide. They did, but they signally failed to consult those in the best position to know — experienced railway managers. Not only were they not consulted, but their advice was studiously rejected and ignored, as though the authors of the act were afraid that their assumptions might be found to be seriously flawed, which they were. And that rather than reducing costs, they might lead to cost-escalation on a grand scale. Which of course they did.

The act introduced changes that were far more fundamental than any previous act, and certainly none that have been discussed in these pages. It threw open to franchise or sale the entire railway industry, but then had to introduce a number of regulatory bodies to control it. The government, though wedded to the concept of freeing the shackles of industry, was not prepared to give the same freedom to the railways — that would have flown in the face of nearly two centuries of tradition.

Before the act came into force, British Rail was required to set up a company, still state-owned, to own the infrastructure — the track, signalling, stations, structures, etc, in fact everything that was necessary to allow trains to be operated. It became known as Railtrack and was born on 1 January 1994, becoming a separate state-owned organisation three months later. It was initially planned for it to remain in the state sector, but the government was persuaded to sell it off by means of a share issue in 1996, so that any losses would not be borne by the Treasury. In order to facilitate the sale,

Under privatisation, the freight business was not franchised but was sold outright and bought by Wisconsin. It immediately ordered Class 66 diesels in bulk and one is seen here with a train of china clay hopper wagons at Lostwithiel in May 2000, No 66191. *Author*

£1.5 billion of debt was written off. BR would have been in a much happier financial position if it had received such largesse.

For a few years, Railtrack was financially very successful, but its profits were achieved at the expense of the maintenance of its assets, and the whole enterprise foundered when a broken rail caused a Great North Eastern Railway express to be derailed near Hatfield, resulting in four deaths. As railway accidents go, it might not be considered to be especially serious, but it revealed an alarming decline in the condition of the track. Railtrack's share values plummeted and the government stealthily placed the company in administration, replacing it with a not-for-profit organisation with no shareholders, called Network Rail, which then had the task of over-taking, at great expense, the arrears which had accrued during Railtrack's reign.

BR was also required to set up all its infra-structure maintenance operations into zonal companies, and these were sold off to the private sector. The act required Railtrack to contract out all its infrastructure maintenance operations to these companies, but the contracts were unsatisfactory and initially badly performed. Ultimately, after a series of accidents caused by faulty maintenance, Network Rail took the bold step of bringing all infrastructure maintenance in-house. It was a major change, which was per-formed flawlessly and has been very successful.

The separation of track and trains was one of the most controversial parts of the act, but it was believed to have been done in accordance with a European Community directive. However, the directive only required the accounts of the two functions to be separate, so that they could be transparent to open access operators. There was no overriding requirement to physically separate the two functions.

The most revolutionary part of the act concerned the operation of passenger train services. It was decided that the country should be divided into 25 routes or areas, and that the operation of trains within those areas should be done under franchise. These were put out to tender, and usually awarded to the franchisee which required the lowest financial support (or offered the highest premium). Franchise terms were usually seven years. The take-up of franchises went very slowly at first, but then a rush occurred with bidders offering unrealistic promises, which in the event many were unable to meet. The act provided for failed franchises to be taken over by the franchising authority, but this was rarely done, and it became customary for failed franchises to be retained by the origi-nal franchisee on a management contract basis. The act also allowed British Rail to bid for fran-chises, but the franchising authority exercised its powers not to invite BR to do so. This was despite pleas by MPs that BR were the only ones who knew how to run the business!

In many ways the franchising system for oper-ating passenger trains has been one of the successes of privatisation, because the relatively small companies thus formed are able to con-centrate on their core business within their areas, and just pay a track access charge to (now) Network Rail. Because they are close to the customer, they can read the market more quickly and accurately, and respond equally quickly. In many cases, franchisees have ordered new trains, which are often superior to anything that BR could have persuaded the government to approve and are effectively funded by higher subsidies.

At privatisation, all passenger rolling stock was grouped into three companies and offered for sale, at a price which was well below their real worth, another major government blunder. The new Rolling Stock Companies (ROSCOs) were snapped up by knowledgeable buyers, often railwaymen, and were quickly sold on, mainly to banks, at a large profit. The trains are leased to train operating companies.

The freight business was offered for sale outright, organised in a number of companies, but was bought as a job lot, except for Freightliner, by Wisconsin Central Railway, under the redoubtable Ed Burkhardt. He looked at BR's freight locomotives, didn't like what he saw, and immediately ordered 260 machines from General Motors in Ontario. These new locomotives, Class 66, have worked remarkably well. The new company was named English, Welsh & Scottish Railway (EWS).

How successful was privatisation?

The Treasury had hoped that privatisation would reduce the annual support to the railways, which was running at about £1 billion in the early 1990s. It is now costing in the region of £5 billion, and that can only be accounted a lamentable failure. And it was inexcusable, because the government rushed ahead with its proposals, ignoring all advice. However, it has to be accepted that BR's economy regime could not last for ever, and troubles were being stored up for the future. The problem was mainly lack of investment going back to the 1970s, which had caused Richard Marsh to resign in frustration, and caused Peter Parker to talk about 'the crumbling edge of quality'. Matters improved somewhat during Bob Reid I's years of austerity, but the need to virtually renew the West Coast main line and its infrastructure was looming ever closer, with the Treasury completely unsympathetic.

For the passenger it might be considered a considerable success. There are fleets of shiny new trains (although there were initial problems with reliability — not unknown in BR days), improved services and train operating companies (TOCs) which on the whole attempt to be more responsive to passengers' needs than BR could ever have hoped to be.

For the industry it has been a series of upheavals. Railtrack considered itself to be a property-owning company, and it looked after its property very well, typified by its station regeneration scheme, but it failed to ensure that the infrastructure was being properly maintained and renewed, leaving that to the contractors. It was not a wise policy. Railtrack's relationships with the TOCs was one of landlord and tenant and was unsatisfactory. It felt itself to be superior because it was a permanent entity, whilst the TOCs were transient, with lives only as long as their franchises. But the TOCs were the engine that drove the railway industry and brought in the money. Railtrack should have been an equal partner with the TOCs.

Ultimately Railtrack was replaced by Network Rail, a unique body lacking the financial discipline of a normal company. However, the 2005 Railways Act has given it more authority over the running of the railway, again ignoring the reality that it is the TOCs that fund the whole enterprise, and should be allowed to use their commercial judgements to the maximum extent. That is unsatisfactory, and a millstone.

A body known as the Strategic Rail Authority (SRA) was established by the government because it realised that the flawed privatisation model had left the railway industry without a common focus, and with no one in charge at the helm. The SRA was supposed to give a strategic direction to the industry, so that all parts of it could plan and proceed along a common path, but the government wasn't prepared to allow that to happen because it gave too much financial power to the SRA. The SRA was therefore reformed and paradoxically given greater powers, but it ignored its strategic role and began to micro-manage the TOCs, which was absolutely the wrong policy. Indeed, the chairman of the SRA had more authority than any previous railway chairman, whether nationalised or private.

Bitter squabbles broke out between the SRA, the Rail Regulator and the Department for Transport, which the latter solved by the simple expedient of abolishing the SRA (rather than retaining it with a strategic role) and abolishing the statutory post of Rail Regulator because it didn't like the occupant of that post. He was replaced by a committee. Having thus vanquished its enemies, the DfT took unto itself the strategic direction of the railway industry, including decisions on its size and funding. So for the first time in railway history, a government department is running the industry. Is that likely to result in a better-funded railway able to handle efficiently the increasing demands placed upon it? Or is it a millstone? Only time will tell.

Chapter 13

Trains, traction and investment

The Advanced Passenger Train (APT)

One of the many fruits of the 1968 Transport Act was an undertaking by the government to give financial support to selected areas of engineering research, and one of the early beneficiaries was the Advanced Passenger Train which had been quietly under development for some time. 100mph line speeds were becoming common (the first stretch had been at Lolham on the East Coast main line in 1964), and whilst passenger business managers would have liked higher speeds, these were often limited by curvature of the track, which was a particular problem on the West Coast main line. The East Coast main line was more fortunate. Not only did it have more straight stretches over the flat country through which it ran for most of the way from King's Cross to Newcastle, but for some years civil engineers had been quietly straightening out some of the more severe curves.

In the early 1960s the research department had been carrying out studies into the wheel/rail interface, which led to the concept of a high-speed train capable of running at 155mph on existing tracks. Initially it was intended to use gas turbines for propulsion, but this was discarded in favour of the tried and tested electric method. Progress was rather slow, and eight years elapsed before an experimental train,

known as APT-E, was tested on the Old Dalby test track near Melton Mowbray. During these trials a speed of 153mph was reached — a British speed record — and the construction of three pre-production 14-car trains was authorised, known as APT-P.

One of the several unusual features of these trains was a tilting suspension to enable them to negotiate curves much faster than conventional trains, which enabled almost an hour to be cut from the existing Euston to Glasgow times. And in order that the trains could use braking distances provided by the existing signalling, they had a new form of hydro-kinetic braking. However, despite the 155mph capability, it was planned to adhere to a 125mph speed limit for the time being until cab signalling and tilt supervision (C-APT) had been installed.

Another five years went by, and eventually it was possible to conduct trials on the West Coast main line, during which a speed record of 160mph was reached north of Carlisle on 20 December 1979. There was considerable impatience both at the BRB and the Department of Transport for the introduction of the trains into revenue service in order to test public reaction, and perhaps this was done prematurely, because it was little short of both a technical and public relations disaster. There were a number

On 17 February 1982 APT unit No 370001 leans through Oxenholme with a test train. *Melvyn Bryan*

Universally regarded as one of the finest (and most popular) trains ever produced in Britain, the High Speed Train, which revolutionised travel on the East Coast and the Great Western main lines in the 1970s, is still rendering yeoman service. One of the East Coast sets, headed by power car No 254021, speeds through Wood Green with the 16.00 'Talisman' King's Cross to Edinburgh on 14 September 1978. *J. G. Glover*

of breakdowns and even a derailment and the BRB lost patience with the entire venture. All work was stopped and the trains were shunted into the sidings, there to remain.

What went wrong? Too many technical innovations were included. Most of the work was done by research department staff, rather than in the mainstream of railway mechanical engineering. The latter had quickly produced a world-beater — the 125mph High Speed Train (HST) with a diesel power unit at each end. BRB approval had been given for the design of a prototype HST in 1969 and the first fleet of trains was introduced on Western Region services from Paddington in October 1976, long before APT was ready. HST was a success from the start, and having diesel traction gave it greater route availability than APT. And it has to be said that the Mk3 coaches with which the HSTs were equipped were far more comfortable than the coaches on the APT, the sides of which had to be tapered in, causing a loss of seating space which became marked at shoulder level. Operators regarded the 155mph capability of the APT as a liability, because it would have caused considerable pathing problems at that speed with other trains having to be kept out of the way. And finally, and perhaps most damning, was a belated realisation that the London-Glasgow market for rail had shrunk, and reducing the journey time by an hour to about four hours would make little difference. It was a brave but ultimately unnecessary venture and it is clear that it did not have wholehearted support in some railway quarters.

The High Speed Train

When the HST was introduced into squadron service on the Western Region in 1976 it was a major milestone. It was immediately a success with the travelling public and has remained so ever since. The concept was brilliant. A fixed formation train with a power unit at each end, giving a colossal 4,500hp. It was also very popular with the passenger business and with operators. It could go virtually anywhere on existing track and could stop quite happily from 125mph in existing braking distances. It outshone the West Coast electrification, which was pegged to 100mph, later raised to 110mph on certain sections. The Mk3 coaches quickly became popular with passengers and the only major criticism that one could make was the absence of power-operated doors, allegedly due to government parsimony.

Construction of the prototype train began in 1970 and it went into service in 1972 to begin a long period of tests and trials to ensure that all the problems were ironed out before fleet production began. During these trials the prototype train achieved a speed of 143mph on the 'racing track' between York and Northallerton. The train was built in BR workshops: Crewe built the power cars and Derby the coaches. It was a magnificent tribute to BR's mechanical engineers and their genius.

The Western Region, which had received neither electrification nor the 'Deltics', was the first to benefit. 27 sets were introduced on services from Paddington to Bristol and South Wales in 1976, followed by a further 14 sets for the West of England services. The Eastern Region made a case for HST introduction on the King's Cross to West Riding services, and on the East Coast main line to Edinburgh and Aberdeen, receiving 32 sets in 1978/9. More sets were introduced later and the Midland line from St Pancras to Sheffield received several sets. Finally, 18 sets were introduced into the NE-SW cross-country services, which received a much-needed boost.

The cross-country services, running through several Regions, had been the Cinderella of BR's InterCity business and had been quietly languishing for years, a sad reflection on regional management, which was more interested in its own domestic services. The real resurgence came eventually with the creation of an InterCity business, and ultimately with Virgin Trains' cross-country revolution (see below).

The HSTs are still the mainstay of much of the passenger business even today, up to 30 years later, and many passengers would prefer to travel in Mk3 HST comfort than in more modern creations, which they regard as inferior. The Mk3 coach is only disfigured by a shortage of seats at tables, which correspond to the windows. Passengers entering a Mk3 coach will almost always choose a table seat in preference to an airline-style face-to-back seat. They vote with their feet, and it is a sad reflection on BR management (and to their shame, its commercial successors) that it has failed to recognise that need, and provide passengers with seating of their choice. Airline-style seating is a wretched millstone. Most passengers want seats at tables so that they can spread out their belongings, and they want to be able to see out of the windows, which means arranging the seats to match. They will put up with cramped seating in an aircraft (and windows are unnecessary for most of the journey) because often there are no alternative means of transport or the journey is of short duration, but there are powerful alternatives to the train. As the old maritime adage has it, 'a good ship spoilt for a ha'porth of tar'.

One of the huge benefits that came in 1971 was the introduction of Mk2 carriages with air conditioning, a major step forward in the passenger environment with a constant temperature range and greatly reduced external noise. These benefits were incorporated into the HST Mk3 carriages. Unfortunately, air conditioning has not been as reliable as one might have hoped, and despite all the steps that have been taken in the last 30 years the problem has not yet been completely solved. It is an odd paradox that whilst mechanical engineers can design the most advanced forms of traction, they seem incapable of designing a foolproof air conditioning system. Perhaps they will reply that you get what you pay for.

After 30 years of faithful service, the HSTs are coming to the end of their serviceable life, and the search is on for a replacement, but preferably an HST Mk2, not a completely new design such as the Class 180 'Coradias' and the Class 220/1/2 Virgin Cross Country trains, the 'Pioneers' and the 'Meridians'. One might well ask, 'Why change a winner?'

West Coast electrification to Glasgow

Electrification through to Glasgow had always been the ultimate aim for the West Coast main line, dating back to 1957, and taking advantage of the highly successful 'sparks effect' the British Railways Board put forward a proposal for electrification through to Glasgow Central from a junction with the Liverpool line just north of Crewe at Weaver Junction. It quickly became known as the 'Weaver to Wearer' scheme, based on a well-known (at the time) chain of men's clothing shops. Development work started almost immediately after the opening of the Euston-Manchester/Liverpool/Birmingham scheme and the Glasgow scheme was authorised in 1970. As with other such projects, its extent was curtailed, and there was no room for electrification of branches such as Blackpool and Windermere, not to mention Barrow-in-Furness, which unfortunately led to a worsening of the services to those not unimportant traffic centres. Blackpool and Barrow had in fact been included in the original West Coast electrification plans, and it is salutary to recall that Barrow used to have its own through trains (and sleepers too) to Euston.

The operating floor in the Glasgow signalling control centre. *BR*

Work on the Glasgow extension began in 1971 and was completed in 1974, which was quite a remarkable achievement, and a new class of 4,600hp electric locomotives was provided, the Class 87, of which 36 were built by BR, with GEC equipment (including one Class 87/1 which was a test bed for thyristor control).

There was no diesel locomotive of such power available, and it would have been unthinkable to have run HSTs, of similar power, through from Euston to Glasgow. The 1976 timetable shows seven weekday services from Euston to Glasgow, between 07.45 and 17.45, all taking a few minutes over five hours. By 2003 there were nine departures, between 06.20 and 18.30, but decelerated to five and a half hours, or even six hours, by the inclusion of intermediate stops, clear evidence of the decline of the London to Glasgow traffic, but giving an improved service to intermediate points, such as Preston, Lancaster, Oxenholme and Penrith, which have become important railheads. Their importance was not so evident in 1976. Only the 'Royal Scot' retained its 5hr 5min timing.

The 'Pendolino' revolution has kept nine trains, and since December 2005 several have a timing below 5hr, with a fastest journey of 4hr 24min. Whether the full benefits of upgrading will make significant inroads into the London-Glasgow traffic remains to be seen. It will depend more on marketing skills than on reductions in journey time.

The millstone of the West Coast main line upgrading

As we saw in Part 3, the government took no interest in the renovation of the West Coast main line when it became due in the late 1980s, and nothing was done until privatisation rather forced the issue. The government had no intention of footing the bill and hoped that private capital would plug the gap. Railtrack's initial plans were costed at under £3 billion and included an advanced form of signalling known as 'moving block' and 140mph running, but it was living in dreamland. Moving block was light-years away in the future and the plans had to be hurriedly revised, with the awkward result that the costs eventually rose to £13 billion. That included all the cost of resignalling by conventional means and a speed limit of 125mph. No detailed work is being done anywhere on the development of moving block.

Crisis time had arrived, but the work had to be done if the line were to remain usable, and the government, to its chagrin, found that it was having to fork out more than if it had accepted the challenge in British Rail days, when it would have been done much more cheaply (and quickly). Virgin Trains was the company involved in association with Railtrack, and the prolonged negotiations involved both the Rail Regulator and the Strategic Rail Authority (SRA). Finally, a renegotiated settlement was reached at about £4 billion cheaper. Nonetheless, the whole affair soured the government's relationships with the railway industry, and was the main cause of the reorganisation under the Railways Act 2005, which had the disastrous effect of abolishing the SRA and transferring all responsibility for railway planning to the Department for Transport. Nothing like this has ever existed in the whole history of railways.

It is a sad commentary that whilst our continental neighbours France, Germany, Italy and Spain have all been engaged in building many hundreds of miles of high-speed lines, all that we in Britain have achieved (not quite yet) is the Channel Tunnel Link.

'Pacers' — a horrible millstone

'Pacers' are those two-axle monstrosities, railbuses that infest our northern towns. And as might be expected, your ubiquitous civil servant figures largely in their genesis. In the late 1970s, mechanical engineers began to consider replacements for the first generation diesel multiple-units which were already over 20 years old. Based on their experience, they produced an excellent three-car diesel multiple-unit, Class 210, with above-floor engine and sliding doors. The passenger environment was improved and it would have made a very satisfactory replacement. However, the ubiquitous civil servant took one look at it and, having been told the weight of the train per passenger seat, its total seating capacity and its production cost per passenger seat, held up his hands in horror and declared it much too good (and expensive) for its potential customers who, of course, mainly lived in the north of England. He asked the simple question — why does a bus cost so much less, and why don't you put a bus body on a rail chassis? That question overlooks one simple answer, that the production run for a Class 210 would be numbered in hundreds, whilst a bus body is manufactured in many thousands. It also overlooks another simple answer, that bus passengers generally travel short distances and are content to put their shopping on their knees as well as being crammed in, but train passengers often have bulky luggage, bicycles etc, and travel much greater distances. Being crammed into a rush-hour 'Pacer' for half-an-

Surely the nadir of BR's fortunes. The Department of Transport thought that bus bodies on a railway chassis would be ideal as a replacement for the Modernisation Plan diesel multiple-units of the 1950s. They may have all the advantages of a bus, but they have few of a real train, where passengers travel longer distances. With cramped seating and no provision for luggage, bicycles, prams, etc, they are quite awful. One of the early models visits Stratford-on-Avon station on trial in July 1981. The trial should have amply demonstrated their unsuitability, but BR placed volume orders. They became known as 'Pacers'. 'Cattle trucks' would have been a more appropriate appellation. *T. W. Moore*

Above: The Class 210 diesel-electric multiple-units were intended to be a replacement for the 1950s DMUs, but the Treasury mandarins thought them to be too expensive and too good for provincial passengers, so they had to put up with 'Pacers' instead. *Jeremy de Souza*

Left: Class 210 DMU brochure

Driving Trailer - 4 car set

ℛ10.001.

Prototype Class 210 Diesel Electric Multiple Units

Two prototype sets of the Class 210 train have been built for evaluation as replacements for the ageing fleet of diesel multiples units which will soon reach the end of their useful life. Although many DMUs have been refurbished to prolong their operational life some are approaching the condition where economic repair is no longer possible and the passenger environment and riding performance unacceptable to the traveller.

The new diesel electric multiple units (DEMUs) are designed with many features common to the newest Inter-City coaches with double glazing air conditioning and secondary springing for greater passenger comfort. The intention is to provide a far higher standard of passenger comfort and between the three and four car units a range of facilities suitable for both commuter journeys and for longer secondary and cross country routes. These trains will have a performance superior to established DMUs and can achieve 90 mph.

hour might just be endurable, but that is surely the limit of endurance.

However, BR was compelled to have 'Pacers' and most of them are still there 20 years later. Their crashworthiness is a minus factor, and yet the scrapping of perfectly good Mk1 trains on the former Southern Region was required because they were deemed to fail the crashworthiness test by the Health and Safety zealots. They, too, do not have to travel in 'Pacers'.

There were 20 twin-sets of Class 141 'Pacers', built in 1984 during the nadir of BR's fortunes, and they consisted of a Leyland National modified bus body on four-wheeled underframes. They were followed by the slightly improved Class 142, of which almost a hundred twin-sets were built at Derby during 1985-7. One wonders what the coach builders thought about these vehicles, given Derby's long tradition of turning out splendid, comfortable coaches. Most of them went to Lancashire, which perhaps typifies the BRB's attitude to that fine county, as its suburban services and stations and infrastructure plunged ever deeper into decrepitude. Andrew Barclay & Co produced 25 similar

Above: The Class 156 'Super Sprinters' have long been used on the West Highland line. In BR days the 14.20 from Mallaig to Glasgow leaves Banavie station, with Ben Nevis in the background. Metropolitan-Cammell built 114 units between 1987 and 1989. *W. A. Sharman*

Left: The Class 158s were intended for cross-country services but the interiors were originally too cramped for such traffic. Derby Works built 182 of these units between 1989 and 1992. The fleet now provides the backbone of the recently formed Trans-Pennine franchise, until a new design is delivered. In BR days a smart-looking Class 158 unit stands in Shrewsbury station on 16 February 1991. *Peter Marsh*

sets during the same period, with bodies built by W. Alexander & Co. They went to the unfortunate North East. Finally, BREL built a batch of 25, again during the same period, with W Alexander & Co's bodies. It was Yorkshire's turn to suffer.

'Pacers' might be considered suitable for short journeys on quieter routes, but the peculiar mechanics of privatisation have seen them used on much longer, and busier, routes. One of the worst examples must be Leeds-Morecambe, almost two hours on mainly jointed track. No wonder the trains are so empty.

Electrification of the East Coast main line — a milestone?

After the completion of the West Coast electrification it was time to resurrect the plans for the East Coast. The 'sparks effect' was still strong and it was felt that only electrification could provide sufficient power to haul heavier trains at higher speeds than the HSTs which were just being introduced on the route. The electric trains which were designed were capable of 140mph and were known as 'IC225s', the rather more eye-catching metric equivalent. Unfortunately, service speeds in excess of

Planning the extent of electrification ran into the same problem as had plagued the West Coast. Electrifying the spine — King's Cross to Edinburgh — was an obvious requirement, but the more difficult decisions concerned all the branches. Doncaster to Leeds was an obvious choice, but what about Leeds to Bradford, Leeds to Harrogate, Doncaster to Hull, Newark to Lincoln, around the coastal route from Northallerton to Newcastle, and Edinburgh to Aberdeen? Ideally, they should all have been electrified but the investment funds were not available. And, unlike the West Coast, electric haulage was to be restricted to passenger trains. Freight would continue to be diesel-hauled, a sensible decision because virtually all the traffic arose and terminated at points off the East Coast main line.

The branches that were not electrified suffered in consequence, with a reduction in through services to King's Cross, although a minimal service continued to be provided from some places by HST, except for Aberdeen, which retained its well-established through HST services. Some short branches in the West Riding were electrified through unusual circumstances. The original timetable of the King's Cross-Leeds services allowed sufficient layover time at Leeds for the trains to run through to Bradford Forster Square via Shipley, and this 13½-mile section

Above: Electric locomotive No 91001 emerges from Welwyn South tunnel on 25 March 1989 with the 13.20 King's Cross to Leeds. GNER would like to widen the two tracks to four through this area but it would be extremely expensive. Continental governments would just get on with it. *David Percival*

Right: Two Class 91s stand side by side at King's Cross awaiting departure in 2004. *Author*

The GN suburban electrification came several years earlier. Unit No 313012 coasts to a stand at Wood Green on a Moorgate to Hertford North service on 14 September 1978. *J. G. Glover*

was quickly electrified, supported by the PTE. Present-day timetables do not allow such a generous layover time at Leeds, with the result that there are only two through services each way daily. Shipley has become an important railhead for prosperous residential areas to the north, and whilst these developments were being planned, the PTE desired to improve the suburban service between Leeds/Bradford and Skipton/Ilkley in view of the growing commuter traffic. As a result, another $15^1/_2$ miles of electrified line were added to the system. And to complete the picture, a daily through train was added from Skipton to King's Cross and return.

Trains had traditionally run through from King's Cross to Glasgow Queen Street via Edinburgh, mainly to provide a through service from intermediate stations on the East Coast main line, and it was commercially important to retain this facility. However, the cost of electrifying the $47^1/_2$ miles from Edinburgh to Glasgow Queen Street ruled out this option in favour of electrifying the $28^1/_4$ miles from Edinburgh to Carstairs, joining the already electrified West Coast route at that point. It is ironic that although this added 10 miles to the journey, it was still for some years as quick to travel from King's Cross to Glasgow via Edinburgh as from Euston direct to Glasgow.

With the electrified route thus pared to its essentials, Bob Reid I persuaded the government to approve the scheme in 1984, and it was completed in 1992, just in time for the teething troubles, which tend to infest new schemes, to be mainly corrected before privatisation. The East Coast franchise was won by Sea Containers and operates under the trade name of Great North Eastern Railway. It quickly became one of the most successful of all franchises, both financially and from a customer viewpoint. GNER increased the service frequencies considerably and has fully maintained the long, proud tradition of the East Coast express passenger service. Its Chief Executive, Christopher Garnett, is not a fan of electrification, especially when faults in the overhead line equipment (OLE) cause considerable delays to his trains, and he has his eyes on the projected HST Mk2 when the existing electric trains are approaching the need for renewal.

So, the big question remains. Was electrification the right answer or would it have been better to have a fleet of HSTs? When it was being planned, the groundswell of opinion pushed electrification, but it should be remembered that the LNER, in its postwar programme, had plans to convert its East Coast express services to diesel haulage. However, in the 1970s, electrification was seen as merely the final step in a process that dated back to the 1955 Modernisation Plan, and HSTs had still to prove themselves. They were not at that time regarded as the best trains ever built, a view that is now commonly held. And turning back the clock is not an option.

Three EMUs of Classes 304, 312 and 310 line up at Birmingham International station during the Motor Show. *Chris Morrison*

Birmingham International — Britain's newest main line station

In the early 1970s, when West Midlands industry was very prosperous, the idea arose of building an exhibition centre in open country about halfway between Birmingham and Coventry. At that time, the West Midlands was the centre of motor vehicle production which was probably its most important industry, and there was some dissatisfaction with the London exhibition facilities for the annual Motor Show. Hence, the idea of being able to stage the Motor Show on the industry's doorstep was very attractive, and it quickly expanded into the concept of a general exhibition centre. The result was a series of excellent exhibition halls, with all the facilities that both exhibitors and visitors would want. The location was chosen because of its proximity to the trunk road and motorway network and to Birmingham Airport, but also for the availability of space for extensive car parking. It was also located next to the main railway line because it was assumed that many visitors, especially those from overseas, would travel by train.

The design of the station was based on a number of factors:

- It was expected that special trains would be run for major exhibitions, starting and terminating at the station.
- Large flows of passengers were expected when major exhibitions were being held.
- The West Midlands PTE planned to run a shuttle service to and from Birmingham New Street station during major exhibitions.

The exhibition centre, which became known as the National Exhibition Centre (NEC), has been a great success and it is fortunate that the architect designed the station on a grand scale. It has two, long island platforms reached by escalators and stairs from a very large, airy and imposing concourse with a range of facilities and a pas-

sageway giving direct access to the exhibition centre. It is a station to match the exhibition centre and not just be its poor relation. It opened on Monday, 26 January 1976, a milestone, just in time for its first major exhibition the following Sunday, when six special trains ran from London. It was later used by the Royal Train and has been one of BR's great success stories.

'Operation Princess' — Virgin's new cross-country service

It is a sad comment on railway affairs that Britain had never had a really good cross-country express passenger network linking the North East and the North West with the South East and the South West. In the former company days there were well-known daily services, such as Newcastle and Leeds/Bradford to Bristol; also longer distance named trains such as the 'Devonian' (Bradford Forster Square to Kingswear), the 'Pines Express' (Bradford Forster Square, Liverpool Lime Street and Manchester London Road, via Bath to Bournemouth West), and the longest-distance train in Britain, from Aberdeen to Penzance via Banbury and the GWR. And there was a profusion of through carriages, but no real semblance of a comprehensive cross-country network. There was little or no improvement in BR days, mainly because the through carriage facility had been largely abandoned and the individual Regions were more interested in their own domestic express train services. Improvements were a long time coming and had to wait until Virgin introduced 'Operation Princess'.

Operation Princess introduced a huge network of regular interval high-speed services criss-crossing the country and reaching out almost to its farthest extremities. But its planning overlooked some essential points:

- Cross-country services by their very nature travel several hundred miles and have to negotiate a number of congested areas. They are the most difficult of all services to operate punctually.
- In the new regime, signallers no longer give automatic priority to express passenger trains. Congested lines mean that they have to juggle paths (timetable slots) to accommodate stopping passenger trains and freight trains, otherwise those trains would be seriously delayed.
- Cross-country expresses which lose their paths are more likely to suffer further delays.
- Late running jeopardises tight turnround times at destinations. This was the Achilles' heel, and meant that trains had to be

hurriedly turned round short of destination in order to regain their return path, or they just started the return journey already late.

Virgin quickly reacted to increase turnround times, but could only do so by cutting out the last legs of journeys, which deprived many quite important towns of the benefits of Operation Princess. A new timetable was introduced to regularise the situation, but it produced imbalances which have not been cured.

So far as the trains were concerned, they were technically excellent, but internally they were far less so. The planners appear to have overlooked two cardinal points.

First, much of the service was based on four-car trains. The planners appear to have believed that a frequent service would avoid overcrowding, but that assumption was based on the faulty premise that passenger loadings at individual stations are equal throughout the day. That, of course, is not the case. Peaks arise at particular times, and have caused appalling overcrowding.

Second, cross-country passengers by their very nature are likely to carry a lot of luggage and they need somewhere to put it. The planners, obviously more accustomed to air travel, must have assumed that passengers' luggage would be carried in the hold (or in a separate luggage van) and made little or no provision for it. The inevitable result was unimaginable chaos as passengers with luggage attempted to join crowded trains whose aisles and vestibules were already jammed with luggage. How could any planner have made such a fundamental mistake? Virgin quickly responded by removing some seats and replacing them with luggage racks, but it is hardly adequate. Part of the problem was the inability of the overhead racks to accommodate anything other than hand luggage.

And there are too many airline-type seats, and too many seats with restricted views of the outside world. Cross-country passengers tend to want to see out.

So, was it all a disaster? Operation Princess certainly got off to a bad start, but at least some remedial measures were quickly taken, and now that the service has settled down it is excellent when not overcrowded. And its frequency is a bonus. But the timetable needs revision to bring back into the fold those far-flung stations that were jettisoned. And something needs to be done about short distance commuters who swarm aboard to the discomfiture of longer distance, possibly less agile, passengers. Perhaps impose a minimum fare, or a supplement. Or is Virgin somehow quietly benefiting from the distribution of revenue via the system known as ORCATS? That's a little-known game for the experts to play. Finally, all the trains should have a minimum of five coaches.

The Channel Tunnel, Eurostar and the high speed rail link

Within a year or two, the high speed rail link from the tunnel to London will be completed and the new station at St Pancras will be opened. The celebrations of such an achievement can then begin, with the running of the first train being a major milestone. Britain's first high speed line will then be in business. The important but unanswered question is — will it be the first and only, or will the government come into line with our European partners and build others? A question for the future.

After a long, long trawl through the whole history of railways in all its manifold activities, it is inevitable that one should be left with a number of impressions and conclusions. What follows are the more outstanding and/or important.

The railways have been blessed with some excellent engineers of all disciplines. Men of vision, foresight, skill and determination bordering on genius. Admittedly, some pursued an aim beyond reasonable grounds, but they were searching for the holy grail. Some inevitably fell by the wayside, but those who found it by sheer determination became the giants of the industry. For many railwaymen, of all grades, their industry fostered a degree of loyalty and dedication rarely found in any other industry, and such feelings were necessary to enable the railways to face and attempt to overcome all the many and varied problems which confronted them throughout their history.

Railwaymen did not ask for any thanks for their endeavours, but it might be borne in mind that without the railways there would have been no industrial revolution and Britain's history would have been quite different. Britain's railways also gave splendid service to the country during two world wars, and the only thanks they received from the government were to be driven almost into bankruptcy after World War 1, through government mismanagement during the period of state control, and to be blatantly robbed after World War 2 of funds built up to pay for postwar reconstruction. No other industry has ever been treated in such a shabby fashion.

Indeed, no one reading these pages can have escaped a feeling that governments of all hues appear to have done all they can, either deliberately or through sheer incompetence, to make life as difficult as possible for the railways. Almost every government initiative or action has been to the railway's disadvantage, and no other European railway has suffered in this manner. It is difficult to understand why governments have been so hostile to the railways, because throughout the 20th century the railway companies acted in a responsible and mature manner.

Undoubtedly there has always been a degree of antagonism between railways and the government. The latter were always uneasy about the monopoly powers of railways and did not trust them. They were happy to see the rise in the interwar period of a road alternative that was not highly trade unionised, and to nurture it. Government memories of being held to ransom, as they saw it, by railway strikes in the first three decades of the 20th century died hard. But equally the government's failure to ensure that the railways would be able to meet all the demands that would be placed on them by World War 2, and to deliberately allow them to be weakened in the years preceding the war, was both foolhardy and reprehensible. It allowed its hostility to railways to override proper considerations of national defence.

Since World War 2, matters have gone from bad to worse in respect of government actions.

Nationalisation in 1948 was an organisational disaster, all advice from railway sources being disregarded. The government accepted the BTC's 1955 Modernisation Plan, but then could not wait for the benefits to accrue, despite its being a 15 year plan. The Beeching axe was unnecessary — BR had been closing branch lines throughout the 1950s and would have continued to do so throughout the 1960s without all the panic that followed the Reshaping Report. And the expected savings from the Beeching-era branch line closures were much less than the country (and the government) had been led to expect.

By contrast, Barbara Castle's 1968 Transport Act was full of good intentions, partly frustrated by the return of a government of a different hue in 1970, but the creation of Passenger Transport Authorities has been a great success. The 1974 Freight Facilities Act was also full of good intentions to influence more freight on to rail, but certain people within the Department of Transport seemed to delight in frustrating those good intentions. There was nothing new in this attitude. It has always been there. Read Ted Gibbins' books on the subject to get the full flavour (see Bibliography).

It is said that the railways were starved of investment funds in the 1970s/80s, but that would be overstating the case. There was *under*-investment, and two chairmen of the British Railways Board, Richard Marsh and Peter Parker, resigned in despair on the issue. Bob Reid I did better by achieving massive organisational savings, and then there was more investment. But things were being done on the cheap and it showed. And there was still no prospect of funding for the essential renewal of the West Coast main line infrastructure.

And now we come to what might be regarded as the greatest absurdity in railway history, and quite unnecessary too — the 1993 Railways Act. It purported to transfer the railways to private enterprise and lead not only to a great inwards rush of private capital but also to reduce the payments of government towards the running of the railways. Can any planners and government advisers ever have been so wrong on any issue in history? It resulted in an organisational nightmare of gigantic proportions, mainly because the authors of the act deliberately ignored all the advice that was given to them by experienced railway managers. It split the railway industry into over 100 separate companies. It introduced thousands of contracts. It required a huge and clumsy government regulation system. It nurtured an army of lawyers and consultants. It was a factor in four serious train accidents. And it now costs the government about three or four times as much as pre-1993.

And yet, paradoxically, there has been an unprecedented growth in passenger numbers and freight to such an extent that the tracks are overcrowded with trains in some areas. The response of any sensible and intelligent government faced with such a situation would be to provide the extra capacity needed and to encourage further growth, to ease road congestion both in conurbations and on the trunk road network. The main success of privatisation has been the creation of train operating companies, who with few exceptions have managed their businesses with great efficiency and entrepreneurial skill, leading to the increase in passenger numbers already mentioned. The obvious response of the government would have been to give them more powers and control over the railway network, but in fact the government did the exact reverse. It gave Network Rail, the infrastructure 'owner', more authority, but kept most of it to itself, creating a new railway department within the Department for Transport. One can only wish them well.

The huge sums now being needed to support the railways cannot be allowed to continue. The solutions are not difficult to find: a minimum of organisational interfaces and unified ownership (or control) of trains, train operation and the infrastructure. To improve efficiency and reduce costs it is essential to achieve a form of merger between Network Rail and the train operators. Network Rail is a permanent, nationwide organisation and should merge with the train operators (the TOCs) in the various areas. Initially, Network Rail could be the franchisee in selected areas, eg Scotland and the Great Western, on an experimental basis leading ultimately to permanent merger. The companies so formed should then be given full entrepreneurial freedom from regulation and control. If costs are to be reduced, it is the only answer. The concept of rolling stock companies (ROSCOs) has also been a success, leading to a major input of private capital, but the system needs modifying to reduce the hiring costs of older stock.

And finally, what stands out as one of the true highlights of railway history? It is the High Speed Train — a great engineering and commercial success, designed and built by British Rail engineers in BR workshops and exploited by BR businesses. Yes, there were some problems with the fleet, but passengers love these trains, and that is the key factor. There ought to have been more of them, but the government in its usual fashion restricted the fleet sizes. They are now nearing the end of their productive lives and we need an HST Mk2. It will be a DfT venture, but it must succeed and the DfT's reputation will stand or fall on it. The specification? Power-operated sliding doors, reliable air conditioning, plenty of leg room (people are getting taller), more tables in Standard class, correlation between seats and windows, adequate luggage space under passengers' control, plus all the technical stuff, with diesel or electric capability.

And the great failure? What happened to electrification, the 'sparks effect'? In order to be really successful you need robust electrification structures and you have to electrify the cross-country routes, the branches and the diversionary routes, together with some of the extremities, such as Aberdeen and Plymouth, to avoid the absurdity of running diesel trains for hundreds of miles under the wires. But our governments have always been too parsimonious to do this, unlike Continental administrations. And electric trains do not need fossil fuels. For example, they can run equally well on nuclear-generated electricity as well as other non-fossil sources.

And the great hope? Western European nations have been building and operating new high speed lines for many years. They total thousands of miles. And what has Britain being doing? Apart from the Channel Tunnel Rail Link — only talking about it. But Britain's geography is not like other countries and it does not lend itself easily to a high-speed network. However, we do need a new high-speed line from London to Birmingham, to relieve capacity problems on the existing route from Euston, and continuing to Manchester and Leeds, with the option of proceeding to York and Newcastle. Similarly we need a new high speed route from Paddington as far as Didcot. And there is still plenty of scope for additional running lines alongside other existing routes, or for the upgrading of diversionary routes, to accommodate more freight trains. However, a better solution would be a new high-speed freight route Glasgow–Edinburgh–Newcastle–Leeds–Manchester–Birmingham–London–Southampton, with a branch to Felixstowe. It would not penetrate to the centre of conurbations but would merely pass close to them and serve them from distribution centres (railheads). It would be built to Continental gauge and be capable of carrying the largest containers, and because it would be built mainly in open country it would be considerably cheaper and quicker to build than a high-speed passenger line. It is a great tragedy that the Strategic Rail Authority did not develop plans such as these, rather than wasting its energies trying to micro-manage the train operators. Strategic planning is now in the hands of the Department for Transport. They must not fail the nation.

Bibliography

Ahrons, E. L.	*Locomotive and Train Working in the Latter part of the 19th century* (2 vols, 1952, reprinted from the *Railway Magazine*), W Heffer and Sons.
Allen, Cecil J.	*Salute to the Southern* (1974), Ian Allan
Appleby, K. C.	*Shildon-Newport in Retrospect* (1990), RCTS
	Britain's Rail Super Centres York (1993), Ian Allan
Bell, R.	*History of the British Railways During the War 1939-1945* (1946), The Railway Gazette
Biddle, Gordon	*Great Railway Stations of Britain* (1986), David & Charles
Bonavia, Michael R.	*The Organisation of British Railways* (1971), Ian Allan
	The Birth of British Rail (1979), George Allen & Unwin
	The Four Great Railways (1980), David & Charles
	British Rail — The First 25 Years (1981), David & Charles
	Railway Policy Between the Wars (1981), Manchester University Press
	A History of the LNER, (3 vols, 1983), Geo Allen & Unwin
Bond, Roland C.	*A Lifetime with Locomotives* (1975), Goose & Son
Casserley, H. C.	*LNER Locomotives* (1977), D. Bradford Barton
Clay, John F.	*Jubilees of the LMS* (1971), Ian Allan
Cook, A. F.	*LMS Locomotive Design and Construction* (1990), RCTS
Ellis, C. Hamilton	*The Midland Railway* (1953), Ian Allan Ltd
Essery, R. J. and Jenkinson D.	*An Illustrated Review of Midland Locomotives* (vol 2 1988), Wild Swan Publications
Findlay, George	*The Working and Management of an English Railway* (1889), Whittaker & Co, George Bell & Sons
Gibbins E. A.	*Blueprints for Bankruptcy* (1993), Leisure Publications
	Square Deal Denied (1998), Leisure Publications
	Britain's Railways — the Reality (2003), Leisure Publications
Goodman, John	*LMS Locomotive Names* (1994), RCTS
Gourvish, T. R.	*British Railways 1948-73, A Business History* (1986), Cambridge University Press
	British Rail 1974-97, From Integration to Privatisation (2002), Oxford University Press
Grieves, Keith	*Sir Eric Geddes, Business and Government in War and Peace* (1989), Manchester University Press
Griffiths, R. Prys	*The Railways Act 1921* (1925), Sir Isaac Pitman & Sons
Hall, Stanley	*Railway Detectives — 150 Years of the Railway Inspectorate* (1990), Ian Allan
	The History and Development of Railway Signalling in the British Isles (2000), Friends of the National Railway Museum
Haresnape B. and Swain, Alec	*Churchward Locomotives — A Pictorial History* (1976), Ian Allan
Hughes, Geoffrey	*LNER* (1986), Ian Allan
Johnson, John & Long, Robert A. (Editor in Chief, Roland C. Bond)	*British Railways Engineering 1948-80* (1981), Mechanical Engineering Publications

Livesey, H. F. F.	*The Locomotives of the LNWR* (1948), London Publishing Co
MacDermot, E. T.	*History of the Great Western Railway*, Vol 2 (1964), Ian Allan
Mason, Eric	*The L&YR in the 20th Century* (1954), Ian Allan
Nash, George C.	*The LMS at War* (1946), LMSR
Neele, G. P.	*Railway Reminiscences* (1904), McCorquodale (reprint 1974)
Nock, O. S.	*William Stanier — a biography* (1964), Ian Allan
	Britain's Railways at War 1939-1945 (1971), Ian Allan
	The History of the LMS (3 vols, 1983), Geo Allen & Unwin
Pearson A. J.	*The Railways and the Nation* (1964), Geo Allen & Unwin
Powell, A. J.	*Living with London Midland Locomotives* (1977), Ian Allan
	Stanier Locomotive Classes (1991), Ian Allan
Richards, E. V.	*LMS Diesel Locomotives and Railcars* (1996), RCTS
Sanderson, H. F.	*Railway Commercial Practice* (2 vols, 1952), Chapman & Hall
Sherrington, C. R.	*The Economics of Rail Transport in Great Britain* (2 vols, 1928), Edward Arnold & Co
Simmons, Jack & Biddle, Gordon	*The Oxford Companion to British Railway History* (1997), Oxford University Press
Simnett W. E.	*Railway Amalgamation in Great Britain* (1923), Railway Gazette
Thorley W. G. F.	*A Breath of Steam* (1975), Ian Allan
Whitehouse, Patrick and Thomas, David St John	*The Great Western Railway — 150 Glorious Years* (1984)
	LMS 150 — A Century and a Half of Progress (1987)
	SR 150 — A Century and a Half of the Southern Railway (1988)
	LNER 150 — A Century and a Half of Progress (1989) — All David & Charles
Williams, Geoffrey	*Stars of Steam, Classic Locomotives and their Engineers* (2000), Atlantic Transport
Wood, W. V. and Sir Josiah Stamp	*Railways 1825-1928* (1928), Thornton Butterworth
Wragg, David	*Signal Failure, Politics and Britain's Railways* (2004), Sutton Publishing
Yeadon, Willie B.	*A Compendium of LNWR Locomotives* (Several vols), Challenger Publications

abc series of locomotive stock lists and shed allocations (various dates), Ian Allan

Acts of Parliament, various

DMU and EMU Pocket Books, Platform 5

Government White Papers and reports, various

Locomotive Stock Books, various years, RCTS

Magazines — *Modern Railways, Rail, Railway Gazette, Railway Magazine*

The Railway Observer, Journal of the Railway Correspondence and Travel Society

Railway timetables, various years

Railway Year Books, various, The Railway Publishing Company

Reports and booklets issued by the Railway Companies, the British Transport Commission and the British Railways Board, various

Report — *The development of the major railway trunk routes* (1965), BRB

Report — *Modernisation and Re-equipment of British Railways* (1955), BTC

Report — *Financial and Operating Results of the British Group Railways in 1938*, Railway Gazette

Report — *The Reshaping of British Railways* (1963, BRB) HMSO

Index

Two railway icons, the Forth Bridge and an HST – both long-lived and both symbolic of the great railway age. *John Peter*